WHAT READERS SAY ABOUT THIS BOOK

God bless you, I do too.

"Evelyn has been a great help to the women in our shelter ... Being a survivor myself, I very much identified with her words, the pain and suffering, the difficulty in leaving because of fear ... and being unsure where to go or how to provide for my children [if I went] ... I know how painful it must have been for Evelyn to put these words on paper ... I hope this book will reach battered women [everywhere] and lead them to seek their own help and healing." -*Paula Marshall, Director of a Mountain Home Arkansas battered women's shelter*

Evelyn Hart Stewart

"[I] read your book and I was spellbound. I had a hard time putting it down ... Every woman should read it... and maybe they can see through [Evelyn's] experiences...what to look for in a [potentially] abusive situation. I'm going to ask my granddaughters to read it [to let them know] there are ... signs they can look for .. .to avoid a bad relationship ... Thank you for sharing your story." - *Letha Artacho, San Jose, California*

"I challenge the reader to get this book and be sure to set aside plenty of time...because you won't be able to put it down! [It] is sure to become a movie some day and, after you read it, you will understand why!" -*Laurie Geroux, Hesperia, California.*

Behind Closed Doors, Copyright © 2007 by Evelyn Fort Stewart. All rights reserved. Printed in the United States of America. No part of this book may be used or reproduced in any manner whatsoever without written permission except in the case of brief quotations embodied in critical articles or reviews. For information, address Evelyn Fort Stewart, 412 Cooper St., Mountain Home, Arkansas 72653.

Library of Congress Cataloging in Publication Data

ISBN 978-0-9794189-0-7

Behind Closed Doors is a new version, revised by Evelyn Fort Stewart, of *My Miracle, One Woman's Journey From Tragedy to Triumph* by Evelyn Fort Stewart, and *Totally Discombobulated* by Evelyn Fort Stewart (Author's Online, 1998).

Printed in the United States of America

*To my children Harvey, Dean & Bev,
and to my Lord Jesus Christ.*

Evelyn Fort Stewart

Foreword

I was honored and humbled when Evelyn asked if I would write the foreword for her book, 'Behind Closed Doors". I remember clearly the day I met [her] and how it was like the hand of God had reached out to grab me from the whirlpool tempest that was threatening to take my own life. Her down-home, soft-spoken words were the salve my heart desperately needed. It was as though she had the perfect, angelic insight to save my life. And she did just that. How do I repay her? How do I do justice to the work of love and kindness enclosed within the covers of this book?

The legacy she could have passed on to her children is a far cry from the one she did pass on ... Her legacy is to arm yourself with the strength of God and know that one day the abused will be the victors, and the abusers will be judged according to their deeds. It is a subtle message [and] a powerful truth. Evelyn not only knows it, but she believes it, because she is living proof of that truth, and her story is the proof of her profound faith ... How she kept a pure heart after all that happened to her can only be understood after reading "Behind Closed Doors".

Thank you, Evelyn, for saving my life ... I am honored to be a small part in your plan for survivorship, and I pray that others find the same heart-light that you offer through sharing your life.

Morgan Chai
author of "Retrieved"
Retired Intelligence Officer
www.FurtherBeyond.com/authors

Preface

In December of 1986, my son Dean came to South Carolina to pack me up and move me to Scottsdale, Arizona to be near him. He had always known of my passion for writing, but I had long given up on ever being able to realize my dream of becoming a journalist. No matter how much I planned, and longed, to go back to school, something always interfered. It seemed that it just wasn't in the cards for me.

On our trip to Scottsdale, I said to Dean, "You know, son, if I'd had an education, I could write a best seller." He was kind enough not to laugh. Instead, he replied, "Yes, Mother, I know." He grinned at me, but he was serious when he added, "All you'd need to do is write the story of our life." And that seemed to end the subject.

One day about a year later, my daughter Bev walked into my house, carrying a computer. "Brother said to tell you to start writing," she said as she dumped the thing on the table. I was dumbfounded. I'd never actually seen a computer up close before.

The next day I started hunting and pecking on the keyboard, just to see if I could actually make letters appear on the screen. I'd heard that writing was good therapy so I began, on that day, ten years of self-induced psychotherapy. It took that long for the story to begin to unfold. There were many stops along the way to dry my eyes or simply to walk away and try to collect my thoughts. Everything came back to me so clearly, images I thought I'd buried away forever. Sounds, words, songs, screams, pleas and, along with that, the happy memories ... the good times. Life, even a rough one, can't be all thorns, there are indeed some lovely roses along the way.

Telling my story became an obsession with me. I knew I needed to use it to reach others, to assure those going through what I went through that they are not alone. I had to find a way to help break the chains of violence.

My dream now is to get this story in the hands of every female from ages thirteen to ninety-nine. At least one copy must go to every domestic violence safe-house in America. I will keep saying it until I run out of breath: Abuse breeds abuse. And then I'll add, "Keep the faith; in yourself, in good, and above all, in God."

Evelyn Fort Stewart
Mountain Home, Arkansas
July 12, 2006

Acknowledgments

I want to thank my son, Dean, for his never-ending faith and for believing I could write what he referred to as "our story". He was right. Here it is, against all odds. He never gave up on me.

I thank my daughter, Bev, and her husband, Don, for their love, time, patience, and support. I couldn't have done it without them.

A personal thanks goes to my friend, Joe Jacoby, who encouraged me to tell my story. Joe was a press agent for Hubert Humphrey during his years in the White House as Vice-President. It was my pleasure to have shared a portion of my story with a man of his magnitude while I was living in Arizona. He even wrote a letter to a major publisher on my behalf, but the notion was rejected because of my lack of command over the English language.

Thanks to all of my Internet friends around the world who have given me moral support and who kept me from giving up on my dream. There are too many of them to name individually, but they know who they are and I love each and every one of them.

Most of all I want to thank the good Lord, Jesus Christ. I try to live as He showed us how to live. God impressed me with telling my story. I argued with Him many times. I said, "Lord, you know I don't have the education." But God never let up on me. Getting this book published surely proves that all things come to those who believe.

Thank you to my friend Robbie Hensley. She came into my life soon after I lost my beloved Dean, and has been a real blessing and encouragement to me ever since.

My friend, Jim Bakker, may not realize it, but he has really touched my life and encouraged me in so many ways throughout the years. God bless you, Jim.

My nephew, Durwood Forte, has provided me with a wonderful website. Thank you, Durwood, for not giving up on me. Neither your broken neck, nor your wheelchair, has slowed you down. I appreciate you more than I can say. I love you and I thank you.

And now, a deep, deep thank you to *you*, the Reader. If you're going through tough times, know that others have been there and they've survived. Not just survived, but thrived. You can win, you can come out of the situation you're in whole and sane. I hope this book has helped if only a tiny bit in proving that point to you. I pray it gives you the encouragement you need in order to fight the good fight.

Evelyn Fort Stewart

Behind Closed Doors

Behind Closed Doors

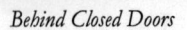

1

Spring seemed to come early to the South Carolina swamps in the year of 1940. Momma and Daddy's favorite place in the afternoon was on the front porch, sitting in their old wooden rocking chairs. Even after all those years of being married, even after raising twelve children, they still enjoyed their afternoons of quiet talks. It seemed that more and more lately, though, the subject was about an impending war. They were overcome with fear about the possibility of one or more of their sons being killed in battle. However, today's topic concerned their baby girl, child number twelve, me.

I heard Daddy say to Momma, "I think it's about time you started teachin' Evelyn how to cook and sew, so she'll know how to take care of her man when she gets married."

"Well, my heavens, Marion," Momma responded indignantly, "she's been makin' your biscuits since she was nine years old. The child knows how to cook."

"You know what I mean, Elma." He only called my mother by her first name when he was dead serious about something. "In no time a'tall she's gonna be sixteen."

"That's a whole three years off," Momma said, rocking. "She'll be ready."

I remember that conversation as if it were yesterday, even though it was nearly sixty-nine years ago. I had seven full-grown, robust brothers, six of them between my next sister and me. Back then, living near the swamps, it was like existing in a different dimension compared to the world today. Daddy was worried that time was running out for me. He wanted me to be prepared to be the kind of wife that my mother had been all those years. Momma, on the other hand, was more concerned with the fact that since we lived in such a remote place, I'd find a potential spouse at all. Just about everyone living in our community was related to one another and Momma didn't cater to the idea of me marrying up with any of my kinfolk. The place had been settled in the 1800's by two families. One of them was on my mother's side, the other was on my daddy's side. The only road in existence at that time, separated the two. That property line today is a major highway.

Although the area had been given Mother's family name, or version of it (her maiden name was Shuler; our community was called Shulerville), Marion Fort was its leading citizen. I grew up in a very sheltered environment. I was never allowed to play with my brothers and the only times I even got to play with my sisters was briefly on Sunday afternoons. Once in awhile, after church, I was allowed to join girls my own age, and almost every one of them was a relative. Other times, I would have to stay on the sidelines, watching the boys play games. I liked listening to them make small talk about girls. I found myself growing up acting more like them, and turning into what was referred to in those days as a tomboy, defying my parents' wish that I would somehow mature into a Southern Belle.

As Momma and Daddy sat in their rocking chairs, discussing my future on that long ago day, my thoughts were, "I may be thirteen, but the idea of gettin' married sure never crossed my mind." My thinking was more along the line of going back to school. I'd been a straight A student the entire seven years I'd attended, but then Daddy put his foot down; education was a waste of time for a woman, he said. To me, turning thirteen hadn't been a big deal. There was no celebration or birthday cake, but I didn't think anything of it. There wasn't money enough for all those birthdays and Daddy made sure that all twelve of us were treated the same. Even though he'd reached a place where he could afford some kind of gift for me, my folks were strict in their belief about fair treatment. None of the other siblings had birthday celebrations, so what would lead me to believe that I was more special than the rest?

It was on this same day that I overheard Momma say, "My Lord, Marion, what would we do if one of them boys got to Evelyn?" I don't remember her exact words after that, but I sure understood that she was afraid one of my brothers or their friends might get me pregnant. God forbid that should happen. Back in those days an unwed mother was scorned for life. I guess that was a major reason they kept such a watchful eye on me. No man would marry a girl unless he knew for sure she was still a virgin. Daddy had already married off four of them.

My heart was burning with desire to go back to school, but the chances of that happening were pretty slim. My father made it plain to all of us that he earned a good living in spite of the fact he had only a first-grade education. He finally conceded that it might be good for all of us to go until at least the seventh grade. After that, he needed us working the farm. Growing food was our number one priority.

Now that I'd graduated from the seventh grade, I was at home all day being taught to cook and sew by my Nanny Eve. Listening to my parents plan my life, I began to wonder what it would be like to reach that much-talked-about magical age of sixteen. Sixteen then was about what we think of when we think of age eighteen today. Once you reached your sixteenth birthday, you were considered to be your own person. I began looking forward to the birthday that was supposed to perform miracles in my life. I had to accept that school was no longer an option for me. The marriage seed had been planted.

Growing up, seeing and feeling the love my parents shared, I truly believed that all marriages would be like theirs. Never in my wildest dream could I have guessed what a cruel world I would soon face. I often ask myself if it would have made a difference had I known what the future held in store for me.

I had another desire, too. I wanted to become a writer. With this kind of thinking, and the way my father felt about me getting married the instant I was eligible, I knew I'd have to keep that ambition a secret. I understood that making a living was critical. If I could earn a living, then put myself through school, I felt sure my parents would be proud of me. Even though I was young in years, I was a very grown-up and responsible thirteen.

After we returned from church the Sunday following their porch talk, and we'd finished eating dinner, Mother and I cleared the table and washed up the dishes, as usual. This day she seemed somewhat different than most other times. It was as if she wanted to talk about something, but was afraid or just couldn't find the right words. I wasn't much help to her in that department, being still pretty naive about life even though I was a head taller than all the other girls and boys in my class. Our entire family was tall with big bones and hardy frames. My mother told me it's the Scottish blood that makes us as big as we are. I've since learned that Momma was wrong. Mother and Father were of French, not Scottish, extraction. But back to my story about doing dishes on that Sunday afternoon.

Daddy decided to make his usual trip to the barn to check on the animals when Momma walked out on the front porch where my brother, Stanley, was enjoying the afternoon sun. She reached out and gently tapped him on his shoulder as she went down the steps, into the yard. Then, almost in a whisper, I heard her say, "Come along, Stannie. I want to talk to you." Stanley got to his feet and followed her around to the side of the house.

At first I paid little attention to what was going on between them until I realized that she must have had a secret she wanted to share with him. Momma and Stanley shared a lot of secrets, which made me curious, so immediately my ears perked up. My big, handsome brother had lost his left hand to a sugar cane machine when he just two years old, but it never seemed to bother him and no one gave him special privileges because of it. In fact, I hardly noticed anymore. What I was noticing just now, was that Momma wanted to tell him something that was on her mind, and she wanted to do it while Daddy was out of earshot. That was the way she handled things when she didn't want him to know what she was up to.

Pretty soon she called me over. My heart jumped with excitement to know that I was about to be included in their secret. I approached enthusiastically, jumping from the porch onto the ground. Stanley's back was to the chimney. Mother's back was to the wild plum tree; its lush green splendor was covered with beautiful white flowers that would soon produce small, sweet fruit.

I didn't have the least idea of what to expect. My first thought was that she was going to scold me for something I'd done, even though I couldn't think of any wrongdoing. Despite the fact Mother seemed nervous, there was great certainty in her voice when she told me, "Evelyn, you're going to Charleston to work in the cigar factory. At least you're going to go and try to get a job there."

I'd never seen my mother that agitated. I wasn't quite sure if she was trying to keep Daddy from knowing what she had in mind for me or if maybe they weren't in complete agreement about it. Mother pretty much knew how to work Daddy when she wanted things to go her way, even though she hadn't been able to convince him to let me continue my schooling. He reminded her that he had made my sister, Margie, turn down a scholarship when she graduated from the seventh grade; there was no way he was going to show partiality toward me.

Getting on that train at my young age and going to Charleston to find work was definitely food for thought. I was filled with mixed emotions. This was going to be my first trip away from home other than when I visited one of my sisters. I was excited about the thought of earning money, having my own to spend. I kept wondering when Momma was going to make this happen. It would be two weeks before she filled me in on the details.

Many years later, when I thought back on how it all came about, the new world that was about to open up to me, the shock of a marriage unlike anything I'd ever known, the horror of what awaited that innocent thirteen-year-old, I often reflected on the fact that Mother was forty-eight years old when I was born. Daddy was seven years older. And I marveled at their sixty-three golden years of wedded bliss.

2

Even at thirteen I understood my parents deserved some time for the two of them. Mother had thought this through very thoroughly. Little did I know she had some way, somehow, figured every tiny little detail. How she accomplished this during that era, I still don't know. I guessed that Stanley was instrumental in this amazing feat. He was staying in a Charleston rooming house owned by a Mrs. Clark, and Momma trusted Stanley to see after me. Going to work at thirteen wasn't a big deal back then, but none of us was aware that a law had recently passed stipulating that a person had to be sixteen years-old in order to work on a public job. Nobody bothered to inform my mother of this earth-shaking information, though it probably wouldn't have mattered to her. With her strong belief in God, she accepted without question that all things were possible. We'd known our entire life that if Momma said something was going to happen, it would happen. No Doubting Thomases were allowed to live under my parents' roof. Momma said I was going to Charleston and that I was going to work and that was that.

My parents were believers in the Bible. My mother's interpretation of the Bible, her reason for sending me off to go to work, was that Jesus became accountable for his own actions at the age of twelve. Since my father could neither read nor write, Mother read to us from the Good Book while we all, including Daddy, listened. The only book in our home, other than a few textbooks, was the Bible.

Everything that I knew about the outside world was straight out of either the Bible or the swamps. I was as naive about city life as a person could possibly be. I didn't know about streets, let alone about street life.

Momma made me three new dresses with matching aprons. A couple of days before time to leave, she called me into my bedroom where she had the clothes spread out across the bed so I could see them at a glance. I let out a squeal of joy like you never heard before.

"I always want you to look nice," she said. "And I want you to wear the matching apron to protect your clothes so they'll last longer."

She told me to get my other things packed.

"You need to take everything that's yours. I don't have any idea when you'll get to come back home, not with the way the government's got gas rationed. Lord only knows what else is going to happen with this war the way it's goin'. I've made arrangements with Vernie to come take you to Jamestown. She'll get you on the train, so there's nothin' for you to worry about. Between the two of us, we've taken care of everything." I noticed that her voice was trembling.

Vernie was the wife of my brother Raymond. She was a good Christian woman who wore her hair in a bun on the back of her neck most of the time. I don't think she ever learned to say no to anyone, especially to my parents.

I stammered, "B-b-but how will I know where to go, or when to get off the train?"

"Now don't you fret, Evelyn. Didn't I tell you it's gonna be all right?"

Sunday morning arrived much too soon. In one way, I was excited. In another way, I was scared out of my wits. I'd heard my brothers talk about how big the city of Charleston was. There were more ifs running through my mind at that moment than pigs had piglets. What if I got off the train at the wrong place? What if I got lost afterward? I knew every person that lived in our small community, but I didn't know anybody in Charleston except Stanley. Momma assured me that he would stay close to make certain I was okay.

Just as Mother instructed, I packed my bags. It was time to make the seven-mile car trip to the train. At one-thirty I heard Vernie's old Ford approaching. Then I heard her voice as I was closing my luggage. We had gotten home from church, like always, just after twelve noon. Momma's plan was to get me on the train that came through Jamestown, seven miles down the road, at two o'clock. Then the fifty-mile journey to Charleston would begin.

"My, my, Evelyn, you sure look pretty today," Vernie said, looking me over.

I kind of shrugged my shoulders, then blushed and thanked her. I was feeling more scared than pretty at the moment.

Mother said to Vernie, "I sure thank you for gettin' Evelyn to the train for me."

Vernie said not to worry about it, she was glad to do it. "Well," she said to me, "grab your bag. We better get going. By the time we get to Jamestown and I buy your ticket, the train'll be there."

As we were approaching the car, Momma called out, "Now don't you worry none, Evelyn. Stanley's gonna keep an eye out to make sure you're all right."

I swallowed real hard. I was on my way. There wasn't any turning back. The funny thing was, though, that I still wasn't sure what brought on this sudden change in my life. I wasn't given any explanation and I had no idea what to expect. Suddenly, I got very cold feet. I wanted to jump out of the car and run back screaming, "No! I don't wanna go! Don't make me go!" I would have loved my first train ride had I not been going alone.

From the time I was a small child, I had accepted without question rejection from my siblings. The older ones resented me because they were tired of my mother having babies. Another girl in our large family wasn't welcome and they let everyone know it. I never was one to have pity parties, though. I was taught to be a good listener and to do as I was told. Yes meant yes, no meant no; patience is a virtue. In those days, children were brought up to be seen, not heard. So, even though I never questioned my parents, I wondered what this was all about and I tried to understand the why of it. My mind went back to Nanny Eve. I was hardly on the road and already I missed her. To my understanding, Nanny Eve had either been one of the original slaves brought directly from Africa or a daughter born soon after reaching this country. She had gotten too old to keep on working, though she stopped by to visit from time to time, especially on her way to the post office to check her mail.

When I was about three years old, Nanny Eve told me that every person has a Guardian Angel.

"Nanny Eve, where is my Guardian Angel?" I asked.

"My child, your Guardian Angel is right there on your shoulder."

Immediately, I looked to try to see where my Guardian Angel was. Nanny Eve was smiling as she said, "Child, you can't see the angel, but if you listen very closely, your angel will speak to you in a wee small voice. God has given each and every one of us a guardian to watch over us and to protect us. It don't matter where we go, or how far we go, our Guardian Angel is with us. Child, you must always listen to that quiet voice within yourself for guidance. That's the way God protects us in life. Now, when you get to the place you think you know more than the angel that God has sent to protect you, that's when the devil gets his turn with you. That's the time people get themselves in trouble. You just remember what I'm telling you. It will help you through many a trial that you'll come to face in this life." Those words have given me the courage and strength to meet a lot of my problems through the years.

Sitting there, listening to the hum of the car's motor, my mind had gone back to the spring of 1940 when everyone was so upset about World War II. I thought about the primitive part of the country where I was born, near the swamps. I'd spent thirteen very happy years there. Even though Shulerville was remote, one thing we were proud of was the fact we had a post office. It was operated out of one of the bedrooms in a private home. I was daydreaming about my beloved Nanny Eve and her walks to the post office when I realized that Vernie was speaking to me. I glanced at her and she grinned.

"Welcome back to the real world. Don't be scared. There's not any reason for you to be scared. It won't be long until you're going to meet some nice young man who'll want to marry you and take care of you. You know there aren't any boys in Shulerville except your cousins. One day you'll look back and thank Mrs. Fort for seeing fit to do this for you. You'll see, once you get there and you find a good job and start making your own money. You'll be glad it happened this way. Just you wait and see. By the way, when we get to Jamestown, I'll go in the depot to get your ticket for you and I'll make sure the conductor puts you off at the right stop. You're going to like being in Charleston. I just know you will."

It wasn't that I was afraid of work. The scary part was just the fact of getting there, finding my way around.

"Evelyn, when you get off the train, go to your left and walk fifteen blocks. You be sure now that you count the blocks. When you get to the fifteenth one, you'll see a sign that reads 'Meeting Street'. Here." She handed me a piece of paper with a number written on it. "You'll see there's not going to be a problem. Just leave your suitcase here in the car till we hear the train coming. We'll be able to see it in plenty of time to get your suitcase. Oh, my goodness, I almost forgot to tell you something."

"Tell me what?"

"When you get to the cigar factory, tell them you're sixteen years old. If you say you're thirteen, they won't hire you."

This was one I had to ponder, this was definitely food for thought. My entire life I had been told over and over again *Thou shalt not lie*. It's one of the Ten Commandments right along with *Thou shalt not kill*. Now that I was being pushed out of the nest, why was it all right to lie to get a job? Was God going to overlook a lie if it was to get a job? I had been in that little Pentecostal Holiness Church twice on Sundays and every Wednesday night, not to mention going every night of the two-and three-week-long revivals where every sermon pounded home that it was wrong to lie. It is wrong to kill. It is wrong to commit adultery. I'd been taught to memorize those ten command ments from a very early a.ge Now, all of a sudden, I was told to lie to be able to get this job. Despite the fact I had no choice in the matter, I felt a deep sense of guilt. What I couldn't comprehend was that the same people who drummed those commandments into me were now telling me to disregard the one about lying. I sure didn't get it.

At that moment I heard the train whistle in the distance. It was time to stiffen my back and prepare myself for what I would be facing. Was I going to be mature enough to handle it all? I wondered.

By the time the train arrived, there were a dozen people loitering around the station. That was an exciting event in those days, at least in my part of the country. A favorite pastime, especially for the older folks, was to meet up at the depot to see and hear the old iron horse chug its way in and out of town.

This time the steam engine pulled up with a loud screeching sound. I was in awe, absolutely spellbound, to see the "old iron horse" for the first time. The conductor stepped from the train wearing a black suit with a long coat that came down about six inches above his knee. He had on a black cap with a bill on it that was made pretty much like an army cap. He reached into the train and took out what looked like a homemade set of steps. They were just the right size to make it so that people could board the train. Vernie walked up to the conductor and said something that I couldn't hear because of all the noise the train was making. Then the conductor yelled out, "All aboard for Charleston!"

He took my suitcase, slid it onto the train, then reached out to take me by the arm and help me board. I made my way to the first seat that I could find. My stomach was churning. My knees almost went out from under me. This was one of the greatest fears I'd ever had to experience alone. All of the other rides I'd ever taken were on wagons and buggies. In a few minutes the train whistle blew, then we started chugging along very slowly. About a quarter of a mile down the track, the train began to pick up speed. I felt as if I was in a fog with not a clue as to what was going on around me. It was as if I was dreaming, or in another world.

I made my head comfortable against the cushioned seat, trying to focus on my surroundings. Acres of freshly-plowed fields flew past the window. They looked as if they had been made ready for spring planting. Just a little farther up the track, I saw swamps with shiny black water that glistened in the sunlight. There were lots of cypress trees laden with Spanish moss. From time to time, I could see the

South Carolina state flower, the yellow jasmine, ready to burst out in full bloom. Suddenly, in the middle of the woods, the train jerked to a halt. Seeing my concern, the conductor hurried to reassure me.

"It's all right, Miss. It's only some cows on the track. Nothin' to worry about. We'll be on our way shortly."

True to his word, in a matter of minutes the old iron horse began lumbering along as if it had more of a load than it was capable of carrying, rocking back and forth through the beautiful scenery.

I closed my eyes, wondering what was going to happen to me. I felt like I imagine a baby bird must feel when pushed from its nest. I felt so lost and alone without anyone to turn to. Then I thought about how a small bird, when forced, was able to fly when it didn't even know it could. *Here I am now*, I was thinking, *a big girl. With the help of the Guardian Angel on my shoulder, I can make it on my own. I can.*

A great wave of self-assurance came over me. All at once I was thankful that my parents had taught me about God. They and Nanny Eve had assured me that God would always be in my heart to guide and protect me. Just thinking about that seemed to give me a sense of peace. Time flew and it wasn't long before we reached our destination.

As I started to exit, the conductor took my arm to steady me. "Good luck, young lady," he said as I stepped from the train. "You take care now, you hear me?"

I stood looking around, feeling peaceful but somehow odd, too. I took from my pocket the piece of paper that Vernie had given me and studied the directions she'd written. I had to get them straight in my mind before setting out. Half dragging my heavy suitcase along beside me, I was too mixed up emotionally to realize what a beautiful day it was. My arm began to ache from tugging the luggage. I spotted a park bench up ahead and made my way to it. I needed to rest and also to think things over. Not that I had any expectations about what I was getting into, I didn't. I had none whatsoever. But it was as if I was being haunted by every day of my past life. I knew there was no hate or malice in my mother's reasoning, but at that moment, sitting in a very strange place fifty miles from home, facing only God knew what, my mind was going in circles. I didn't have even a nickel in my pocket.

I wondered what the place where I was going to room and board was like. I wondered if I'd be able to get a job. My breath caught in my chest. What if there wasn't a job? How could my mother possibly know that I was going to get a job? I began to hyperventilate.

Hearing footsteps approach, I glanced around and saw two unshaven individuals. Their clothes were worn, torn, and dirty. They looked as if they hadn't had a bath for quite some time. I watched as they drew closer. Finally, I picked up my suitcase and moved on. "Hey there, pretty girl!" one of the men called out. "We didn't mean to run you off."

I didn't turn to look at them, I just kept on walking. I hurried as fast I could, dragging my suitcase against the blacktop.

A few blocks away I spotted a sign that read Meeting Street. I double-checked Vernie's directions to make sure that was what I was looking for. She hadn't said whether I should go to the left or to the right. For no reason I could explain I went to the right, though it didn't take long for me to realize I'd gone the wrong way. I turned around and went in the opposite direction. I was becoming paranoid. My heart was pounding furiously, but I kept on walking. Finally, on a big white house, I saw the number I'd been looking for: 518. Somehow, I got up the courage to go knock on the door, asking myself the entire way, *What'll I say when somebody opens the door? Good Lord, what if nobody asks me in?*

Then I began to have another conversation with myself. *Evelyn, you won't get the answers to all of your questions until you walk up those five steps and knock on that door.*

The wood door to the house was open, only the screen door was closed. I was rather surprised to see screen doors and windows because we didn't have that luxury in Shulerville. I forced myself to climb the steps, but my knees were trembling and my suitcase seemed to have gotten twice as heavy as when I first started out.

Once on the porch, I sat my baggage down and knocked gently. I could see a lady inside, sitting in a rocking chair. She had something in her lap, but I couldn't make out what it was. She was so engrossed in whatever it was she was doing that she didn't seem to hear me. I wanted to turn and run away, but instead I knocked once more.

That's when I saw her stand up and approach. She had a startled look on her face, as if to question what this young girl with a huge suitcase was doing on her front porch.

After some hesitation, she said, "Yes? What can I do for you?"

I began shyly stuttering, trying to find a way to handle the situation in a mature fashion. "I'm-I'm-I'm Evelyn F-F-Fort."

Her expression changed as if she recognized me.

"In that case," she said, "why don't you just come on in here? I'm Mrs. Ellen. Everybody calls me Mrs. Ellen."

"Yes, that's what my brother, Stanley, told me to call you."

Then, with her slow southern drawl, she asked, "You are Mr. Marion and Mrs. Elma Fort's daughter from Shulerville, aren't you?"

"Y-y-yes, yes, Ma'am–Mrs. Ellen, I am." I was standing there like my feet were glued to the floor.

She pushed open the screen door.

Once I was inside, she said, "Bring your suitcase." She made a pointing gesture, then she added, "You can put it there." *There* meant a place by the staircase.

I did as she asked, then stood watching as she took her time moving back to the chair she'd been sitting in when I arrived. She picked up her knitting. I heard the clicking of her needles as she said, "I been expecting you. Stanley doesn't live here anymore, I guess you know, but he came by and told me you'd be getting in today. I'd expected you to be here earlier though. I've made arrangements for you to stay here with me, that is, if you're willing to follow my rules."

"Y-y-yes, Ma'am. I won't give you any trouble, I promise."

"In the morning, I will wake you at five o'clock sharp. Breakfast will be at six. That will give you enough time to get dressed, eat, and get to work by seven. You'll be at the cigar factory when the personnel office opens. Supper's served promptly at six o'clock. You'll eat then or you don't eat at all. Bedtime's eight o'clock. You'll pay me ten dollars a week for your room and board, and you'll share a bed with my daughter."

Rising to her feet, she motioned me to follow her.

"Come. I'll show you where to put your things."

When we reached a tiny square of a bedroom, she said, "You can hang your dresses there in that closet, but everything else stays in the suitcase. You can use the dresser mirror. When you finish, everything goes back into your suitcase until you need it again. You mustn't be leaving things lying around." Then, as if talking to herself, she said, "Now that should take care of that."

"But-but, Ma'am, I-I-don't have ten dollars to pay you with."

"Not to worry. You'll pay me when you get your first paycheck."

I felt as if I were on a roller coaster headed straight for hell. I'd never had ten dollars at one time in my entire thirteen years. I'd never even seen ten dollars all at once in my entire life. This was certainly giving me something to ponder. I'd been taught to speak when spoken to; that piece of advice was coming in handy. I was out of the frying pan, but I didn't know how to handle the fire. This had been a traumatic experience for me from the get-go. For some reason I remembered Daddy saying, "When you think you're doing bad at home, you need to go visit your neighbor. Once you do, you'll see things in a different manner." I never understood exactly what he meant until now. Spending that short time with this lady, I realized that truer words were never spoken. Every complaint I'd had as a child seemed to suddenly vanish.

I put my suitcase away, trying to remember all of her rules. Then I sat on the side of the bed, careful not to wrinkle the bedspread. I didn't move until seven o'clock when she stuck her head in and said, "You best go take your bath. You wouldn't want to break your eight o'clock curfew your first night here, now would you?"

The bathroom was kind of small, but it had a nice big tub, the kind with bear paws on its legs. It felt wonderful to soak in warm, sudsy water. All we had to bathe in at home was a number three zinc tin tub. Mrs. Ellen had hot and cold running water. This was a luxury to be remembered.

My landlady had given me very strict orders to use only what water I needed; none was to be wasted. That wasn't a problem. I was accustomed to the waste not-want not rule. As my mother used to tell us, "All good things must come to an end" and the bath had to come to a close. When the water started cooling down, it was time to make ready for bed. I toweled myself off, reached for the floor-length nightgown that Mother had made for me, slipped into it and made my way to the bedroom. Once under the covers, I was asleep much quicker than I ever thought I could be, in a strange bed.

Next morning, I was awake before the alarm went off at five. The first sound to greet my ears was that of clinking pots and pans in the kitchen. That told me that my landlady was cooking breakfast. Quickly sliding out of bed, I washed my face and got dressed. I combed my hair and put on just a touch of pink lipstick that my sister-in-law Bernice had given me a long time back. My church frowned on girls, and even grown women, wearing any kind of make-up, claiming it was a tool of the devil. When Bernice gave it to me, she told me to keep it until I was old enough to wear it. I had hidden it away so Mother wouldn't find it, knowing that she would have thrown it away. I had to hurry. In only a few minutes I would have to leave to find my way to the cigar factory.

I hurriedly ate breakfast, dreading the thought of having to ask Mrs. Clark for directions. I finally screwed up the courage.

"It's fourteen blocks from here," she said. "You need to get there a few minutes before seven. That way they just might be able to talk to you first. Being early will make a good impression."

3

I left with a lump in my stomach as large as a grapefruit, but I found the cigar factory without a problem. It was a huge brick building with several steps leading up to the main entrance. I went through the front door with no clue what to expect. To my left I saw a sign on a door that read Personnel Office. I stopped to take a deep breath to try to slow the pounding of my heart. Knees shaking, I knocked on the door. A deep, masculine voice on the opposite side called out, "Come in." I hesitated. The voice said, "Come on in." With trembling, sweaty palms, I pushed the door just enough to be able to see inside. Once again, I heard the slow voice with a thick southern drawl. "Please, do come on in."

I was eye-to-eye with a tall, dark, very handsome man who had salt-and-pepper hair, making him appear to be quite distinguished. There was definitely an outdoors look about him. His dark brown eyes shone with gentleness. An aura about him made me feel as if I'd known him for a long time.

"Hello there, young lady. Could it be possible that I know you?"

Stammering, as if my tongue was stuck to the roof of my mouth, I said. "I-I-I don't think so. I-I'm-I'm Evelyn Fort–from Shulerville." I repeated myself, "I-I-I don't think so, Mister."

"You don't think soooo–what?"

"I-I don't think you know me. I've never been here before."

"Ahh, young lady, but I just might know who you are." He

flashed a big smile. "If not you, then I'll bet I just might know your father and mother."

This was a bit too much to reckon with. Neither my father nor my mother had gone anywhere other than to church, with few exceptions. Momma had gone to Charleston only once that I knew of, and that was to get her ears checked by a head specialist. If she went anywhere else while she was in town, it was more than I knew about.

"My goodness," he said. "You're even prettier than I could have guessed."

I was stunned, to say the least. I actually reached up with my right hand to close my mouth, it had dropped wide open. It was easy to see that the gentleman was getting a kick out of the expression on my face as I blushed deeply.

"Ah, yes, " he continued, mysteriously. "I've been to your house several times. I've even been deer hunting with your father and I must tell you, he's the best. You're a very lucky young lady to have those two fine folks for parents." He hesitated a moment. "I only remember seeing you once. That was a long time back. With my job here being what it is, I don't get away too often. My, my, how you've grown up to be such a pretty young lady! The last time I was in Shulerville, we took a tent with us. There were four of us. We camped out near your Uncle Richard's place. Do you remember that?"

"Yes, sir, I remember the tent. I don't remember seeing you."

"I'm sure looking forward to doing some hunting with Mr. Fort again in the near future. Matter a fact, the last time I was there I asked Mrs. Fort when was she was going to send me some good help. Help's short with everybody going to the defense plants. The demand for cigars and cigarettes to send overseas is greater than ever. I need all the good workers I can get. When I saw you at your house that day after we came in from hunting, you were hustling around pretty good. Truth is, you're the one that gave me the incentive to ask your mother to find me some good help." He flashed another smile. I began to feel somewhat more relaxed. *So, I thought, this was how my Mother could be so sure I'd get the job.*

He became more serious. "Evelyn, I'm glad to have you here with us. It never ceases to amaze me how fast you pretty country girls grow up nowadays. You know, I might have the perfect job for you." He hesitated as if thinking for a moment before he continued. "Yep, you just might be perfect for the job I have in mind."

It was easy to see that he sensed my nervousness and was trying to put me at ease the best he could. Without a doubt, he would had to have known that I was a total country bumpkin.

Trying to hold back the excitement I was feeling, I blurted out, "Do you really mean it? You're really going to give me a job?"

"Yes, I am. That is, if you're ready to go to work."

"Yes, sir, I am."

"Then follow me. We'll just go see what we can find for you."

Following quietly beside him, I realized that he had made me feel the best I'd felt since learning of my move to Charleston.

When a lady came over to meet us, I heard his name for the first time: Mr. Bentley. He introduced the woman to me as my floor lady. I was told that her job was that of supervisor of my department. She would tell me what to do.

Mr. Bentley told her, "How about you showing this pretty young lady around? I know her folks personally. I know she's going to do a good job, so take your time showing her around the place. Let her decide if she thinks she's going to like it here. When you've finished, bring her back to my office. I need to make out the paperwork so she can get started."

My job, it turned out, was to weigh out the right amount of tobacco then see it got evenly fed down a trough to a girl sitting at the end of the machine. When a metal arm would swing out, the girl placed a leaf of tobacco across a square object. The machine would cut the leaf the correct size to create a cigar wrapper. The machine followed through with wrapping the cut section around the tobacco that I had placed in the trough. This was now a cigar ready to be smoked and it fell into a box under the machine. It was child's play compared to what I was used to doing at home. *Yes,* I thought, *this is going to be a piece of cake.* I knew that my mother had made the right decision for me.

The tour took about an hour, at which time the floor lady escorted me back to Mr. Bentley's office. He handed me a work application to fill out. It was a simple form. When I got to the space that asked my age, I quickly wrote in "Twenty." If I was going to tell a lie why not tell a good one? I finished filling out the resume and slid it across his desk. He glanced at it then at me. "From what I see here, it looks like we just found ourselves a real hard worker."

"Yes, sir," I beamed. "I'm going to work real hard for you."

By this time, I was feeling much, much better. As I turned to begin my official job, he called out, "The lunch bell rings at twelve noon. Take thirty minutes for yourself."

"Sir, I won't be able to eat lunch for a while. I don't have any money."

"Oh, no, young lady. That just won't work."

My heart sunk. I'd gotten fired already!

"We can't have people working here with a hungry stomach. People can't rightfully turn out a good job when they have a hungry stomach."

I could feel the tears well up in my eyes. The last thing I wanted to do in front of this nice man was to cry, but here I had a great job then I lost it just as quick, if not quicker, than I found it.

"Sir, I want this job, but please, I don't have any money at all."

He saw a tear slip down my cheek. With his thumb, he gently wiped it away.

"Oh, come on, it can't be all that bad now, can it? There's nothing for you to worry your pretty little head about. Hmmmm, now let me see what I can do here to make things better for you. I could never let Mrs. Fort's pretty daughter go hungry. As I remember, she fed me really well when I was there. Just thinking about her collard greens and corn dumplings makes my mouth water."

Somewhere in my throat, I found a small voice with which to make a final plea. "I promise, I won't be very hungry."

He reached in his pocket and took out two one-dollar bills along with a fifty-cent piece. I backed away from him a step or two, appalled. "Sir, I don't think my father would like it if I took your money. I don't think he'd approve of that at all."

"No, no, young lady, now you listen to me. You don't understand. This is nothing for you or your father to be upset about. It's just a loan. I'm not giving this to you. I'm going to have it deducted from your first paycheck. Now, do you think that will be satisfactory?"

"Oh, thank you, Mister Bentley! Thank you very much."

I reached to accept the money, but he tucked it into my apron pocket. This was an amazing turn of events, one I'd have to reckon with. I had left home at one-thirty the day before without one penny in my pocket and already I was in debt twelve dollars and fifty cents. The job paid twenty-seven dollars and fifty-cents for a full forty-hour week. That was the first time I had ever held two dollars and fifty-cents in my hand.

On that date in April of 1941, every able-bodied person old enough to help our country wanted to do their part. In order to keep this type of plant operational, personnel was hiring anyone and everyone willing to work. Neither Mr. Bentley, nor anybody else, cared about my age so long as I gave him eight hours each workday in return for the company's money. Most of the women old enough to work, and who could leave their children, had jobs in defense plants. It was a breakthrough of sorts. For the first time, women were allowed to wear long trousers and were given jobs that usually went to men. The whole thing would expand enormously once the Japanese attacked Pearl Harbor, but this was only April and we wouldn't bear the burden of actual war for another eight months yet.

That afternoon, when I got to the boarding house, Mrs. Ellen stopped knitting to lower her glasses to the end of her nose so that she could see over them.

"Sooo," she said, "I take it you got your job."

"Yes, Ma'am. I did."

"Did you work today?"

"Yes, Ma'am, I did, after they got all my papers filled out."

"Good, very good."

Now that I had a good job and good people to work with, I figured I'd have to be patient with a landlady who made me uncomfortable. Everything was so much different than I had been accustomed to. She seemed to be so cold, so withdrawn. My parents were outgoing. They'd never met a stranger in their life. People were drawn to them. Also, I still hadn't heard from Stanley since my arrival. According to Momma, he was supposed to be seeing after me. Not that he could have made any difference, but still, Momma said he was supposed to watch after me and I'd expected it. Of course, I knew, too, that Stanley was working long hours at the navy yard since there was a drastic shortage of electric welders.

Weekends were painfully long. I could hardly wait for Monday morning so I could go back to work. During that first year and a half, I saw very little of Mr. Bentley and mostly when I did, it was just in passing.

One Saturday I decided to go downtown to check out the main thoroughfare, King Street. My dresses were beginning to look worn. I didn't have my mother to depend on for making new ones. I was fifty miles away from her and without transportation. Even if I'd known someone with a car, they probably wouldn't have had ration stamps to buy gasoline. Or even, if they had the stamps, there would usually be no gas to purchase.

On this particular Saturday, I put on my best dress and walked to town. I did more window shopping than anything else because in those days window shopping was a wonderful experience. All of the displays were simply beautiful. I had money in my pocket, but I was shy. I'd never shopped and didn't know how. I thought maybe it would be best if I took my time and watched how other people went about buying store-bought things.

My shopping trip ended without a single purchase.

On my way back to the rooming house, I spotted a restaurant across the square from the All-Men, Military Citadel, on Meeting Street. A sign in the café window read "Help Wanted." It was the first fine restaurant I'd ever seen. My heart raced as I peeked inside to see the splendor of the place. It was the prettiest thing this little country girl had ever laid her eyes on. I stood there for a moment savoring its magnificence. I felt as though I was looking into a fantasy land. Somewhere along the street, the Andrew Sisters sang their top hit warning: "Don't Sit Under the Apple Tree with Anyone Else But Me". It seemed that every jukebox was playing the same song at the same moment. The sound of the music made me feel as if I were floating on a cloud. In my young years at home, we didn't have a radio. This was when jukeboxes and radios were just becoming popular. Never in my life had I witnessed seeing so many people listening to such a beautiful melody. I can't remember hearing anything other than the Andrew Sisters' tunes that day.

With Charleston being the port of embarkation, streets were crowded with servicemen from every branch of the military. The ambiance was a little reminiscent of Las Vegas today. No matter what hour of the day or night, you could hardly get up or down King Street without bumping into people. Most of the servicemen and women were on their last furlough before being shipped out. I was in awe of the whole situation and found myself a spot, backed up near the wall of that beautiful restaurant, where I could take it all in. As I listened to all those wonderful songs, it put me on a natural high. I had to pinch myself to see if I was dreaming. Once more, I looked at the Help Wanted sign taped to the window. Eventually, I got the nerve to open the door, then ease myself inside the restaurant that turned out to have a Greek theme. I felt like children today feel when they visit Disneyland for the first time.

A bald headed man with black eyebrows saw me and came up to me. When he spoke, he had a thick Greek accent. I think it amused him to see someone so awestruck over his establishment.

"Miss," he said at last, "how can I help you?"

I was as dumbfounded as a country person could be, fighting myself to think of something to say without looking like a complete idiot. Finally, I stammered, "I-I just wanted to ask about the job." I meekly pointed to the sign on the window.

"You want job, eh?"

He took a couple of steps back to look me over from head to toe. Then he nodded and scratched above his right ear. "I tell you what, I give you job. One condition: You go home, come back work two o'clock today. I need help. I furnish you clean, white, starch-ironed uniforms straight from the laundry. I pay you two dollar a day plus tips. You work hard, you make not less than eighty dollar a week, even more if you try."

"Yeah, uh, yes, sir. I do want the job. I'll be back. You did say two o'clock?"

"You be back, ready to go to work at two o'clock. You get here in time to get dressed. You start work two o'clock sharp. Yes?"

He seemed to be having as much trouble with my southern drawl as I was having with his Greek accent. I later learned that his name was John and that he hadn't been in the United States very long. He was beating the English language to death.

I didn't have any idea of landing another job when I went inside, but with that much difference in money, I couldn't refuse his offer. I liked my job at the cigar factory, though. My first thought was to take this part-time job, but what a difference there was between twenty-seven dollars a week and eighty, plus all my meals and those white uniforms.

John waited for my answer, then added another incentive.

"You work seven days a week until more help come. Then I give you one day a week off. Awright?"

"All right."

"What dress size?"

I shrugged. I'd never had a store-bought dress. I didn't have the foggiest idea what size to tell him.

"Never mind," he said. "I have nice white uniform for you when you be back."

By two o'clock that afternoon I was dressed in my white starched uniform, ready to go to work. Waiting tables turned out to be a breeze. There were people to talk to and they seemed to like the service I was giving them. I made twelve dollars and seventy-five cents in tips my very first day. I loved the idea of working seven days a week. It kept me busy so that I didn't have to contend with Mrs. Ellen, who still made me uncomfortable even after a year.

Two weeks later, Stanley came to see me.

He'd heard that I'd changed jobs, though he didn't seem to care one way or another. I wasn't too concerned about what he thought, anyway. I cared about what my mother and father would think. Being on my own, I had to do what was best for me, and what was best for me was to make as much money as I could make.

During Stanley's visit, I asked if he'd help me find another place to live.

"Yeah, sure. I'll see if Agnes will rent you a room."

Agnes, the daughter of the midwife who had delivered ten of my brothers, was now living in Charleston. I had totally forgotten about her. I thought that being with her would be more like living at home. My parents had more or less adopted Agnes after her mother died. When both of my folks, plus eight of my brothers and sisters, came down with typhoid fever during the epidemic in the early nineteen hundreds, it was Mrs. Bradwell, Agnes's mother, who stepped in to take care of everyone. Stanley was just a baby when it happened. Without any medical training, Mrs. Bradwell called on her own experience as a mother and did such an outstanding job that Momma said God had blessed her with the gift of being able to take care of people. My mother also told me that Mrs. Bradwell stayed with them day and night until their fevers had broken. The epidemic was so widespread that the entire community was quarantined, that's how contagious it was. Quite a few neighbors died during the epidemic, but that didn't stop Mrs. Bradwell from doing what she could to save my parents, as well as my brothers and sisters. Tragically, Mrs. Bradwell herself came down with fever and died. In her grief, Mother had remarked that "the Death Angel came and refused to let us keep her".

A week after my asking him to help, Stanley moved me into Agnes's place on America Street. Most of the houses in Charleston were old, but in great shape. Agnes's home was built so that one room was located next to another, much like today's motels. It had a long porch, which allowed me to have a private entrance. When I first saw my room, I exclaimed, "Ah, man, this is great!" Even though Agnes had two young sons, I knew that when I came home from work at two a.m., I could go to my room without disturbing anyone. I was thrilled to have such a nice room with a private bath and a good-size closet. For all this splendor Agnes only charged me ten dollars a week, which was the going price at that time.

A couple of weeks after that, another girl applied for a job in the restaurant. John hired her. With a staff of seven waitresses, it would be possible for each of us to take off one day a week.

My secret passion was still to find some way to enroll in a class of some sort. I was determined to do whatever it took to better my education. Working sixteen hours a day wasn't allowing me enough time to pursue my dream. I kept telling myself that if I worked hard and saved my money, someday I'd be able to take advantage of some sort of education. In the meantime, I would read books every chance I got. It was a twelve-city-block walk home, so between that and the job, plus the reading I was trying to squeeze in, I stayed exhausted most of the time.

One day, I finally reached that magical age of sixteen. Since I'd lied to everyone about my age, they thought it was my twenty-first birthday.

"Evelyn," John said on this grand occasion, "today is your twenty-first birthday. We have only one twenty-first birthday in our entire life, so for you this day, the sky is the limit."

His dark eyes were beaming.

I wasn't sure I heard right.

"I'll see to it that you have the best twenty-first birthday dinner any girl has ever had. I am going to have it prepared especially for you by my chef."

I was so surprised that my reaction bordered more on shock. I'd never had a birthday present and I'd sure never had anyone offer me a sky-is-the-limit dinner. Maybe it was a joke.

"You're teasing me, aren't you?"

"Not on your life. Do you really believe that John would kid a pretty girl on her twenty-first-birthday? Just to prove to you I am not kidding, right now you go back to the kitchen. Give your wishes to my chef. He will take care of it for me."

I should have felt guilt, I suppose, letting these wonderful people think I was turning twenty-one when I was just turning sixteen, but I was too excited to think about it.

The twenty-four years old chef looked like pictures of Greek gods I'd seen in magazines. He was also one of the greatest chefs in the world. Or at least in Charleston. In his broken English, he told me, "You our Queen for this day. I hope you have many more special birthdays. You are more beautiful than any Queen."

The meal he prepared was indeed fit for royalty. Thank you didn't seem adequate for such a wonderful gift. I simply couldn't find words to express my appreciation.

My first Wednesday off was a day I'll never forget. There are times in our life when one incident will change it forever, and this was to be one of those times, though I would hardly have suspected it from its innocent beginning.

I slept until ten a.m. When I finally got up, I did my laundry, tidied up my room, and ran a tub of water. I sprinkled in a bit of bubble bath, then I eased my body down into the fragrant warmth and settled back to enjoy a new book. After about an hour, I got out of the tub, wrapped a towel around my head, then slipped into my floor length housecoat. I felt happy inside. Everything had been going my way for a change. I had a nice room, a good job, I was making money and building up some savings.

The last time I saw Stanley, he told me that he was saving to buy a car. It wouldn't be a new one, of course, but he was going to shop around until he found a good used one that he could afford. Only seconds after getting into my housecoat, I heard a car door slam out in the street near the entrance to my room. I peeked out of the window to see Stanley walking toward the house. Seeing the unfamiliar car parked at the curb made me happy for him; he'd finally gotten himself an automobile. The tomboy that still lived inside me was jumping for joy and I was ready to go out and play.

4

I bolted into the street to check out what I thought was Stanley's new car, a spiffy 1936 Plymouth. "Your car!" I blurted out excitedly to Stanley before I realized that a stranger was sitting behind the wheel. He was a handsome fellow with a beautiful smile that showed even, white teeth. Embarrassed to be on the street in my housecoat and with my hair in a towel, I turned and ran back into my room faster than I had run out. According to the times, a young girl dressed the way I was dressed didn't run headlong into a street on a warm spring afternoon. My church insisted that it was downright unthinkable, even degrading. I sure didn't want to destroy my reputation. It was important that I keep the moral values I had been taught. Lord knows Nanny Eve had taught me better than to do a thing like that. I was eaten up with guilt. God forbid that Stanley would go home and tell my parents that I did such a thing. The Pentecostal Holiness Church dictated most of what women should, or should not, do and even what they should, and should not, wear in our little community.

Stanley followed me back to my room. "Evelyn, if you'd have given me time, I'd have told you it wasn't my car."

"Oh, Stanley, please don't tell Momma or Daddy that I run the streets in my housecoat!" Never mind that the housecoat was down to my toes and had long sleeves with a collar up to my chin.

"Don't worry about it," he replied easily. "I just stopped by to see if you wanted to go with us to the movies tonight."

Before he had the words out of his mouth, I was accepting the invitation. "I'd love to. Who's us?"

I had never been to a movie and even though our religion frowned on it, I was overjoyed. It never crossed my mind at the time, but there was more to a little introduction to the handsome owner of the Plymouth than Stanley was telling me.

"He's a buddy," Stanley explained. "Name's Larry Barkley. Works in the navy yard with me. Since he has his right hand off above the wrist, and I have my left hand off, the yard wanted us to share a pair of welding gloves. Says it saves them a lot of bucks to do it that way." Stanley grinned. "Works out real good."

"Yeah," I said. "I guess it would."

"Well?"

"Well what?"

"You want to go to the movies with us or not?"

"Yes, sure, I'd love to!"

"Great. We'll pick you up about seven. Be ready when we get here."

The excitement of going to the movies for the first time was staggering. When they came back for me, I went out to meet them like the best mannered lady they'd ever met. Stanley got out of the passenger side of the car. He motioned for me to get in between them.

"Larry," he said, once I was settled, "this is my sister, Evelyn. Evelyn, meet my friend and roommate, Larry."

Larry nodded and sort of grunted an acknowledgment. He seemed rude, but I didn't care. I was going to the movies!

We hadn't gone very far when Larry asked my brother, "Is your sister always this quiet?"

"'Fraid not," Stanley chuckled. "In fact, sometimes she gets started and it's hard to get her stopped."

Once inside the theater, I again found myself sandwiched between them. A couple of times during the movie, Larry rested his arm on the back of my seat, being careful to not touch me. After the show was over, we went out for burgers and fries, then they dropped me off at home. It was all harmless enough. All three of us seemed to have had a good night out. I remember thinking how well everything was going. I loved my job. It had taught me to be independent and showed me that I didn't have to depend on anyone else. Also, I was in a position to mingle with people. Mixing with others was an education in itself.

The next day when I got off work at two in the morning, my regular time, I changed from my uniform into my street clothes, put on my favorite pink lipstick, picked up my purse and waved goodbye to the others. Outside, I recognized the 1936 Plymouth that had taken me to the movies the night before. My first thought was, What on earth are Stanley and Larry doing up this late? I knew they had to be at work at the navy yard at seven in the morning.

Larry stepped from his car and motioned to me. When I saw that he was alone I asked about my brother.

"Stanley knows I'm here to pick you up and take you home."

"Are you sure he said it's okay?"

"Sure." I thought he seemed kind of nervous. "Stanley said he needs his sleep, so he stayed home." I wasn't sure I liked what I was hearing, but I'd never argued with anyone older than me and I wasn't sure how to respond. Finally I said, " I don't think my parents would approve."

"Ah, come on now," he pleaded. "Just you come on and get in the car. I promise I'll take you straight home. I don't have any ulterior motives."

I was dead tired on my feet. It was pretty scary that time of night on those dimly lit streets crowded with servicemen from everywhere. Most of them were on their last leave before shipping out to Germany, with no idea if they would make it back alive. Newspaper accounts made it sound like more of them were getting killed in battle than were making it through the war. Everyone's heart was going out to these young people. That made it easy for the men to get the girls to give in to their needs. Sometimes it backfired on them, though, and the girls finagled them into quickie marriages to get their allotment check. Some girls just wound up pregnant. Taking all of that into consideration, I made the decision to get into the car.

He took me straight to my place. I thanked him, went inside and crawled into bed. Even though Larry had been quite the gentleman,

I couldn't shake the feeling that something was not as it should be. He'd treated me like any good brother would treat a sister, so why was I feeling uneasy about this person? Why was that Guardian Angel on my shoulder so uncomfortable?

The next night when I came out from work, Larry was parked in the same exact spot. This made me feel even more uneasy about him for some reason. Looking back, I know that the little voice within me was trying to give me a warning. I pushed the feeling aside and got into the car, just as I'd done the previous night. Again, he took me straight to my room, dropped me off the same as the night before with one exception. "Who was that man you were talking to in the restaurant?" he asked.

I was stunned that he would know or care that I talked to anyone. "Which man?"

"The one I saw you talking to."

"I guess it was a customer. I talk to all of my customers. Why do you ask?"

"Uh ... no reason, just wondered."

"Talking to customers is how I make my tips. If you give them good service with a friendly smile, they appreciate it."

This routine repeated itself night after night. It wasn't that I was ungrateful, because I was more than thankful for the ride home. He was trying to get his point across that his only concern was getting me home safe. I was trying to get my point across that he needed to be rested in order to turn out a good day's work. I'd gotten by for three years before he came along. It didn't make any sense to me that he would place himself, as well as his job, in jeopardy. Why was it so important for him to sit out front of the restaurant hour after hour, watching me? I told him I'd feel terrible if he got fired because of me.

"Don't you worry," he said. "I can't get fired."

"What do you mean?"

"The government has froze us to our jobs."

"How can the government do that?"

I could tell he was getting real upset with me.

"Stop your worrying. Anyway, I sleep in the car while I'm waiting for you."

"Just the same, I'd rather you stay home and get some decent rest."

"All right. If that's the way you're gonna be, I won't come around tomorrow night."

There wasn't another word spoken on the drive home that night.

Next time I got off work, I was surprised, and relieved, to see that his car wasn't parked in the same familiar spot. I looked around to make certain then started walking. I hadn't gone more than a couple hundred yards when I heard footsteps behind me. Someone was walking fast and gaining on me. My heart was pounding so hard that it seemed to be in my mouth. Moments later, a sailor stepped up beside me.

"Hello, beautiful lady," he said. "Can I walk you home?"

I didn't want to be rude, but I didn't know him, or what his intentions might be. "No, thank you."

He repeated, "Can I walk you home?"

"My parents wouldn't approve."

After about fifty or so yards with him walking silently beside me, I stopped and turned to him. "Listen, I just finished working a sixteen-hour shift and I'm tired, so please, mister, I'm not being rude, but I want you to leave." I started walking faster, thinking he might go away. After a couple of minutes, he turned around and walked in the opposite direction. I was grateful he didn't argue with me and that he respected me enough to be on his way.

Just before I got to the entrance to the house, I heard a car. I glanced around, but I didn't see any headlights. A couple of seconds later, I recognized Larry's Plymouth easing along with its lights off. He pulled alongside of me.

"What you doing?" he asked.

I was so upset at seeing him that I had a hard time being civil.

"I'm going inside. What else could I possibly be doing at this hour of the night?"

That was all the conversation we had except for his curt goodbye as he drove away. Much later, he told me that he'd parked up the street so I couldn't see his car when I came out from work. He knew that I was up to something, he confessed. He was certain there was a reason I didn't want him to pick me up after work.

"I knew if I sat there and waited long enough," he would eventually tell me, "I'd find out what you were up to. I had to see for myself why you didn't want me taking you home. I found out okay when you met up with your sailor."

I was shocked. "I wasn't up to anything except wanting you to get your rest so you could put in a good day's work. I haven't got the foggiest idea who that sailor was. Evidently he saw me walking alone and wanted to walk me home."

"What'd you tell him?"

"I told him that my parents wouldn't approve. When he understood that I wasn't going to let him walk me home, he left. You said you followed me so you must have seen for yourself what happened. For Pete's sake, what reason would I have to lie to you?"

Larry had never actually asked me for a date, but evidently he took it for granted that, since he was going out of his way to pick me up, he had some sort of ownership over me. The scarey part was his persistence. I began to resent him. What right did he have to question me? He was forcing me to let him pick me up when I didn't want him to. There didn't seem to be any way I could stop him from coming around night after night. It was as if the only thing that mattered to him was to sit outside that restaurant and watch me work. Then he would take me home and drop me off. There wasn't even any conversation. He was the quietest, strangest person I'd ever known. Had I been older, or if I'd had even one person to instruct me along these lines, I would have coped better, I'm sure. I'd never had anyone I could turn to for advice.

All during this time my inner feelings were trying to warn me that something wasn't right. I didn't have the experience to handle it. What few words Larry did say, he used to his advantage. He was right in thinking that it was dangerous for a sixteen year-old girl to walk home alone on those dimly lit streets in the wee hours of the morning. I didn't know then that he was only using that line as a ploy to get me to yield to his way of thinking. Having grown up with a brother who had only one hand, I knew it couldn't have been easy for Larry to have reached the goals he'd reached. After I got to know him better, he told me something of the battle he fought after getting his hand shot off. This made me sensitive to his experience. If the war hadn't been going on, neither he nor Stanley would be working in the navy yard. I didn't want it on my conscience that I cost him his job. I was getting more and more confused. I couldn't make any sense out of the way he was behaving. None of my brothers had acted that way. My father hadn't acted that way.

One night he asked me what one thing I wanted most in the world. It didn't take a lot of thought to come up with the answer.

"It would be nice to go visit my parents."

"Then why don't you go?"

"The hours that I work? I don't know when that could ever happen. I even work Sundays, you know that."

Since the navy yard operated around the clock, twenty-four hours a day, Stanley was pretty much working as many hours as I was, and I rarely got to see him anymore. That made it even harder for me to understand how Larry got so much time off. He seemed to be free every weekend, which was odd since Stanley was putting in seven-day weeks.

I may have only been sixteen with a seventh-grade education, but the arithmetic didn't add up.

Two weeks later I got a day off. I heard an unexpected knock on my door at eight o'clock in the morning, interrupting my plan to sleep until at least noon. When I opened the door, Larry was standing there, flashing his pearly whites. I couldn't believe what I was seeing. How could I possibly make this man understand that it would be best for both of us if he would just go away? I was so tired of his pressing questions, which seemed to always end with more nagging about the unknown sailor who almost walked me home. Seeing Larry on my doorstep, I must have shown the disgust that I was feeling.

"Aren't you supposed to be at work?" I asked, trying not to yawn.

"I came to take you to see your parents. You did say that you want to go see them, didn't you?"

That was a matter of a different color. The little immature girl in me took over. I had been homesick for so long. My heart leaped with joy at the thought of being able to see my parents, but something in me turned suspicious. "Don't tell me you stayed out of work to take me to Shulerville?"

He just stood there smiling. "It don't matter why I'm not working. All that matters is do you or don't you want to go to see your folks, like you told me you wanted to? If you do, then get yourself ready and let's go."

Regardless of why he was missing work, the truth was he wasn't going to work anyway, so why not take advantage of getting to see my parents? I began rushing around getting dressed. The thought of going home blocked every other thought out of my mind. I didn't stop to question myself about how my parents would respond to my showing up with a strange young man they had never seen before. It was unheard of for a sixteen-year-old not to have a chaperon when in the company of a male, but my situation was a bit different from most girls'. I had a job and I was living an independent lifestyle. My parents were strict, but I had never known them to be unreasonable.

I got dressed as quickly as I could and soon we were in the car, making our way down Lee Street and across the Cooper River Bridge. Past that point, there wasn't much to see except the countryside. I settled back and listened to the hum of the motor. I was enjoying the trip when, out of the blue, Larry said, "So, you didn't know who that sailor was, huh?"

I sighed a long, weary sigh. I was sick of the question.

"No, Larry, I didn't know who he was. I never saw him before or since."

"Why would you talk to him if you didn't know him?"

"Oh, for heaven's sake, why can't you put it to rest? The only thing I could, and did, tell him was to go away."

"Why'd he want to walk you home in the first place?"

"Dear God in Heaven, Larry, what's wrong with you? I don't know. I suppose the same reason you want to drive me home every night."

"Just what the hell do you mean by that remark?"

"Let me put it this way. You told me the only reason you keep picking me up after work is to get me home safe. So maybe, just maybe, that's what he also had on his mind. Not to be rude, but quite honestly I don't have the foggiest notion what he wanted. I was too tired to really care. All I had on my mind was to get home, get a bath, and go to bed." That's what I said, but what I was thinking was, *Lord, show mercy on all of us. Enough is enough.*

He was getting on my nerves. I'd learned that when he was irritated, or starting to lose his temper, he'd clear his throat. That's what he was doing now, meaning that he didn't like my answer. His face was getting red, another sure sign he was ticked off. I didn't have a glimmer of what kind of mountain he wanted to make out of such a small molehill. I couldn't see that I had done anything wrong.

I laid my head back against the car seat and drifted off to sleep. I don't know how much time went by before he nudged me. "Hey, you better wake up. We're almost there."

I sat up straight and looked around. Sure enough, he was making a left at the place that had once been my school bus stop. It brought back such memories. The mere sight of our old house with its imitation brick siding, set my heart to pounding with excitement. I couldn't wait to put my arms around Momma and Daddy. Larry had hardly come to a stop when I threw open the car door and leaped out. I was a little kid again, running for the house. Momma came to the door. I gave her a big hug before Larry had a chance to catch up with me.

I was amazed to hear Mother say, "Hello, Larry. How you been? Good to see you again." Then she turned to me. "What in the world have you done with your manners? That was very rude for you to run off and leave Larry behind. I thought I taught you better than that."

Daddy gave me a great big hug, then he shook hands with Larry. After that, they went about doing some small talk, leaving me to wonder how well they knew this young man. I thought he was coming to my parents' home for the first time. Finally, my father said, "Come on Larry. Let's go in the living room where we can be more comfortable."

Mother and I were alone in the kitchen. From where I was standing, I could see Larry reach up on the mantle over the fireplace to pick up a framed picture of me. Evidently Mother had seen him too, because she got a funny little look on her face and said, "Just as I thought."

"What did you think, Mother?"

"I thought Larry would be back."

"What do you mean? Are you saying that he's been here before?"

"Not more than three weeks ago. It was on a Sunday. Stannie finally got a day off from the navy yard, so Larry brought him to spend a few hours with us." She smiled and nodded toward Larry in the other room. "He sure took a good look at your picture when he was here that day."

I couldn't help but notice how Momma looked like the cat that swallowed the canary. She was a romanticist at heart and now that I had reached the magical age of sixteen, she was putting two and two together, realizing that Larry wasn't our blood kin. I was thinking *so that's why Larry and Stanley showed up so mysteriously that Wednesday with their invitation to the movies*. Knowing what I know now, the movie had been Larry's way of manipulating my brother to get to meet me. I was too naive to see that he was a wolf in sheep's clothing. Larry had gotten me so upset on the drive there, making a big deal about the sailor, it hadn't registered that he never asked me for directions. It was nice spending a few hours with my parents. Then the time came to get back to Charleston.

"Momma," I said, then turned to my father, "Daddy, it's been wonderful to see you. I've missed you so much." I didn't want to leave. "It's getting late, though. I have to get to work early in the morning, so we'd better get started back."

Mother gave me a long look before she responded. "Do you really have to leave so soon?"

"Well, Momma, today's my day off. It's the only time I have to do my laundry."

It was already five o'clock. The most speed that cars could reach in those days was about twenty-five or thirty miles an hour, and that's if you were driving fast. We were looking at a two-hour trip back to Charleston. After tearful goodbyes, we left.

5

We made fairly good time until we got within two miles of the Cooper River Bridge. That's when I heard Larry say, as if talking to himself, "I hope that right back tire holds up."

Larry had seemingly had a mood swing and was trying to be funny. My gut feeling was that he wanted to get a rise out of me by saying a thing like that.

"You're kidding, right?"

"No, no. I kinda wish I was."

We couldn't have gone more than three hundred yards after that when the right back tire blew. It sounded like a shotgun blast. After I got over my scare, I took a deep breath.

"Now isn't that great?" I said, disgusted. "That's just peachy dandy!"

"It's not too far on to the general store. I think we can make it that far on the rim."

"It's sure a good thing it happened before we got middle ways on the bridge," I remarked.

Cooper River Bridge was something like two miles long, a toll road that was unforgiving. If you had a car problem on it, you were up the creek without a paddle. The general store Larry mentioned was just this side of it, but I knew that at this hour of the night it would be closed, so I didn't see what good it would do to get there. Then I thought of a new problem.

" Do you have any tools to change a tire?"

"Tools? What good's tools when I don't have a spare?"

This was much, much more than I was able to comprehend. Why would anyone in his right mind attempt to go across Cooper River Bridge knowing he had a bad tire? What's worse, knowing he didn't even have a spare tire or tools to change a flat. I counted to ten under my breath before I said, "Pray tell me, just what are we going to do now?" I was losing patience and losing it fast.

"I was waiting for payday to buy a new tire."

"Oh my Lord. You must be insane to come this distance on a bad tire."

"Okay," he said. "What do you suggest we do?"

"I haven't got a clue."

"I guess maybe I could flag a car down. Maybe somebody'll take me across the bridge to someplace I can get a tire."

"What about money?" I only had a couple of dollars with me and he'd said he was waiting for payday.

" I've got enough to buy a tire."

We made it to the general store, but just as I thought, it was dark and there was no one around. Larry parked about midway down the long driveway, then he just sat there. I didn't want to upset him further and had no hankering to make matters worse. What I didn't understand was why he didn't try flagging down a motorist.

Also, I was seething because he hadn't told me about his visit to my parents' house. Here he questioned me about talking to a sailor I didn't know, but who gave me no problem, and yet Larry was keeping a secret from me about meeting Momma and Daddy. The more I thought about it, the madder I got. At the same time, I realized this wasn't the right time to start an argument. He was so strange, so different from anyone I'd ever known when he got upset. He would clam up, get very quiet. He was never irrational when he questioned me. He spoke in a slow, quiet, monotone. Underneath, I could sense a burning inferno of fury within him. My feeling was that he was trying to keep that fury smothered by being soft spoken.

I just had to say, "Why don't you try to stop a car to take you across the bridge so you can get another tire?"

"Nope. I'm not in that big a hurry to get home."

"How can you say such a thing? You know you're supposed to be at work at seven in the morning."

"What's your worry? You don't have to be anywhere 'till ten."

"What's that got to do with the price of eggs?"

He started in with that peculiar throat clearing thing he did when he was on the verge of anger. "We're gonna spend the night here in the car. Everything's gonna be all right."

"You're out of your cotton-picking mind. I want to go home."

Instead of getting mad, once again he laughed. I wanted him to flag down a car and get across the Cooper River Bridge to find another tire. In those days, people were very accommodating. It was possible that the first car he hailed would stop to pick him up and help us out.

"What if my parents find out I spent the night with you in this car? I don't even want to think about what Daddy might do."

"Now how's anybody going to find out unless you take it upon yourself to tell them? Oh, come on, Evelyn. Nothing's going to happen to you, I'm going to see to that. I promise nobody's going to hurt you."

I'm thinking that the somebody I was worried about was him.

"Larry, you know how people look down on situations like this. Will you please think about what you're doing?"

"What do you mean situations like this? The only situation that we have here is a tire that's blown out. That's the only situation I know about."

"Well, I don't know how it is where you come from, but my father told me once that my reputation would go farther than I ever would. If it gets back to Shulerville that I spent the night in a car with a man, I'll be branded for the rest of my life."

"Will you shut your mouth and settle down. "

It didn't make any sense whatsoever that he wouldn't at least try to find a way to get us across that bridge so we could get to work the next morning. I knew he wasn't going to try to molest me. My feeling was that since he hadn't even tried to kiss me, he certainly wouldn't try anything else. I knew that, but those passing by didn't know it. My reputation was at stake.

When he realized how anxious I was, it seemed to trigger in him a challenge that he could make me do what he told me to do.

"I tell you what," he said at last. "How about you crawl over there in that back seat and try to get yourself some sleep? I never have figured out how you manage to put in all those hours."

I shrugged. "I love my job. Anyway, it's work that makes the world go 'round. It sure has kept a roof over my head these past three years, without any help from anybody else."

He had me where he wanted me. There wasn't anything I could have said or done to make one iota of difference to him. I was tired. I was scared of him. Reluctantly, I climbed into the back seat and stretched out as best I could.

"How do you think you're going to get across the bridge in the morning?" I asked, yawning.

"I'll think of something."

Every instinct told me that if I antagonized this short-fused man, it would be inviting more trouble than I'd be able to handle.

"When you do get someone to take you across the bridge, can I go with you?"

"I'm just going to get a tire. I'll be right back. Now how about you stop your damn worrying? Try to get some sleep."

"I don't mean to be a pest, but my street's on the other side of the bridge. If I went with you, I wouldn't have to wait or come back here. I could just go on home."

"I know you could do that, but I don't want you to. It's too far for you to walk. Don't forget, I promised I wouldn't let anything happen to you."

I was beginning to feel woozy, then I realized we hadn't had anything to eat. Worse yet, we wouldn't get anything to eat until God sent a miracle to get us back across that Cooper River Bridge.

"The general store'll open at six. We'll get help then."

Larry had won his battle.

I turned and twisted until I finally drifted off to sleep. From time to time a car would come by and blow its horn, jolting me awake. Just as I would start to drift off again, another car would toot in passing, no doubt people thinking we were parked to make out. It was around three o'clock in the morning before traffic quieted down. At six-fifteen we awoke to the sound of a car pulling in the driveway next to us. We sat up at the same time. It turned out to be the couple who owned the general store.

A lady got out and glanced in my direction, then she went to the front door, unlocked it and proceeded to go inside. The man with her came over to us. He looked Larry up and down.

"How you doing, young man?" He leaned back to look at the busted tire. "Looks like you got a serious problem."

"Yes, Sir, sure do." Larry got out of the car. He rested the elbow of his artificial arm on the window frame.

The man nodded toward me. "This your wife?" All the time he was talking, he never took his eyes off the hook that replaced Larry's hand.

"No, sir. This here's my girlfriend."

That was my first time to hear anything about me being a girlfriend.

"I took her over to Shulerville yesterday to see her parents. She works all the time, hadn't got to go home to see them for quite awhile." He nodded toward the road. "Back there, my tire blew. I managed to make it this far on the rim."

"That was pretty decent of you to take her to see her folks."

The man scratched his head as if searching for something more to say. I'm sure he was concerned about us being there overnight, so close to his business and me being so young.

Finally, he had another question for Larry. "Where you from, Mister?"

"Walhalla, South Carolina." Larry looked sort of embarrassed, then held out his good hand. "Sorry. I should have introduced myself. I'm Larry. This is my girlfriend like I told you. Evelyn here's from Shulerville."

The man said to Larry, "You work around here?"

"Over at the navy yard in Charleston. Electric welder. Evelyn waitresses downtown on King Street. Sure looks like I missed work again today, but Evelyn might be able to make it on time, that is, if I can get another tire to get us over the bridge."

The gentleman gestured toward the hand hook. "You say you do electric welding with that thing?"

"Yes, sir, I do. Vocational Rehabilitation sent me to school. When I finished my six weeks, they got me the job at the navy yard. It's been rough working so many long hours." With that, he changed the subject. "Sir, you wouldn't happen to have a tire of some kind around here that'll fit this old Plymouth, would you?" The man was slow in answering, so Larry continued, "Just anything that'll get me across the Cooper River Bridge to where I can buy a new one."

From his expression I could tell the proprietor was having trouble making up his mind. He didn't know how to go about dealing with this problem of ours. Then, in a slow southern drawl, he said, "Let me go check to see. Sometimes I find things around here I don't remember having. I need to let my wife know that everything's all right out here."

He left and went in the store. It wasn't long until I saw him checking out some old tires in back. Pretty soon he returned empty-handed. "There's nothing here that'll work, I'm afraid." He glanced again at Larry's artificial arm. "Looks like you been in some sort of accident. That didn't happen in the war, did it?"

"Oh, no, no, sir, it didn't. I wanted to go in the army. They wouldn't take me on account of this, but they sure enough got my two brothers. No, sir, I got this in a hunting accident one day while me and my best friend was out rabbit hunting." Seeing he had a fascinated audience in the gentleman proprietor, Larry began to elaborate. " We came to this small stream of water. Well, I jumped across the creek first, then I reached back when my buddy handed me the gun, barrel first. I started pulling it towards me when some kind of a vine caught the trigger. The gun discharged and shot my hand right off. Vocational Rehabilitation fixed me up with this here artificial arm. Without it I'm pretty much helpless."

"I just can't understand how you can do electric welding with a gadget like that."

They both laughed.

"Yeah," Larry said, "but it sure does work."

I nudged him. "The tire, remember the tire."

"Well, Mister, my girlfriend here's getting impatient with me. All she ever thinks about is work, work, work. Do you think you might be able to run me across the bridge to get a tire and bring me back?"

The man thought a few seconds. "I just might have time to do that since the store don't usually get too busy this early. Let me see if my wife thinks she can handle things by herself." He went back inside. In a couple of minutes he came out and went to a new Ford station wagon in the driveway. He got in and pulled up alongside us.

Larry told me to stay with the Plymouth until he got back. Then he got in the man's car and they drove away.

I was thinking, *Good Lord, that conversation was the most talk I've heard him engage in since I met him.*

They were gone only long enough for me to get rested a bit, then they came back with a tire. Fifteen minutes later we were across the bridge. When he stopped at the curb in front of my rooming house, I quickly got out. Before I could even get to my door, Larry caught up with me.

"Hey, hey you. What's the big rush? I don't see any fire anywhere, do you?"

"I want to hurry and get my bath so I can get to work."

"Ahh, come on now; why would you want to do a thing like that?"

I was losing my patience with him.

"If you don't understand," I said, as if speaking to a child, "then I'll tell you. My boss won't put up with people staying out of work. If I don't work, I won't have a place to live."

I watched him transform in front of my eyes. His eyes were pleading. His voice was that of a young boy, not a twenty-two-year-old man.

"Evelyn, please, they won't fire you for missing one day. There's too big a shortage of workers. Besides, if they do fire you, there are plenty of other jobs you can get. You can get a job anywhere, as conscientious as you are."

"I don't want another job. I want to keep the one I've got."

I opened the door and started in, but he went ahead of me. I was stunned. This was a definite no-no, it was an unthinkable thing for a man to do. He wasn't showing any respect for me. Today nobody thinks twice about a situation like this, but in 1943 it was quite a different story.

The angel on my shoulder was getting restless. I had a gut feeling that something was just not right with Larry.

"Look," I said, as reasonably as I could manage. "I really do appreciate you taking me to Shulerville, but if Agnes finds out I have a man in my room, she'll make me move."

I was tired. He was pushy. I began feeling disgust and I knew it was showing. Suddenly, he snapped, "Just what the hell is it with you?"

I stood looking into fiery dark eyes as he lifted his artificial arm up and down.

"Are you acting this way 'cause I have to wear this?"

"Oh, come on now, Larry. Don't you think you're being ridiculous? You know better than a thing like that. I grew up with Stanley having one arm, remember?"

"Well then, what is it? You just want to get rid of me?" He stared at me with a hard look in his eyes. " I'm right, aren't I? And I'm not wrong about that damn sailor you're so crazy about either, am I? That's it, isn't it? You can't wait to get back to work so you can see him. Or could it be that damned bald headed boss of yours? What the hell's your problem?"

That was it. "Just leave so I can get ready for work."

"Evelyn, if you're so upset about one day's work, then what the hell do you think about me? I've missed two days just to take you to see your folks."

"Just you wait a cotton-picking minute, Larry. If you've missed two days of work, that's your own fault. I never asked you to take me anywhere in the first place. I would never ask anyone to leave their job for something like that. Don't you even try to put that kind of a guilt trip on me." I was so tired of arguing with him. "I'm real grateful you were kind enough to take me, but you were wrong to stay out of work, especially as much as the Navy needs you on the job. Aren't you afraid you're going to get in trouble? I certainly would be if I was in your place."

"Like I told you, they have us froze to our job."

"You don't look very froze to me. Putting a freeze on your job doesn't mean you can work when you want to and stay out whenever you get ready."

With fire in his eyes, he leaned close. "Freeze or no freeze, they can't make me do a damn thing I don't want to do. If I don't want to do it, then dammit, nobody's going to make me do it."

With that he left, slamming the door behind him.

I was much too upset to make a mad rush to get to work. Chances were my boss lucked out and found someone to work in my place, anyway. So, now what should I do, I wondered? I gave in and did exactly what Larry had done and that I had criticized so harshly; I took the rest of the day off. Then I took all of my frustrations out on the rub board in the bathtub, doing my laundry. Momma and Daddy always preached, "If you lay with dogs, you're destined to get fleas." Larry confused me. I'd never been treated like he treated me and I didn't know what to make of it. I felt that something had to be wrong with me, not him. What had happened, and I wouldn't realize this for a very long time, I had let him weaken me to the point I succumbed to his tactics.

I thought I'd probably never hear from him again and I fervently wished that he would just disappear. I never wanted to see him again. My big fear was that I would lose my job. I knew that my boss, John, was upset with me, I just knew it. I prayed he wouldn't fire me. I vowed to myself that if it came down to it, I wasn't too proud to beg. With that in mind, I was at work the next morning at nine-thirty sharp. I explained to my unhappy boss the best that I could about the flat tire, but it didn't even sound believable to me.

"Yah, yah," he said in his thick Greek accent. "Now I've heard 'em all."

"John, please believe me. As crazy as it sounds, it's the truth."

All he said then was, "Don't let it happen again."

I promised it wouldn't, and I meant it.

6

That night when I got off work, I looked around to see if the Plymouth was in its familiar spot across the street. It wasn't. I thought, *Great. Maybe I've finally gotten him to understand that his job should come ahead of flirting with me.* I didn't see him again until the following Saturday, or actually Sunday, since it was after two in the morning. Just as I stepped out of the restaurant to go home, I saw him standing in the street next to his car, motioning to me. As I approached, he said, "You sure do look tired."

"It's been a hard sixteen-hour shift. Saturdays are always busy, all day long."

In a sweet, gentle voice he said, "Come on. Get in the car. Let me take you home. You look to me like you need all the rest you can get."

Driving to my place, he told me that he'd gotten a letter from his mother saying that she needed him to come home for a visit. He was going to see if his boss would let him off to go the last weekend in May. By this time we were in front of my rooming house. I got out and was walking away when he called after me, "See you later." Even though he'd been nice, and our conversation was just a normal conversation, I was coming to realize that he was possessed by the thought of me. I don't mean to sound conceited, but it was looking like a plain and simple fact. I was still that naive child when it came to this kind of situation. I was taught to give my work my all, that I could handle whatever was required of me. And that's the way it had been–at least until now. Around this twenty-two year old man I was lost for an answer or even a way to stand up to him.

The next night he was there, waiting again, and every night after that. It was the second Saturday in May, when he asked if I'd go to Walhalla with him, to see his parents. He took me completely by surprise.

"The offer sounds nice, but you know how I feel about time off, Larry."

"Evelyn, you can't keep on working yourself to death the way you've been doing."

I was reminded of something Momma used to tell me: "The devil never sleeps. He is always there to tempt us."

"Larry," I said, with all the patience I could muster, "we never have enough help the way things are. We're lucky to get even one day a week off. How can I make you understand that?"

Then, in his most charming, teasing way, he said, "I'm quite sure the restaurant won't go out of business if you don't show up for a couple of days."

The very thought of taking a long trip like that appealed to me, especially since I'd never been anywhere except to Charleston. I was so tempted. I really was tired most of the time. I told myself that I'd been working sixteen-hour shifts for more than two years now. *Shouldn't I be entitled to take a trip every once in awhile like everyone else?*, I reasoned with myself.

"What if I ask my boss for the time off and he says no?"

He flashed his pearly whites. "How could you ever know the answer to that if you don't ask?"

I didn't respond right away.

"Where is this Walhalla?" I finally asked.

"Well, it's in the upper part of South Carolina, not far from the Blue Ridge Mountains, in the foothills, actually. I can tell you this, there's nothing like it in Charleston. It's a little over three hundred miles." Then he started painting beautiful word pictures. "This time of year the wild flowers are in bloom. In the middle of October, the leaves, as you ride across the North Carolina mountains, are every color in the rainbow. I want to take you there at that time of the year.

Evelyn, you'd just love it, I know you would. I don't think there's any other place like it. There just aren't words for me to express to you how beautiful, how breathtaking, the mountains are when the leaves are in full color."

Just as the devil himself tempted Jesus, Larry was tempting me.

I got home, took a bath and went to sleep. I dreamed of being in those beautiful mountains. Never to have seen mountains, or even a picture of mountains, everything I dreamed was fuzzy and muddled, except for the lovely flowers surrounding me. There were acres and acres of gorgeous flowers in blossom. In my dream, I became a princess surrounded by wild flowers. The next few nights, as the dreams continued, I would find myself among wild azaleas. I was always surrounded by God's breathtaking beauty. I would awaken in the mornings still feeling the beauty of what I dreamed about, but there was a kind of sadness that followed. I had trouble shaking the feeling. Hindsight is twenty-twenty. I know now it was a whisper from the Guardian Angel on my shoulder that Nanny Eve told me about. Nevertheless, in the end I agreed to ask my boss for the weekend off.

Here's how I deluded myself into believing I had my reasons for such a decision: Larry had never tried to kiss or to seduce me, so it wasn't like I would be going off with a sex maniac. The memory of the dream where I was a princess was exciting. Everybody loves princesses. In one particular dream, I realized what it must be like to know real happiness. Then I remembered another dream of wanting to go to school, but not getting the opportunity. The sadness that I felt was tremendous. I'd always felt alone, not only did I feel alone, I felt as if I were invisible. During that era, elders believed that if you hugged or petted children it would spoil them. Most everyone's attention was on how to have enough nourishment to stay alive. Those years, if you didn't grow food, you didn't eat. Our survival depended on the products of the land. No one had any real farm equipment. My father and my grandfather owned plow mules for the most part.

So many times during my life, when things seemed to be more than I could handle, I've let my mind flash back to those tender years. They were, and are, my safety blanket. Those were the happiest of times because there was so much love. Those working the fields would sing and chant tunes and when they did, my little heart would sing with them. As a child, I wanted to be in the middle of it. I asked myself how it was possible that despite all of the love around me, I still felt so alone and so isolated. I didn't understand it then, but I do now. As I look back, I think about how imperative it was that everyone did all they could to work the farm to its fullest potential. Momma used to say it was how we kept the wolf from the door.

Now that I was working and living on my own, without seeing my family for months at a time, I came to feel a great sense of independence, and yet my mind was going in circles. All at once I wasn't clear about what was right or wrong, good or bad. I was being sorely tempted. I wanted to go on the trip with Larry. Then, on the other side of the coin, I also knew that I needed to stay home and work. I remembered what he'd put me through when the tire had blown out.

I wasn't immune to the fact that he had a marvelous smile and was handsome enough to charm a rattlesnake. When I later met his father, I realized that Larry came by that charm naturally. Women were drawn to them even though they were both a bit cocky at times, more so when there were females around.

I truly battled with the devil, weighing all of the pros and con's. And I let the devil win. I ended up paying the price–for the rest of my life.

I was seeing less and less of my brother Stanley. It was as if he had turned me over to Larry to see after me. Nevertheless, I told Larry that we'd have to get my brother's permission before I could give him a definite answer. It was also a cop-out on my part. I was too weak to resist the trip, but I felt sure that Stanley would have no trouble saying no.

That night when Larry came to pick me up, he was in a very jolly mood. "Guess what?" he said.

"What?"

"I talked with Stanley last night. He said it'd be all right for you to go with me to meet my parents."

I was shocked.

"Are you sure? Now, Larry, don't you tell me that unless Stanley really said it."

"Yep, he said it. Even told me to tell you to have a good time."

Had I stopped to take that one remark into consideration, I would have known that he wasn't telling me the truth. Stanley would have never told him that.

He looked me straight in the eye. "Evelyn, one thing you're going to learn about me is that I'm not a liar."

The angel on my shoulder evidently had gotten tired of my indecision and had moved aside to let the devil take over. He had placed candy in front of the baby. The baby had slowly but surely taken the bait, even though a warning was screaming in my brain: "DON'T GO!" Another voice was talking inside my head. It was asking about the seven-year age difference between Larry and myself. I could hear what Momma once said about the difference in age between her and Daddy: "It's better to be an old man's darling than a young man's slave."

The next time Larry picked me up after work, he said his boss had given him time off to make the trip. That was on a Tuesday night. He had plans to leave the following Thursday. My boss had told me already that I could take time off as well, but with the nagging feeling in my gut, I wasn't ready to tell Larry. I got ready real fast when he finally exploded.

"What the hell kind of hold has John got over you to make you afraid to ask him to let you take a day or two off?"

This got a rise out of me. "Oh, for heaven's sake, the man has a business to operate. The reason he hired me in the first place was that he needed help. But," I took a deep breath before I said it, "I asked and he said I could go." Larry knew how to scare me into telling him anything he wanted to hear. For some reason, he could put fear in me like no other human had ever done.

He calmed down immediately. "Then we'll be leaving when you get off on Thursday night."

"I'd rather go in the daylight. I've never been on a three-hundred-mile trip before. It'd be nice to see what the country looks like."

When time came for us to go, Larry picked me up at the rooming house. I closed my weekend bag and handed it to him, then we were on our way. Every time I got in his car I would sit as close to the passenger door as possible. Larry looked at me and smiled. He was happy. He felt he had all the control over me that he wanted.

We had gone a couple of miles when he said, "Why the worried look?"

"I don't know. I just have a feeling that something's not right."

"I bought new tires so you don't have to worry about a blow out."

"Are you going to be on your best behavior?"

He laughed. "I guess, something like that."

By ten o'clock that morning we were approaching Columbia, the capital of South Carolina. I began to notice the beauty of the rolling hills. All I knew about before was the flat, sandy swamps around Shulerville. As close as I'd always been to the ocean, I'd never seen it. I was all eyes, taking in everything.

"If you think this is pretty, " Larry said, "just you wait; you ain't seen nothing yet. When we get closer to the mountains, you'll see what I mean."

I couldn't even imagine what mountains could possibly look like. Larry was watching my every move the way you watch a child on Christmas morning. He was getting a real kick out of my "Oooohs" and "Ahhhhhs."

During the drive he talked some about his mother and his baby sister, Laura Mae. He mentioned having an aged grandmother who came to stay with them from time to time. He also told me that he had dated his sister-in-law, Edith, before she married his older brother, Albert. Then there would be long periods when he would just sit quietly, watching the road.

It was nine hours later when we pulled into his parents' driveway. By the time the car came to a complete stop, his mother and fourteen-year-old Laura Mae were running out to greet us.

"We've been waiting for you two to get here," Mrs. Barkley exclaimed, smiling brightly.

Suddenly I felt cheap and degraded having come so far from home, not married to the person beside me, not that I ever would want to be married to him. I had committed the unpardonable sin of traveling with him, not being his wife. A sixteen-year-old girl going across the country with a man seven years older was unforgivable.

Mrs. Barkley said to Larry, "I just got your letter yesterday telling us that you were bringing Evelyn."

So, this was one of his reasons for being so determined to have me go with him; he'd already told his momma that I was coming along. My mind was racing. I didn't even know it myself when he wrote the letter. How could he have possibly known when he wrote it? Back then it took a letter four days to go from Charleston to Walhalla. He would had to have mailed it the previous Monday. I made up my mind right then, that as soon as I got myself back to Charleston, he'd have to go his way and I'd go mine. He had managed to take all the joy out of the trip for me.

About then his father came out to meet us. Mr. Barkley was more reserved than his wife. He was a small man in stature, measuring five foot six or eight inches in height and weighing about a hundred and forty pounds. His skin was beautifully tanned, no doubt due to the hours he spent farming in the sun. He had remarkably piercing black eyes. When he looked at me, he made me feel he had completely undressed me. He had the smile of a snake charmer, the same pearly white teeth as his son. I later learned that he was a share cropper farmer. That meant that, unlike my father and my grandfather, Mr. Barkley didn't own his farm. At harvest time, the landlord got a share of the crop for rent. Although Larry's daddy was extra nice on the surface, I began to get bad vibes about him. There was often a cold strangeness about him, while other times he was warm and friendly.

I thought my parents' home was primitive, but the Barkley's lived in an old, run-down farmhouse. Mrs. Barkley had tried to make it homey with what she had to do with. The living room had a bed with two wooden rocking chairs and a fireplace. The floor consisted of eight-inch-wide boards that appeared to have had the rough part smoothed off from where the wood was originally sawed at the mill.

There was only one bedroom with two full-size beds. An old-time organ went up almost to the ceiling, but I never knew the brand name. The kitchen-dining room was about twelve feet wide and at least twenty-six feet long. The homemade eating table had a beautiful tablecloth spread over it, just as all three beds were covered with lovely hand-crocheted bedspreads. Under each bedspread, I soon learned, was a bright-colored sheet. They had gone out of their way to make the house look as good as they possibly could for me. Later, the women brought out a few more of their sewing creations. Each garment was breathtakingly beautiful. It was evident that many hours of hard work had gone into the fine thread used to create those masterpieces.

By now it was late afternoon. The sun had already gone behind the mountain range in the distance. Soon it would be dark. While it wasn't cold, there was a definite chilling sting in the air. Mr. Barkley started a fire in the wood cook stove, then he went into the living room to get a fire going in the fireplace.

As Mrs. Barkley tied an apron around her waist, she said, "Evelyn, I got a big, old, home-cured ham I've been saving for just such an occasion as this."

She got out a dough tray and made a huge pan of homemade biscuits. She cooked large, lean slices of home-cured ham and the red-eye gravy that always goes with it. On the table was a great display of homemade butter with several different kinds of homemade preserves and jellies. She also scrambled up a batch of eggs. What more can I say other than that woman could cook! It had been so long since I'd had that kind of good country cooking, I pigged out.

After we got through eating, then washing and putting the dishes away, I went into the living room. I put on my jacket to go out and sit on the porch. A full moon was just rising. It seemed to beam its light over everything. The Blue Ridge Mountains in the distance looked as though they surrounded the whole countryside. There was a swing on the front porch along with several wooden rockers and some straight, cane-bottom chairs. In the front yard were two large chinaberry trees draped in all the splendor of the beautiful moonlight.

I heard the screen door open then close behind me. Turning to look, I found that everyone had decided to join me. Larry went over and sat down on the swing. After standing there in awe of the beautiful mountain ridge, I looked around for some place to sit.

"Evelyn," Larry said, " why don't you come over and sit by me, that is, if you're not too scared."

I reluctantly sat on the swing next to him. He put his arm up on the back of it. After a few minutes, he let his arm slowly fall across my back, then around my shoulders. I wiggled around, indicating he should move his arm, without drawing everyone's attention. He chuckled to himself before moving away.

The chinaberry trees appeared to glow as if silver dust had been sprinkled over them. They stood glistening in the moonlight. Their shadows threw off silvery beams. It was a perfect night for lovers. Only thing was, there weren't any lovers. I never once considered Larry a boyfriend. As I looked out across the miles of mountain range, there weren't enough words for me to express my feelings for the beauty I saw there. I never dreamed that I could, or would, ever be fortunate enough to experience anything so devastatingly gorgeous.

Then Mr. Barkley asked, "Larry, when did you and Evelyn get married? You didn't say in your letter."

I froze. I didn't say a thing.

Larry let out a bit of stifled laughter, but he didn't answer his father.

Finally I said, "We didn't."

Mr. Barkley frowned, not understanding. "You didn't what?"

"We didn't get married," I said. I thought, *My Lord, why is he asking such a question?* The very thought of getting married to this man sent a cold shiver over my body.

Mrs. Barkley chimed in, "How about it, Larry? The truth."

"Talk to Evelyn. She's doing the talking. Ask her." The fact that Larry was laughing, and the way he was acting, was leading them to believe we were married.

The cool air soon drove us back inside around the fireplace until time to turn in. Mrs. Barkley busied herself turning down the covers, getting all the beds ready for everyone. "Larry," she said, 'you and Evelyn can sleep in here by the fireplace."

Larry burst out laughing about as loud as I had ever heard him laugh.

My nervousness showed in my voice.

"Mrs. Barkley, we are not married. I'm not sleeping with him."

I could see the shocked look on her face, as if I'd slapped her. She couldn't believe we weren't married. You take a long trip with a man, you were supposed to be married to him. I was embarrassed. I felt much worse than these people felt for me. I had to be out of my mind to let Larry coerce me into doing a thing like we were doing. Had one of my brothers brought a girl from out of town home with him, they would have gotten thrown out on their ear by my parents. Momma and Daddy upheld their morals and expected me to uphold mine. That was the moment when I realized why the little nagging voice was getting to me. Deep down I knew better all along.

Mrs. Barkley finally found her voice.

"Oh, my goodness!" she said. "In that case, Laura Mae can sleep in here with you. Larry will have to sleep in the room with Daddy and me."

Like my momma, Mrs. Barkley called her husband Daddy. Most wives did in those days.

After we'd gone to bed, the only noise I heard was the occasional cracking of the fire in the fireplace, until it eventually burned itself out. After that, I lay in the stillness of the night, brow-beating myself for being so naive. Eventually the sandman rescued me into a deep sleep. The next thing I knew a rooster was crowing and, outside, birds were singing. I drifted back to sleep. The next sound I heard was coming from the kitchen. Mr. Barkley was getting a fire started in the wood stove. Then I heard the rattle of the old percolator as he put it on a burner to brew up some of his favorite coffee.

Laura Mae had gotten up without awaking me, but now she was gently shaking my shoulder. "Evelyn, you may as well get up 'cause nobody sleeps in this house after five o'clock in the morning. We all have to get up to get our face and hands washed for breakfast. The only way anybody stays down after five is if they're too sick to stand on their feet."

We had already finished eating and were washing dishes when I heard a noise at the kitchen door. It was Larry's sister, Louise, with her husband, Etley. When they introduced her to me, it took me by surprise. He had told me about Laura Mae and his two brothers in the army, but he hadn't mentioned a sister named Louise.

She was friendly and I liked her right away. It was plain to see that she was heavy with child. Etley was about six feet seven inches tall. At least he would have been tall if he hadn't been somewhat hunchbacked. He looked to be all muscle, weighing at least two hundred and thirty pounds, a typical lumberjack. Both he and Louise were very pleasant–until Larry made his entrance back into the house. He'd been out gathering wood for the stoves, but when he came in and exchanged glances with his sister there was a definite change in his attitude. He spoke to Etley, but not to Louise.

A couple of hours later, I heard more people coming in the front door. One was his oldest brother, Albert, home on a sixteen-day leave before shipping out to Germany. Larry smiled at his sister-in-law, Edith, who had her girls, Betty, eight years old, and Dot, age four, hanging on her skirt. Larry played around with the children, then spoke to Albert before he grabbed Edith in a big bear hug and swung her around in circles. It dawned on me that this was the woman he told me he dated before his brother Albert married her.

As time went on, everyone seemed to drift away, doing his or her own thing. For some reason I found myself alone in the living room. I wasn't used to getting up at five to eat breakfast and I was tired. The bed I'd slept in looked even more inviting than the night before. I stretched out on it. Wrapped up in my thoughts, along with the quiet of the countryside, I soon drifted off to sleep. I couldn't have dozed very long when a movement on the bed woke me up with a start. When I opened my eyes, I saw that it was Larry.

The first words out of my mouth were, "What's wrong?"

"Don't be scared," he said quietly. "I just want to talk to you."

"Now?"

"Yes, now."

"What about?"

"I've been talking to Momma. She thinks we should get married."

At that, I sat straight up on the bed. I didn't believe what I was hearing. I thought, *What in heaven's name has brought this on?*, but what I said was, "She thinks we should get married?"

"That's what I just said. With you coming here and all, we need to consider how things look."

"Larry, did you tell her that we've never even had a date and that we're only friends? How can you two possibly want us to go get married?"

"I know, but Momma thinks it'll be best for both of us. Even if she hadn't said it, I think it'd be a good idea for you to marry me."

I was too stunned to even think straight. The first thing running through my mind was that he was teasing. The second thing running through my mind was too infuriating to put into words. I'd been taught patience and, above all, never to make a scene in public, but Larry was backing me into a corner, a very unpleasant corner where I didn't want to be, a corner I had let my weakness and inexperience get me into in the first place.

"I don't want to get married," I said flatly. "I'm not ready to be a wife."

He had a surge of temper like you read about in a Stephen King novel. He didn't raise his voice; but he was seething like a cat spitting through clinched teeth. "You think you're so damn much better than me, don't you? Don't you?"

I became scared. "No, no, Larry. I don't think that."

His face turned red. I'd never seen anyone go into a mad frenzy like that. I didn't know what to say or do.

"You're nothing but a cheap little slut. Only a tramp would've come on this trip with me. You think just because your family has plenty of money and mine share crops, that makes you better than me." His eyes burned into mine. "I know you don't want me. You want that damn sailor. You haven't been the same towards me since I caught you with him."

What's come over you? I was thinking. You wouldn't leave me alone until I agreed to come with you. Remember? I wanted to scream out at him, but I had foolishly put myself in this position, now I didn't have a clue how to handle it. I didn't know what the words "tramp" and "slut" meant. Whatever they meant, the way he had said them sounded dirty. I made a mental note to check the dictionary.

He was so angry that his whole body was jerking. He was still standing over me, clinching his good hand as if he wanted to hit me. Trying to think fast, I said, "Larry, I'm only sixteen years old. The only possible way I can legally marry you is to have my parents' signatures."

"You can lie about your age just like you did when you wanted to go to work. If you wanted to marry me, you wouldn't worry about that. How's anyone ever going to know any different unless we tell them?"

"My parents will know."

"Your parents are in Shulerville. Now you tell me, how the hell are they ever going to know?"

"Believe me, my parents will know."

"I want you to tell me right now what it's going to be. Are you going to marry me? You tell me right now, yes or no? It's just that simple."

7

It may have seemed simple to him, but he was scaring the living daylights out of me. He wasn't giving me any choice. It was like when he made up his mind for me to make the trip. He had already decided what I was going to do. Now he had decided that I was going to marry him. I was filled with a deep-seated fear of him. All I wanted was to go home.

Out of sheer terror, I mumbled "Yes" to get away from him and to shut him up.

Why do so many young girls mistake this type of display for love? There's not any love about a person who's that possessive. He never once told me he loved me, never declared any love for me whatsoever.

Larry said, "Yes, what? How about you say that again!"

I mumbled, "Yes–I—I will marry-you."

"Damn it, say the words so I can hear you."

"Yes, I'll marry you."

He reached out and gently hit my chin with his fist. Then he smiled and said, "Now that's much better, don't you think? You take my advice and don't you push me, Evelyn. You know all I have to do is walk in that restaurant and tell your boss that you're only sixteen and you won't be working there any longer. What will you do about your fine job then? Not to mention that damn sailor you're so crazy about."

"You couldn't be more wrong. It's legal to work at sixteen."

I didn't have any plans to marry him. I thought that once I got him back to Charleston, it would all be over. I didn't know him well enough then to understand that he always figured his plans well in advance before putting the wheels in motion. I may have been sixteen, but one thing I did know about marriage was that once you went through the ceremony and pledged to love, honor, and obey, you had best be big and strong enough to live up to that commitment. In those days, marriage vows were taken seriously: "until death we do part" meant until death do we part. Once married to a man, you were his property. You belonged to him body and soul. You were his slave to do whatever he requested you to do. The word divorce was never in my vocabulary or that of anyone I knew. If a person was foolish enough to get into a loveless marriage, then their punishment was to stay in that marriage until death. Maybe it wasn't that way in the whole world, but it was where I came from.

Albert, Edith, and their two girls had gone on home. Albert's nerves were real bad due to the fact he was going to the front line in Germany, I was told. Etley and Louise remained a while longer.

Larry eased over to his mother and tugged her sleeve to get her attention. He said, "Momma, I sure hope you're not busy in the morning."

"Why's that?"

"I want you to go to Walhalla with Evelyn and me."

"Sure, but what for?"

"I want you to help Evelyn pick out a blue dress to get married in."

I asked, "Why blue?"

"Well, if you get married in blue, your love will always be true."

"I'll be very happy to go with you," Mrs. Barkley replied.

Louise asked, "Momma, do you think it will be all right for me to go with you'uns too?"

"Sure, if you want to," she said.

I knew for sure there wasn't any thing that was going to stop Larry. My next thought was, *If I have to go, I'm glad Louise will be going with me."*

The next morning, Mr. and Mrs. Barkley, along with Louise, Laura Mae, Larry, and I, were off to do some Walhalla shopping.

Shortly after nine we were pounding the streets in this small farm town looking for that special blue dress; not a wedding dress, only a simple blue dress. We finally found one that would have been beautiful on a sixty-year-old lady. The whole charade made me sick to my stomach. Oh, how I wished I were back in Charleston, working in John's restaurant. I had trapped myself. Now all I wanted was to get this sick mess behind me. Being five-foot-nine inches tall, and Larry being specific about the shade of blue he wanted, left some doubt as to what could be accomplished until we found the dowdy dress that I went ahead and tried on. Mrs. Barkley said she thought it was real pretty on me. I really liked his mother. Laura Mae was a bit more standoffish, we never did bond the way Louise, his mother, and I bonded.

Inside I was crying, but on the outside I tried to smile. I didn't want to do anything to upset anyone. Mother had taught me well.

Larry looked me over, then made his judgment. "Okay. That one's pretty enough. Just keep it on. Have the clerk put the one you were wearing in a bag."

So, once again, I did as I was told. Now I was dressed for my wedding. After leaving the store, we went back to the car. Ten minutes later, Larry parked in front of a sign that read "Office of the Judge of Probate, Walhalla, South Carolina." It was a home. The judge had his office in the living room. This was before the Walhalla courthouse was even in the planning stages. Only the rich and famous had church weddings during that era.

There was another sign on the door that read "Open. Come In." We all went inside. The place was quiet with a desk and a small lamp that gave off a dim light. No one seemed to be around. On the desk another sign read "Ring Bell for Service." Larry rang the bell. In a few moments, a white-haired, fatherly-looking gentleman entered the room.

Larry said, "Sir, we're here to get married." He was wearing his familiar macho cocky grin, a work shirt and overalls.

The judge asked, "Who's the lucky bride?"

Everyone pointed at me. The judge squinted his eyes as he took a long, hard look at me. "Where are you from, young lady?"

I could hardly find my voice. "Charleston, South Carolina."

He adjusted his glasses, checking me out. Then he cleared his throat. With great authority he said, "Young lady, I hope you haven't come all the way up here to tell me that you're only sixteen years old?"

Larry squeezed my hand. I understood it was a warning. Every fiber of my body was screaming, "This is your chance. Go ahead. Tell him the truth." It was as if I was frozen in time. I was too scared to open my mouth. I was that terrified of Larry and so I blew my only chance to get away and end this whole nightmare. I stood there as if I had been condemned. Indeed, I was condemned to a marriage of horrors. "Oh, no, sir," I lied. "I'm twenty."

I did just as Larry instructed me to do. From the expression on the judge's face, it was my feeling he knew that I was lying. Had he pressed me any further, I'm sure I would have broken down and blurted out more truth than he would have cared to hear. I wanted to scream, "No! I'm barely sixteen," but I couldn't get up the nerve.

After that, the judge started writing out the license. There wasn't any waiting period at that time, so he proceeded with the ceremony. I didn't hear much of what he said. I was so scared my knees were knocking. I felt as if I was receiving a death sentence. Then I heard the judge say, "I now pronounce you man and wife. What God hath joined in holy matrimony, let not any man put asunder. You may kiss the bride."

Mrs. Barkley nudged Larry, now my husband, into giving me a peck on the lips, the first kiss I ever had from anybody.

Larry handed the judge a five-dollar bill with a big, cocky grin, as if he was the last of the big spenders. Then we left and went back to his parents' farm.

The day before, when I had stretched out on that bed for a bit of relaxation, I never once in my foggiest dreams realized that Larry could, or would, coerce and bully me into being his wife less that twenty-four hours later. The big question that had entered my mind was *am I really married*? Was I legally married? According to law, I wasn't, because I had lied about my age. Everyone else, I felt was thinking that I was legally married until death do us part, but the very thought left a bitter taste in my mouth. How could I ever be able to care for this man, let alone love him? I was supposed to feel happy on my wedding day. Instead, I felt sick and degraded. With all the newlywed jokes that were being thrown at me, I began to feel even sicker.

It was six o'clock in the evening. My new mother-in-law was in the kitchen preparing our so-called wedding feast. I went into the bedroom and started packing our suitcase to go back to Charleston. I had every intention of being on my job the next morning at ten o'clock sharp. I glanced around when Larry came into the room. His expression was that of a cat swallowing a canary. He eased up behind me and slowly slid his arms around my waist. At his touch, a cold chill permeated my entire body.

"I want you to tell me just how it feels to be an old married woman."

I folded over to prevent myself from upchucking. "I'm not old. I'm not quite sure about being legally married either."

"Oh, yes. I'll vouch for that. You are definitely my wife now. You're legally married to me. You now belong to me. I was there. Remember?"

How could I ever be able to forget, but I mumbled, "I'm glad you're sure."

He reached out, took the dress that I was folding to put in the suitcase from my hands. "Come on now, don't be that way. This is our wedding day. Let's enjoy it. Momma's waiting for us to be seated at the table. In case you've forgotten, we're their honored guests tonight, so straighten up. Don't you go spoiling it for everyone."

He led me into the kitchen where everybody let out a loud cheer. We sat down at the table. My appetite was not as good as it had been that first night we arrived even though it was a wonderful meal. Country cooking didn't get any better than my mother-in-law's. After we finished, I stood up to make an announcement. "I'd best go and finish packing our things. We have to be leaving pretty soon if we're going to make it to work in the morning."

Everyone looked at me like I had lost my mind. I left the table and went straight to the bedroom. Once again Larry followed me.

"Young lady, just what do you think you're doing?"

"I'm packing our things to go home."

"Well, you can just unpack them 'cause I'm not going anywhere tonight."

"You're supposed to be at work in the morning at seven. I have to be at mine at ten. Why do you want to take a chance on both of us losing our jobs?"

"We'll get back when I get ready to get back. Right now this is our honeymoon, in case you've forgotten."

"No, Larry, I haven't forgotten. How could I forget?"

"You have forgotten one thing, though, haven't you?"

"What?"

"You'd best never forget that you married me today and you'll be my wife until death do us part. Get it in your head right now that you're going to do as you're told or else there'll be a price to pay."

I held up my chin in quiet defiance. "Being married's all the more reason for us to get ourselves back to work."

"I'll let you know when I'm ready to go."

He forced his words through clinched teeth, making me think of an old tabby cat that Momma had when I was little. If you made that cat mad, it'd spit at you. I learned to back off after my first encounter with the critter. To me, the tone of Larry's voice was pretty much the same as that cat. When he was upset, you could hardly tell when he ended a sentence; everything sort of hissed together. He used that tone to impress me, to make me understand that I now belonged to him, body and soul. He now owned me, just like the pair of shoes he was wearing on his feet.

Back in those days, women had very few rights. We were taught that once you were married, the man is head of the house. A woman must obey her man. What happened between a man and his wife was private and would be kept private between the two of them. It didn't matter how good or how bad things were, the woman didn't dare breathe a word of it to anyone.

So now Larry was my husband. Even though I feared him, I would have to deal with it the best I knew how.

Later, everyone went back out on the porch just as we did the night before. I sat beside Larry in the swing. The same mountains were in the background, the same moon was as full and bright as it had been the previous night. The beauty that had been so satisfying to me only twenty-four hours earlier, wasn't the same now that the fear of him had so quickly overtaken me.

Not more than a couple of hours after we returned from getting married, my mother-in-law's brother, a man everyone called Uncle Pat, brought Larry's grandmother up from Easley to spend a couple of weeks. She was a sweet woman in her late seventies. Uncle Pat looked at me with pity in his eyes rather than being happy for me. He couldn't stay but a short time. He was his city's magistrate and had something he had to tend to back home.

It was understood with everyone that the bed in the living room was where Grandma always slept when she was there. Nothing or nobody could change that. I was told that the bed agreement was made out of respect for her. Later on, Grandma confided to me that she refused to sleep in the same room with Mr. Barkley.

My wedding night.

Grandma and Laura Mae slept in her bed in the living room. Larry and I spent our wedding night in one of the two full size beds not four feet from the one my in-laws slept in.

The next morning about ten, we left to go back to Charleston. We had gone a couple of miles when Larry said, "Don't you think it's time for you to quit sitting so close to that door? I think you need to be closer, that is, if you're not afraid of me."

I sat up a little straighter and slid a bit closer to him.

"Well, do you feel any different now that you're married?" he asked.

I didn't say anything. I just tried to smile. In my mind this wasn't the time to discuss the subject.

I fell in love with all of his family, other than his father. There was something scary about the man. It was the same feeling I had about Larry. I couldn't put my finger on it, but there was something out of the ordinary about both men. My father-in-law had an even more sinister look about him than my husband had, even though both of them were extremely handsome. Their dark eyes were the real give away to their odd personalities.

John had warned me that if I stayed away from work once more without asking him, I would be looking for another job. I had promised him faithfully that I wouldn't let it happen again after the flat tire deal. That thought burdened me with so much guilt, I became sick at my stomach. All during the trip I silently prayed, "Dear God, please help me know what to do."

When we got to Charleston, Larry went straight to Mrs. Clark's boarding house where he and Stanley were rooming together. Mrs. Clark must have been watching for us. I didn't know she knew I had gone with Larry. He didn't any more than get the car parked then she ran out to us. I just thought she was glad to see us. She grabbed Larry by one arm and me by the other. She was shoving us along toward the boarding house as fast as she could go.

Larry said, "Hey, woman, what's wrong with you?"

Mrs. Clark didn't slow down or answer him.

Larry asked again, "What's wrong, Mrs. Clark?"

About that time she shoved us through the door and into her bedroom.

She turned to face him. "How can you stand there looking so innocent, asking me a stupid question like that when you've taken this child off for the entire weekend?"

Larry gave her a puzzled stare. "What are we doing here in your bedroom?"

"I'll tell you what we're doing here, Larry; I'm trying to keep Stanley from killing you and I'm also trying to keep Stanley out of jail after he does kill you."

Larry turned every color a human being could possibly turn.

Mrs. Clark then told Larry, "Stanley's so mad he's almost foaming at the mouth. I brought you here to warn you that he's looking for you. Lord only knows you deserve to be killed, but I don't want your blood on my hands."

Larry didn't look near as brave or confident as he had back at his parent's house when he laid the law down to me. He began to stammer and stutter. "B-b-but, Mrs. Clark, Evelyn and me, we slipped off and went and got married."

"That don't make a tinker's damn at this stage of your little game," she snapped right back at him. "Evelyn's just a child. Do you understand? She's underage. You're old enough to know better, at least you should."

Larry nudged me. "Get the marriage certificate, Evelyn. Show her that we're married."

Mrs. Clark took the marriage certificate out of my hand and began to read it. As she turned to leave the room, she said, "Stay right there. It doesn't matter how long it takes me, both of you had better be right here when I get back. You do understand me, don't you?"

I didn't want anyone to get hurt. Larry was up against more than he'd counted on. At that moment, it was anyone's guess as to what would happen next. I hadn't often seen my parents' temper triggered, but when I did, it wasn't pretty to look at. My people were easygoing until someone wronged them. In this case, Stanley had to cover his own backside with my parents. I'd seen very little of him after I got to Charleston, but Momma and Daddy thought we were together on a regular basis. They didn't understand how many hours Stanley was working. Still, he was going to be held responsible for my getting married, at least in Momma and Daddy's eyes.

Even though I was still a virgin, this man, my new husband, had labeled me a tramp at both ends of the state. The hurt stung deep within me. There was little doubt in my mind that I would survive long enough to live down the accusations I knew would be facing me.

Larry sat quietly. There wasn't too much else he could say or do to defend himself. We came from two different worlds. We had nothing in common whatsoever. He didn't have any desire to work. I was a workaholic. He wanted to follow in his father's footsteps and be a sharecropper. I wanted to go back to school to be a writer or journalist. If he got his wishes then he wouldn't have to work more than five or six months out of the year. If he chose to do it the way his father farmed, the possibility of not more that three to four months wasn't unrealistic. The worst part of it was, we knew we weren't in love with each other.

It must have been at least an hour before Mrs. Clark returned. She was carrying two plates of food.

"Here," she said, handing them to me. "You must be hungry."

I was feeling a lot of things, but hunger was not one of them. I took the two plates and thanked her. When she turned to leave again, she was looking very grim. "I'll be back before long, but I still want both of you to stay right where you are."

I handed Larry one of the plates, but he didn't appear to be any hungrier than I was.

It wasn't long before Mrs. Clark came back with a ball of heavy cord. She started stringing it between the two beds.

"Why are you doing that?" Larry asked.

Mrs Clark replied, "This is where you, Evelyn, are going to sleep until I get Stanley cooled down. Right now he don't know where you are. You need to take time out to thank God that he don't. Larry, I'm not kidding or playing around with you, this is dead serious. Stanley is threatening to kill you and he's mad enough to do just that."

Larry was dumb enough to ask Mrs Clark a dumb question: "Why is he so mad? I told you that we slipped off to get married."

She was plainly disgustedly. "In the first place, he's mad that you took off from work without asking. You didn't respect your job enough to get a leave of absence. You're not being there made it that much harder on him as well as all the rest of the welders. They had government rush orders to get out and a deadline to meet. When people like you work when they want to and quit when they please, that makes it harder on the rest of them. The next bomb dropped might just be closer than Pearl Harbor. You need to think about that."

Larry protested indignantly. "I told them I was going to be gone."

"Yes, by gracious, you told them. You told a couple of your coworkers that you didn't ask for permission to be off. Now you come back whining and using that piece of paper that says you're married.

Do you seriously think it's going to undo all the problems you've created these past few days? Do you, Mister Big Man?"

Larry took it, but it wasn't easy for him to digest.

She finished stringing the cord, then hung sheets across it to make a curtain that served as a divider between the beds. She didn't let us out of the room until the next morning after Stanley left for work. Evidently, Stanley didn't know that we were back. Mrs. Clark had gotten the car key from Larry and asked one of her boarders to park it where Stanley couldn't see it. When the time came for Stanley to get home after work, she huddled us back into her bedroom. I wondered how long it would be before Stanley cooled down.

My chance of still having a job was about one in a thousand. I didn't have any idea what was going to happen with Larry and his position. I couldn't help wondering if either one of us still had work to go back to.

Stanley had returned to the house to eat, then had gone out again. Mrs. Clark didn't hide Larry's car as well as she thought she had. Stanley spotted it and came looking for us. It was after eight o'clock, a time when most hard-working people were in bed. Mrs. Clark was with Stanley when he confronted us. I think she thought she could help calm the situation, but it didn't seem to me that anything would work. The moment I looked into my brother's face, I knew he was outraged.

"Larry," he began, "I want to know what the hell you were thinking to take Evelyn off like you did."

Larry was very nervous. "Well, it's like this. Me and Evelyn decided to slip off and get married."

"I don't give a good damn if you did, she's only sixteen. She's too young to get married. Anyway, how could she get married without Momma or Daddy's consent? One of them would have to sign for her. Not only that, it's the way you went about it. I still got a good mind to beat the hell out of you right here and now. The only reason I'm not whipping you is that I promised Mrs. Clark I wouldn't. We need you on the job. It's working the rest of us to death because you want to sit on your lazy backside. You've been gone five days. You haven't even stopped to consider Evelyn. I doubt she has her job any longer."

"Oh, come on, Stanley," he pleaded. "We're married now. I'll take good care of her."

Stanley said, "Really? You're not taking too good care of yourself, staying out of work like you do."

I butted in. "Larry, if you two are through fighting, how about taking me to my room?"

Stanley turned as if he'd been hit with an arrow. "What do you mean 'your room', Sis? I don't think you have a room any longer. Agnes is mad as hell."

So now, instead of being a happy married woman, I felt like everything had come to an end. One thing for sure, I'd lost all control over my life. It was now up to me to ask my husband's permission before making any plans about work or anything else. For three years I'd been on my own. I'd made my own decisions and I'd managed well. Even at thirteen and fourteen I'd worked every day like I'd been taught to do. Now that I was sixteen, everything I'd accomplished had been shot to hell in a few short days.

Larry had assured me that he got permission to be out of work for three days. He lied. He said that he talked to Stanley and that Stanley told him that he saw nothing wrong with me taking the trip to visit Larry's parents. Not one word of it had proven to be true. I'm still not sure what brought about his sick reasoning. Could it have been his way of sneaking me off to force me into marrying him? I don't think so. It was easy to see that he had strong feelings for Edith and that she returned those feelings even though she had rejected him for his older brother. Larry had never forgiven her for that. I was a young, pretty girl, with what a lot of people said was the body of a model. I've always believed that he used me to make Edith jealous.

We spent the next two nights in Mrs. Clark's bedroom. Friday morning Larry got up and went back to work at the navy yard. The only reason he still had a job was the drastic need for electric welders. I was told that he was good at his work, what little he was there. The biggest problem was getting him to show up. Just as Larry said, the government had put a freeze on those who worked for defense. If something in the line of an emergency came up, the foreman wasn't allowed to fire anyone. Electric welders were very much in demand to supply war needs.

The next morning I got up and went to the restaurant. I was there at nine-thirty. Believe me, I would beg if it meant keeping my job. John wasn't happy to see me.

"You do understand that I have to have help every day," he said.

"I can't operate my business at your convenience."

I tried to make him understand what happened. That was nearly impossible when I myself really didn't understand it. I told him that I had gotten married. That seemed to somewhat have a little influence on his thinking. Unlike Larry, I was a good and faithful worker, that is, I had been until Larry came into my life. I remembered that my boss once said he would much rather hire married women. He said that he had fewer problems with them than he did with young single girls. He pointed that out one day as a way of telling me that I had been an exception to that rule. Remembering that statement made me reel with nausea now that I had let him down. I could see the disappointment in his eyes. It took a while for him to come around to admitting how badly he needed me. Then he told me how hard it had been on him with the help shortage. One girl had just up and quit, another had called in sick.

What made matters even worse, I had to find another place to live, one where I could cook and take care of my husband.

8

Sunday morning, before going to work, I went into the kitchen to tell Mrs. Clark that I was going to get my things.

"What are your plans now?" she wanted to know.

I shrugged. "Your guess is as good as mine. Larry has to find some place for us to live. He's gotten us into this mess, he'll just have to get us out."

"Just a minute, I might be able to help."

"You've already been a tremendous help." I hugged her.

"I've got an idea. I've got this one big furnished room just off the entrance. I rented it to a young couple about four months ago. It's got a stove and everything you'd need to start out housekeeping. I've been threatening to put the couple out because of their constant fighting, plus they're always late paying rent. I've gone just about as far as I can possibly go with them, I can't tolerate much more of their shenanigans. If they don't pay me today, they're out. If you think you'd like that room, I'll be more than happy to rent it to you."

I got excited at the very thought. Could I be this lucky? "Oh, please, Mrs. Clark, yes. Let me know if it comes available. I'd love to rent it. You won't ever have to worry about my paying on time."

My landlady, Agnes, took the news better than I thought she might.

"I sure hate to see you move, but I do understand. Had I known you were getting married, I'd love to have been at your wedding."

"I appreciate the thought, but we got married in Walhalla, Larry's hometown."

I was actually thinking about how much I didn't enjoy my own wedding. I wished with all my heart that I hadn't been at my wedding. Oh, how I regretted ever making the decision to go to that part of the country. Just like Mother and Nanny Eve always warned me: "Everything that glitters isn't always gold".

Now that I had a husband, it was much harder for me to work the hours I'd been use to working. I was always pushed for time. I had to cook Larry's breakfast then get him up and off to the navy yard. That meant I didn't get to sleep in until it was time for me to get ready to leave for work. I got home after two in the morning, went to bed, and was back up at six.

After I returned to Mrs. Clark's, she told me that the young couple had come in and paid their rent, but they had also given her notice. They were moving out the next day.

After finding a place to stash my things, Mrs. Clark said, "You may change your mind about wanting it once you see what a filthy mess they left the place in. Fact, it's a step or two beyond filthy."

I wasn't a bit discouraged. "If it can be cleaned, I'll clean it. Don't you lose any sleep worrying about that."

She laughed. "Well, it can be cleaned, but it's going to take a heck of a lot of elbow grease."

If there was one thing I knew, it was how to clean.

She continued, "In the meantime, you can stay on like you have been. I won't charge you anything for the time you been here. I'll only charge you for rent on your room after you get moved in."

She didn't exaggerate about the filth. I actually cleaned maggots out of the place, some of them more than an inch in length. It wasn't an easy chore. There was such a limited supply of cleaning materials in those days.

The day before I left to go to work, I felt the need to talk to someone. Who better than that sweet lady?

"Mrs. Clark, I need to get something off of my mind, something I've wanted to tell you, but I've been scared to. You have to promise you won't let Larry know I told you."

"Honey, you go right ahead. You can tell me anything."

"I hope you don't think I'm a cheap tramp, whatever that word means."

"Why, I could never think of you in that way."

"I guess everybody thinks that I went off and had sex with Larry. I just want you to know that I'm still a virgin. I've never had sex with anyone."

"What? What are you saying? You've been married two weeks and you still haven't had sex?"

"That's exactly what I'm telling you. It's the truth, Larry hasn't even kissed me other than a peck on the lips at the wedding."

Mrs. Clark gently pulled me to her and gave me a hug. "Oh my! You poor, poor, sweet child."

I had to back away before the tears came. I felt I had to tell someone. Once I did, I felt better. I wasn't a bad girl. I'd been nearly crazy with mixed emotions. I still had no understanding of what the word "slut" meant.

The one-room efficiency that Mrs. Clark rented to us was fairly roomy. It was furnished with a nice, three-piece bedroom suite, a small eating table with two chairs, a free-standing kitchen cabinet, and a three-burner, kerosene stove with an oven. It also had a large bathroom. My first day off work I had everything cleaned spick-and-span by the time Larry got home from the navy yard. You could have used white gloves and not found a soiled spot. Now that I was housekeeping as a new bride, I'd have to put into practice everything Mother had taught me about taking care of a husband. All of a sudden it dawned on me that I was enjoying the game of playing house. It was hard work, but I felt that I was accomplishing something. Now that I'd gotten married, the most sensible thing for me to do was to try to make the best of it. I wanted to believe so much that all was not lost. If it made people happy for me to be sixteen and married, so be it. We were both lucky that we still had our jobs. He confided to me that he liked electric welding, he just hated the fact that someone was getting paid to tell him what to do.

June sixteenth was two weeks after our wedding. It would be our first night alone in our own one-room apartment. There wasn't any great lovemaking scene, and certainly no flashing lights. It was over within a matter of minutes.

I couldn't help but remember my first menstrual period. I was thirteen. My sister-in-law, Bernice, was at my parents' house that day. I was horrified at what I found on myself when I went to the outside toilet. I ran to Bernice and told her that I was bleeding to death. Bernice wiped my tears away as she said, "Now, now, you're not bleeding to death. From now on, you'll experience this each and every month. It's called menstruating." She went on to give me advice on how to protect my clothes from being soiled and ended with, "You're growing up to be a woman, kiddo."

One thing that was never discussed in our home was sex. I can't remember ever hearing the word or knowing about a girl having her monthly period.

Now I had begun to experience some of what married life was all about. Larry was actually going to work every morning. I had succeeded in talking John into letting me have every other Sunday off, that way I'd be able to spend some time with my husband. I wanted us to be able to go places, see some of the things that I hadn't been fortunate enough to see before. It didn't take long for me to find out that Larry's passion was getting in the car and going for long rides. He wanted to check out all the back country roads, not any one place in particular, but just drive and explore the countryside.

Each Sunday I had off, Larry would have a trip planned. Our first one had been to Folly Beach. I'd never seen the ocean before and I was thrilled at the sight of so much water. Each and every time I've been to a beach since then, I relive the beautiful memory of that first moment I saw the ocean. Another Sunday he took me to Myrtle Beach. He seemed to enjoy bringing out the little girl in me, the child who never had experienced seeing anything like these sights.

Although he liked to drive and look at the scenery, he never wanted to participate in anything. He would stop along a deserted stretch of beach and let me go wading for a few minutes, but he wouldn't go in with me. I would love to have gone to a boardwalk where I could ride the merry-go-round. I was awestruck by the carousel and all of the festivities around it. The little girl in me wanted so badly to go out to play. Then I would remind myself that I was a married woman and any such notion would have to be suppressed.

Nevertheless, one day I got up the nerve to ask him if I couldn't ride the merry-go-round. Not surprisingly, he replied, "That's for children, Evelyn. You're too old for that kind of thing. You want people to laugh at you?"

He made me feel dumb to have even asked. I knew the only grown-ups on the merry-go-round were mothers with small children.

For a couple of short months, we took beautiful sightseeing trips, then all of a sudden, with no warning, his attitude changed completely. Nothing went right on our little ventures. He was argumentative and hateful. He took the joy out of not just our travels, but out of everything. Something was very wrong. He was having too many mood swings. I couldn't put my finger on it. In some ways he was unusually intelligent, but then he'd act as if he didn't have a brain in his head. Instead of bringing out the joyful child in me, he began to scold me as if I were a three-year-old. The trips had turned into misery, not fun. Even when we took rides, I seldom got out of the car anymore. I finally asked John if I could work every Sunday and have a weekday off instead.

We still hadn't faced my parents about our marriage. One day I took a deep breath and told myself that if it had to be done, now was as good a time as any.

Since my father taught me that girls should be married by the time they were sixteen, I figured that having done exactly that, he'd be pleased. If Momma and Daddy ended up being mad at me, it would probably be because I didn't tell them ahead of time. I knew I would never confess the circumstances of the wedding. How could I tell them that I didn't want to marry, or that I had let myself be bullied into something I had no hand in? Those would be my secrets. I was too ashamed to have it any other way.

When we got to my parents' home, they greeted us, but they weren't their usual sweet selves. After we had eaten dinner, Larry made a grand production of telling them his good news.

"I guess Stanley told you that Evelyn and me slipped off and got married."

I couldn't have felt more shocked had he slapped my face. He was repeating the same story he told Stanley. I never dreamed that he would tell my parents a bald-faced lie. He may have slipped off to do that, but God in Heaven knew that wasn't ever in my mind. I would have only said, plain and simple, "We went and got married." That wouldn't have been a lie. It was only a small matter of not telling the whole truth, but it irritated me.

Daddy gave me the same look he'd given me when I was a small child and he was displeased. He motioned me to come with him into a room where we could be alone.

"Young lady," he said in his no-nonsense tone, " you may think you did the right thing, and I hope you did, but there's something I want to tell you; you're the one who made this decision. You've gone and made your bed, so you'd best plan on sleeping in it. Don't you think for one moment that you're going to come crawling back to me. And there's another thing you'd better get through your head, once married, you're always married. Marriage is a lifetime commitment, Evelyn, don't ever forget it. You didn't consider my input about this, so I certainly hope you know what you're doing." He left the room.

That was my father, the man who led me to believe that if I didn't get married by the time I was sixteen, no man would ever want me.

I stood in stunned silence, not knowing what to do or what to expect. After a short time, I heard him talking to Larry about his last deer-hunting trip. As far as he was concerned any conversation about marriage was over and done with. It wasn't the fact that I got married that bothered him, it was the part about us slipping off and going out of town in secret. He felt that I had disrespected him and cheapened myself in the way I went about it. I took to heart what my father said, especially the part about "once married, you're always married." He didn't realize it, but he had just committed me to a life sentence with a man I hardly knew and didn't much like. Still, I was Daddy's baby and I had hurt him. I would do my best not to disappoint him any further.

My husband was most certainly going to be the Lord and Master of my castle for the rest of my natural life. As bad as it was, I still never realized at the time that it was going to turn out to be the nightmare it became. I thought it would settle into a marriage like that of my parents. Daddy believed that all men treated their wives the way he treated my mother.

Seven weeks later, on a Wednesday morning, after having only a couple hours of sleep, I cooked Larry's breakfast and got him off to work, then I straightened up the apartment, planning on going back to bed for another couple of hours before I had to leave for the restaurant. Just as I slipped off to slumberland, I heard the sound of the door opening and closing again. I thought nothing of it. Mrs. Clark was probably doing what she often did, checking to see that everything was all right. To my surprise, when I glanced up, I found Larry standing in the middle of the room, looking around. It scared me.

"What are you doing here? How come you're not at work?" He didn't answer me immediately so I tried again. "Larry, what's wrong?"

Finally he said, "What makes you think there's something wrong?"

"Why aren't you at work?"

"Because I'm here."

"Why are you here and not there?"

"If you must know, I quit."

"You quit your job?"

"Yes, I quit, damn it. Can't you hear? I just got through telling you I quit." He shook his head as if he was disgusted with me. "Evelyn, I swear before God, you never understand anything I tell you. I quit and I don't want to hear another damn word come out of your mouth about it, so shut it before I shut it for you. Get up and get some clothes on. Wear a sweater, it's chilly outside."

"Where are we going?"

"Do you have to ask so many questions? You just go on and do like I tell you for once in your life. Get your sweater like I told you."

"Larry, please, I'm tired. I only got a few hours sleep."

"You don't want me to have to tell you again, do you?"

I got out of bed, changed clothes, took my sweater out of the closet and put it on. Once in the car, he was stone quiet as he headed for the nearest country road leading out of the city. The ones that were the roughest were the ones he took. He drove for hours without speaking a word. Neither did I. With his attitude, I was too afraid to even try to have a conversation. We didn't get back home until after dark.

True to his turn-about nature, the next morning he got up and left. That was odd, but it was even odder that he went without eating breakfast. Breakfast was his main meal of the day. He didn't give any indication of where he was going. I took it for granted that he'd gone back to work at the navy yard.

It still bothered him that I had a job because he never knew who I might talk to. He was equally upset when I took a day off during the week. He had to know where I was, what I was doing, at all times. I understand now it was his sick way of keeping me under his control, but his possessiveness was strange because he never showed any passion toward me. My mind always went back to the way Daddy was so affectionate with my mother. Larry, on the other hand, only showed emotion when nothing was going his way. I had no feelings for him other than fear, and his peculiar behavior was driving me even further away.

For the next four days he got up and left the same as usual every morning then came Wednesday again, my day off. Larry got up and got dressed, but he didn't leave. Finally I had to ask. "Aren't you going to work?"

"When I decide I want you to know what I'm going to do, that's when I'll tell you. Until then, dammit, keep your mouth shut." With that, he crossed the room in a couple of giant strides and slapped me hard across my face. I fell on the bed in a fetal position. He ordered me to straighten up. When I did, he hit me even harder on the other side of my face. He hit me so hard I saw stars. "Now maybe, by God, that'll teach you to not ask me so damn many dumb questions."

I sat there, holding my face. Nobody had ever slapped me before. I couldn't comprehend it. Why would he hit me for no reason? I began to cry. Quick as he realized that I was crying, he caught me by my hair and pushed my head back to where he could see my face. "Damn you, you'd better stop that bawling right now. I mean what I'm telling you. You keep up that squalling, I'm gonna knock it back in you. All the hell you ever think about is work, work, and work. Well, by God, there are other things in life. Now get up from there. Go wash your face. Get your sweater 'cause you're coming with me."

I didn't dare not mind him. Like the puppy dog I was becoming, I followed him to the car.

He went down Bay Street, then on to Lee Street and across the Cooper River Bridge. I thought, *Oh, dear God, please don't let him go to my parent's house today.* That was the last place in the world I wanted to go after he hit me. They would be able to see that something was wrong. If Daddy found out what Larry had done, he'd confront my husband. Regardless of what he had said, Daddy would never condone Larry hitting me. If they asked, I couldn't lie to them. I'd surely burst out and tell them the truth, then it would be anyone's guess as to what would happen when Larry got me back home.

After about ten miles Larry began to calm down. Just as if nothing had ever happened between us, he said, "I thought maybe you'd like to go see your sister, Lena, today. Think you'd like that?" I didn't know that he even knew Lena.

He seemed to be happier now that he had exercised his authority over me. Maybe he considered himself a great husband, the man of the house.

When we arrived in Jamestown, Lena and her husband, Mitchell, were glad to see me. Lena had gotten married before I was born. I had actually spent more time growing up with her children than I ever did with her. In fact, Lena had two children older than me, with Lela Mae being the oldest. It was Lela Mae who noticed that the right side of my face was swollen and red. I acted as if I didn't have the least idea what she was talking about when she commented on it. I touched my face lightly and quipped, "Oh, that. I worked late last night. Got up, stumbled, and hit my head on the door. Is it really swollen?"

"Yeah. Looks more like Larry might have hit you."

I couldn't tell if she was joking. When she saw my expression, she laughed and said, "I was kidding, Aunt Evelyn."

She loved to call me Aunt, because there was only a three year difference in our ages.

After dinner Larry went with Mitchell and Lena to the garage.

When they came back, Larry said we had to be going.

"What's your hurry?" Lela Mae wanted to know.

"Don't worry," Larry said. "We'll be back tomorrow."

My God, I was thinking. *I'm supposed to work tomorrow.* I was afraid to ask why he would make a remark like that.

Larry continued, but this time he was talking to me. "We'll be moving to Jamestown tomorrow. I'm gonna start working with Mitchell."

I thought, this *can't be happening.* He wasn't only giving up his job making good money in the navy yard, but now had made plans for me to quit my job. What on God's green earth could he possibly be thinking? Why would he even have such a thought? Why would he want to move into the depth of poverty? It blew my mind, not being able to understand his reasoning. I was too upset to think straight. I couldn't see that Mitchell had that much business. In that year, 1942, the population of Jamestown was approximately forty. Mitchell eked out a living with his garage, but cars were few and far between. Those who had cars usually didn't have any gas on account of the rationing. Besides, Larry wasn't a mechanic. Why my brother-in-law made a decision to hire him, I still don't understand.

"Larry," Lela Mae said, "if you're moving to Jamestown, where are you going to live?"

The town consisted at that time of two grocery stores and Mitchell's garage. Other than that, it was still pretty much country. It wasn't well known for rental property, that's for sure.

Larry pointed and said, "Right there in those two rooms out by the garage." He turned to me. "They used to be part of the grocery store, but they sealed up the door and made an apartment out of some of it. Not much to look at, but it's clean." He hesitated a couple of seconds. "Well, we'd best get going. I want to get an early start in the morning."

I thought, *Dear God, no! Please don't let him make me give up my job and move here!* Had he not considered the fact that I made more money than he would make in two weeks living here? I knew in my heart that it would be worse for me than when I was a child. At least when I was little my father had provided for us. Even though there were twelve children, he saw to it that there was always plenty of food on the table. The last thing I wanted to do was give up my good paying job to move to Jamestown. I had made my way out of the country the hard way. I didn't want to be dragged back against my will.

I was still wondering about the fact that the government had everyone, including Larry, frozen to their job. How could he leave under those conditions? I'd heard talk that if people tried to quit the navy yard, they would be blackballed. Once that happened, it would be near impossible for them to ever be hired by anyone else. Would he never be able to get good-paying work again because he walked off of his job at the navy yard?

It was going to be very painful for me to have to face Mrs. Clark. It was bad enough having to face Agnes, but nothing like telling Mrs. Clark who'd been so good to me. Nevertheless, the next morning Larry started grabbing up things and loading them into the car.

"Larry, won't you please stop that? At least wait and tell Mrs. Clark that we're moving."

"You're the one who rented the room in the first place without even asking me. It's your place to tell her, not mine."

While he continued putting things in the car, I went to see our landlady. I met her on the way out to do her daily grocery shopping. This was back before most homes had refrigerators and freezers. The moment I saw this dear, sweet woman, I broke into tears. She reached out and took me in her arms. I couldn't get the lump out of my throat.

"Now, now, child," she said, "things couldn't possibly be that bad, could they?"

"Oh, yes. To me it's much worse."

"What are you trying to tell me?"

"Larry quit the navy yard. Now I have to leave my job. He's already loading our things in the car to move to Jamestown."

"Well, all I can say is don't worry. That kind of thing goes along with being married. It's his job to take care of you. Whether you work or not, it's his job to provide for you. He really needed to think twice about quitting his job, though. That could cause both of you a lot of trouble with the freeze the government's imposed."

In no time we were in the car with all our worldly possessions and on our way to Jamestown. Every now and then Larry would look at me, but he kept quiet for a very long time. Finally, he said, "Just what the hell's bothering you?"

I didn't answer him because I didn't know how to answer him.

"Are you worried about leaving that boss of yours behind or is it that damn sailor that's got you upset?"

"I wish you'd give it up about that sailor. You know nothing happened."

The same old repeats. "To hell with you saying nothing happened. I saw you walking with him. How the hell can you sit there and tell me it never happened? I was there. I know what happened."

I wasn't listening. Larry's accusation reminded me that I'd totally forgotten to call John and tell him I wouldn't be back. I had wages coming to me, but I'd be too embarrassed to try to collect. While he went on about "my sailor", I thought *Oh well. It's easier this way*. I felt guilty for letting Larry take over my life. He was heading in the direction of cutting me off from everybody and everything.

9

We moved the few things that we owned into the two rooms in Jamestown. Now I really did feel like a caged animal. The apartment was no more than a hundred yards from Mitchell's garage. There wasn't any back door to the building. There had once been a door that went into the store directly from one of our rooms but, like Larry had said to me before we moved in, it had long since been closed off. With only one entrance/exit, I was pretty much living my wedded bliss as a hostage. We didn't have a radio, newspapers, magazines, television, telephone, or any of the things I take for granted today. The only time I was allowed out of the apartment was when he decided to let me go spend some time with Lela Mae, which wasn't often.

The kerosene stoves of that era were the pits. The one we had was one of the worst ever manufactured. There was no ventilation and in the mornings when I first lit the burners, the smell was terrible. The stench of kerosene mixed with the smell of coffee would give off an unbearable aroma. I had always loved the scent of fresh coffee brewing in the early morning from a wood-burning stove, but this was no comparison.

When I first started getting sick at my stomach, I blamed the odor in the place. The kerosene smell never seemed to go away. Worse, there wasn't any money to buy anything to clean with. This went on, morning after morning, until about one week later when I woke up thinking I was going to die. I thought, *Oh, dear God in heaven, how could anyone be this sick and still be alive?* At that exact moment, Larry shook me by the shoulder, probably to rouse me into fixing his breakfast. I jumped to my feet and ran for the slop bucket to upchuck.

Afterward, I had to lie back down.

"Why aren't you cooking my breakfast?" he asked at last.

I was still so sick I thought my insides were coming up. Before having a chance to answer him, I started vomiting again. Oh, how I vomited. Finally, I pulled myself back to the bed. I knew he was upset with me, and I also knew he wanted me to fix his breakfast, sick or not sick. He eventually gave up and left to go to the garage with a vicious slam of the door. He made sure I knew he had left for work unhappy.

My next trip to the slop bucket, I decided that it would be easier if I dragged the bucket back to the side of the bed. I didn't have the strength left to hobble back and forth and I certainly didn't feel like having to clean up after myself. My vomiting soon turned to dry heaves. I had been sick before with mumps and then measles, and I had my tonsils out, but never before in my life had I ever been this sick. I had heard my mother say that worry could kill you. That was the only thing I could imagine that would make me this ill. It had to be all the worry I'd been doing.

My husband returned for his lunch and found me still in bed. Nothing had been cooked for him to eat. He was so furious he was trembling. He was the man of the house. His felt he was justified in being angry. Me, being his wife, it was my job to cook for him sick or well.

"Evelyn, just what the hell's wrong with you? Why haven't you fixed me something to eat?"

I thought that if I opened my mouth to talk, I'd throw up again. His mention of food wasn't helping matters. For the first time, I was close to having a flare of temper. I fought to keep from saying anything, because I honestly believed that I was doing wrong by not having his meal on the table. Then, through the guilt, I thought, *This man has to be blind if he can't see I'm too sick to stand up, let alone cook.* I finally got up enough strength to tell him as much.

"No, being sick isn't your problem. Your problem is that you're too damn lazy to get up off your backside to do anything." He grew nastier. "I've got news for you. You're going to get up and cook for me like you're supposed to do, and you'll do it when I tell you to do it." He stormed out, slamming the door behind him once more.

That night I felt some better. I put forth every effort to cook his supper by the time he got off work, but no sooner would I light the burners on the kerosene stove, and then the coffee would begin to perk, and I'd all but faint. I doused my face with cool water, and tried again. Eventually I got some biscuits made, but I had to go back to bed once they were on the table. I couldn't understand why he was so mad.

The next morning I was just as sick, if not sicker, than the morning before. When I woke up, I was on my right side with my back toward Larry. Once again, he shook me to wake me up. "Why ain't you cooking my breakfast?"

Before I could answer, he smashed both of his feet into my back. I landed against the wall five feet away. I lay there for a few minutes, stunned. I wanted to get up, but my pain-ridden body wouldn't cooperate with me. The shock and the fear of the unexpected consumed me. I heard him slam the door as he left. I continued to lie there. I couldn't muster enough strength to get up. For the first time since I married Larry, I let the tears flow. I cried and I prayed. I asked God to protect me or, better yet, to simply end it all. I didn't want to go on living like that for the rest of my life. I would rather, much rather, be dead.

Half an hour or so later I tried to sit up. The nausea choked me, then it turned into dry heaves again. I hadn't eaten anything in days. I finally got up and fell across the bed with my head over the slop bucket. I kept remembering how my father looked when he told me, "If you've made your bed hard, then you're going to have to sleep in it. Don't come back to me." What could I do but stay there and accept whatever Larry wanted to do to me? My father could not have made it more plain; I was supposed to do what my husband told me to do. I had promised to love, honor and obey. If I had let him con me into the mess I was in, I could only blame myself.

The next two mornings Larry kicked me out of bed and onto the floor again. He didn't even ask if I was going to make his breakfast. It wouldn't have done any good anyway. Nothing he did could give me enough strength to stand on my feet, let alone cook.

By Monday I'd been sick for over a week. I hadn't been able to keep down any food or water. I was so weak, I was drifting in and out of consciousness. Larry would get up, get dressed and leave, slamming the door behind him, letting me know just how angry he was.

Day after day I asked God to send the Death Angel to get me out of my living torment. I was very much looking forward to crossing over. I didn't feel I had anything left to live for. I hadn't seen or talked to anyone in close to a month. What possible reason did I have to live if this was the way my life was going to be? I began to wonder what heaven would be like. My thoughts were interrupted by the door opening and Larry walking in, looking around, like he'd lost something.

"You're not ready to get out of that bed yet?" he said, still searching for whatever he was searching for.

"I'm ready, but I don't have the strength." I kept an eye on him, not wanting to be caught off-guard by something unexpected he might do.

"Damn it, Evelyn, you're not sick, you're just pregnant, that's all that's wrong with you. You've gone and gotten yourself pregnant. I'm telling you it's time you got your lazy backside out of bed and quit feeling sorry for yourself."

Pregnant? It never crossed my mind. The word took me by surprise. "How do you know I'm pregnant?"

"I just know. Now get up from there."

I'd never been around anyone who was pregnant. My mother had twelve children, but I was the last one born. My mind rambled on, trying to digest what he said. I wondered if all women got this sick when they were pregnant; that is, if I was pregnant.

I never did figure out what he was looking for. Whatever it might have been, he didn't find it because he left empty-handed, slamming the door as usual.

The next morning I could tell that things were building up inside him.

"I want you to tell me this," he said. "Why the hell did you let yourself go and get pregnant?"

Now that was real food for thought, another topic for him to repeat over and over. Here he was, asking me, a naive child who had grown up in a society that, God forbid, never even hinted at sex, let alone ever had a discussion about it. He had the nerve to ask me why I had gone and got myself pregnant. He made it plain from the start that he didn't want children, but he never gave me a reason, and he never gave me any suggestions as to how to avoid it. There was no such thing as birth control at that time, at least to my knowledge. It was taken for granted back in those days that when a couple got married, they had children. Everybody knew that. Having children was the natural order of things. They all went forth and multiplied.

Two hours later, I again heard the door open. Fear leaped up in my throat. I thought, *Oh, dear God, what does he want this time?* I pulled the covers over my head. What I really wanted to do was scream at the top of my lungs. His footsteps were getting closer, coming straight toward me. I lay there with my eyes closed, afraid to breathe. Suddenly, I felt the sheet over me move. Then I saw my momma standing over me. When she saw my condition, she gasped, "My God, have mercy on us!" Then she turned and left without uttering another word.

My heart sank. How could my own mother see me lying there that sick and just walk away? I didn't think there were any tears left to cry, but I was wrong. I cried knowing that the situation would be even worse if Larry came back and caught me squalling. I just couldn't comprehend why my mother would walk out on me. When I heard the door open again, I quickly dried my eyes on the bed sheet, but it wasn't Larry, at least it wasn't Larry alone. Momma was with him. I was so happy to see her I didn't even care if my husband yelled at me for crying; they were tears of joy.

Momma said to me in her gentle voice, "Now, you hush up your crying. Crying isn't going to help anything. You need your strength. I got to get you dressed, so I can get you to a doctor." While she rummaged around my closet for something decent for me to wear, she kept on talking. "My Lord, have mercy, young'un. Just look at you! Tsk tsk ...My God, Child, you're nothing but skin and bones. When's the last time you had something to eat?"

Larry finally said, "It ain't no wonder she's all skin and bones, all she ever does is lay in bed and sleep. I ain't seen her eat nothing in days."

Mother turned on him with a vengeance. "You just wait one minute, young man. If you were as sick as she is, Lord only knows what kind of predicament you'd be in. Don't you have any compassion at all? You're the one that got her in this mess in the first place. I'm going to see to it she gets to a doctor! Now!"

" Well," Larry whined, "I just can't figure out why she wanted to get herself pregnant. Don't make any sense." He was trying to charm Momma, but there was nothing funny about the situation to her way of thinking. In fact, his comments made her even more furious. It was one of the few times I ever saw her fuming like that.

"You come on and get yourself around here and help me get her to the car," she said in a firm voice.

Larry hesitated for a moment.

Mother narrowed her eyes at him. "You need to understand something and understand it well; you got her in this mess, and you're the one that's going to get her out of it. Do you hear me?"

Larry fumbled around, looking as if he would rather be any other place in the world other than where he was. He had run into the one woman he couldn't push around. In my momma, he had met his match.

Mother was helping me into my dress and still lashing out at him. "What's your problem? Get around here and help hold her up. If we don't get her to the doctor pretty quick, she's going to die. You should have already taken her to see somebody before this. If you'd done that, she wouldn't be in this condition now." She grabbed up a pillow on the way out.

The two of them helped me into the back seat of Larry's car. Momma tucked the pillow behind me so that I could sit up. I just didn't have the strength to do it alone. Five miles down the road,

I started heaving again. Momma ordered Larry to stop the car. When he didn't do as fast as she wanted, she said, "Larry, I told you to stop this car. Can't you hear Evelyn? She's sick. Now stop and tend to her."

He stopped the car.

I crouched on the side of the road, heaving, but there was nothing left to come up. Mother helped me back into the car. She had a wet washcloth with her and she wiped my face with it. While she was getting me settled down, Larry remained behind the steering wheel. Our next stop was the doctor's office. The first thing the doctor said when he saw me, "Good heaven, Elma, why'd you wait until she was practically dead to bring her in?"

Momma cast an accusing glance at Larry, before she said, "I found her in this condition a few hours ago. I got her here as soon as I could."

"Well," he said, "it seems your baby's in the family way, but she's very dehydrated." He gave me a shot for the nausea and Mother instructions on how to take care of me.

Despite the fact we had to stop once along the side of the road so that I could dry heave, we made the twenty-mile trip back to Jamestown in record time. We had just crossed the railroad track, and were within yards of our apartment, when Momma said to Larry, "Don't stop here. I'm taking her home with me. I'll take care of her until she's better." She didn't ask him, she told him.

He didn't like it, but he knew he couldn't do anything about it. Without any argument, he drove on to my parents' place. He even helped Mother get me into the house and in the bed. Then he left without saying a word. I felt as if the weight of the world had lifted from my shoulders.

The next morning Momma killed a chicken and made a pot of her cure-all chicken soup. Neither she nor Daddy had anything good or bad to say in front of me about Larry or my predicament. Momma came into the room from time to time to check on me, but I don't remember Daddy ever coming to my room. It was the only time I felt my father had ever shunned me.

Larry was six miles away, in Jamestown. He didn't come back that night after work and he didn't come back the next night. In fact, he didn't come back until the following Saturday. He got out of the car, came straight into the house, to the bedroom and said, "Get yourself up and get your clothes on 'cause I'm taking you home."

Momma and Daddy remained in the kitchen while he was there. I reached for the clothes I had worn to the doctor's office. I was shaking and weak, but I got dressed like he told me to do. He never offered to help. When I got myself put together as best I could, he walked behind me to the car. My feet felt like I had lead in them. How I dreaded to go back to those two rooms and their smell of kerosene. I felt like I was being marched to a gas chamber. I was scared of what he might do once he got me alone again. He'd had time to think over the fact that my mother had taken the control out of his hands for a few days. I could tell that he was seething, fixing to erupt. I'd come to realize that once we were behind closed doors, he was capable of almost anything. I was terrified. He'd had four days to dream up ways to figure out what kind of punishment he wanted to use on me.

Inside our apartment, I tried to sit up, but I was in no condition to do so for more than a couple of minutes. I had to lie down. Larry got a straight-back chair and sat down with his right foot across his left knee. He sat there for at least an hour, staring blankly into space, never speaking a word. Suddenly he said, "Guess what?"

I was startled by his voice. "What?"

"I got a letter today from the navy yard. They think they're going to force me to come back to work. I've got news for them. I don't want to go back and they sure as hell can't make me."

I didn't really feel like making conversation, but at least his attention was on something besides me. "Why don't you want to go back to your old job?"

"Nobody's going to make me do anything I don't want to do." He went on for another five, maybe ten minutes, moaning and groaning about how the navy yard couldn't do this and couldn't do that to him. He was pretending that the letter didn't bother him, but if that was so, then why all the whining? He ended his tirade with, "You got anything to say on the subject? You listening to me?"

"It's because the government put a freeze on the jobs. It's not the navy yard itself. Have you stopped to think about all the young Americans getting killed every day? Have you stopped to think that you have two brothers over there fighting? I've got three myself, they're in the army. Electric welders are needed just as much as they need soldiers. Why do you think you and Stanley got that free training? If the country doesn't have anything for servicemen to fight with, the whole cause is going to be lost. It just seems to me they need your help." That was sure more than I felt up to saying, but it seemed to me it needed to be said.

It didn't even make a dent in his thinking. "They can't make me do what I don't want to do," he said again. And again.

By Sunday I was feeling some better, but not good enough to get out of bed. Larry said he was bored and was going to go over to the garage to see what Mitchell was up to. Being left alone, the blues suddenly consumed me. When I was small, I felt terribly lonely at times, but I had Nanny Eve to take me in her arms and give me a hug. I couldn't remember the last time I'd had a hug. Maybe it was when Mrs. Clark took me in her arms the day I told her we were moving. Larry wasn't a hugger. Not that I cared about him hugging me, but I never felt more like I needed affection than I felt at that moment.

When he came back, he talked some more about the letter the navy had written to him. I never saw it, but it must have been pretty stern. A threat. He was surprised they had been able to track him down so fast. That's when a light went on in my head. I understood now why we got out of Charleston so fast. He was running from the navy, or from the government, certainly from his job.

By mid-November I was over the morning sickness. The feel of fall was in the air. Days were warm, but the nights were cool. Maybe the wonderful weather had something to do with the improvement in Larry's disposition. I couldn't help but wonder if he hadn't finally accepted the fact we were going to have a baby. All I knew for sure was that I was glad the meanness seemed to have left his system.

One afternoon I got the urge to get outdoors. Larry had put his foot down about me going up to my sister's house. I couldn't see her unless he went with me. So, I decided I'd like to have some ice cream. I had a little change my purse. The more I thought about it, the more I made up my mind to go next door to the store, and buy me a cup. In those days ice cream came in little round cardboard cups. David and Lottie owned the store. David was my mother's brother's son. Lottie was a distant cousin on my father's side.

I proceeded to make myself presentable, strolled on over to the store, and walked directly to the freezer where they kept the ice cream. I took out a cup of chocolate. As I went to pay my bill, I noticed two well-dressed gentlemen standing near the cash register talking to each other. I assumed they were traveling salesmen. David and Lottie got most of their business from people passing through. There was one other man in the store. Lottie was waiting on him. As soon as she finished with him, she turned to me.

"My goodness," she said, "it sure is good to see you again, Evelyn. I been wondering what you're doing with all your extra time."

"Well, you know how it is. Woman's work is never done."

"Why don't you come spend some time with me in the store? I'm here by myself most of the day. The hours sure would pass faster if I had somebody to talk to."

"Well, thanks, Lottie, but I'll have to see."

I heard a sound behind me, but I didn't turn around. Lottie was saying, "I heard you been sick. It does show a bit. You don't have your right color back. You need to take better care of yourself."

"I'm a lot better now."

"Why don't you sit down over there in that rocking chair? We can talk in-between me taking care of customers."

At that instant I heard Larry call my name. He was standing outside the door, looking at me. That was the sound I'd heard a few seconds before, him at the door.

I said to Lottie, "Your offer sounds good, but I have to run along. I'll get back to you later."

When I cleared the door, Larry caught me by my arm and pulled me toward him. He was shoving me along very discretely, trying to look as nonchalant as he possibly could. Anyone looking on would never have thought there could be anything out of the ordinary going on. They would have thought we were just two young married people.

Once we got to our apartment, he spun me around and, at the same time, took one step back. His face was red with anger. The veins in the side of his neck were throbbing. My knees almost went out from under me, I was so scared. I had no idea what was going to happen next, but I knew it wasn't going to be good.

I heard my voice tremble and I wasn't able to stop it. "Larry, what in heaven's name is wrong with you?"

"You want to know what's wrong? It's you! That's what's wrong with me. You have the nerve to ask me what's wrong?"

"What'd I do now?"

"You take me to be a damn fool, don't you?"

"Well, no, no, I don't." My heart was beating faster, "Please, tell me what I did wrong."

I couldn't see that my going to buy a ten-cent cup of ice cream could possibly be all that bad. What I thought had nothing to do with it, however. All that mattered to him was what he thought.

"You don't think I seen those two men in suits go in that store?"

"How would I possibly know if you saw those men go in the store?"

There was fire in his eyes as he stared at me.

"My Lord, Larry, I only went to the store to buy a cup of ice cream. You know I haven't been able to keep anything down. I thought it might give me some strength."

I held the ice cream so he could see it. He slapped it out of my hand.

"Don't you stand in my face and tell me that," he said with his eyes narrowed. "Damn funny you didn't want any ice cream until you seen them two men go in the store. You're handing me the same kind of lie you've stuck to about that damn sailor and you know it. You were trying to lure them after you, just like you did that sailor. You don't fool me for a damn minute. I'm on to you, whore!"

"I told you the truth about the sailor and I'm telling you the truth now."

"One thing for sure," he said as if he hadn't heard me. " I'm going to have to teach you a lesson you won't forget." Then he slapped me hard across my face.

I staggered into the wall, which broke my fall. He stood there in a rage. When I stood up, he drew his arm back again and slapped me with every ounce of strength he could muster. My legs doubled under me and I slid down to the floor. He was seething through clinched teeth, like a frenzied wild cat, when he kicked me. Not hard, but sort of light, to get my attention. Then he said calmly, "I'm going to go back to work now, that is, if you think I can trust you to stay home."

"Yes, yes," I said, crying. "Don't worry. I'll be here when you get back."

Larry wasn't loud when he got mad. He was aware there was only a thin wall between us and the store and he wasn't about to take a chance on being heard. His voice stayed quiet, and he spoke in a monotone. I found myself thinking later that in those days anything a man wanted to do to his wife behind closed doors, was absolutely legal. We'll never know how many women were brutalized during those days. It's taken years for the justice system to finally wake up.

My concern now was my baby. Somehow, one way or another, this baby that I was carrying in my belly had to have a future. My child deserved a good life, whether Larry liked it or not. I loved the little one already. I was looking forward to having a baby I could love and take care of. And this baby was going to love me in return! The thought was so exciting. I had to be careful not to express those sentiments to Larry, still, being so naive, I'd ask myself over and over, *What am I doing wrong to keep bringing out the worst in him? What can I do to change things, to make things better, so he'll treat me better?*

If I didn't do every tiny thing the way he thought it should be done, I was a bad wife. Question after question raced through my mind. I thought husbands were supposed to show some type of love or affection for their wife just as my father did for my mother; that was all the education I'd had about how to be a wife. I was taught as a child to " Do as you're told and ask no questions". At that moment, in my mind's eye, I could see Daddy as he'd looked coming in from working the fields. He refused to sit down until my mother was seated. Once she was in her chair, he knelt by her for a short prayer. He never once forgot to thank God for the family's bountiful blessings. Afterward, he would lean over to kiss Mother on the cheek, and he'd say softly, "I love you, Momma." That wasn't a once-in-a-while thing; it happened three times a day, at every meal. I had forgotten about it until I started writing my story years after the fact. Then I remembered how Father would take my mother's cup of coffee. He'd take a sip and Mother would say to him, "Daddy, you have your own coffee." He just had to have a taste of the food on my mother's plate, the drink in her cup.

Even though, as a child, I often felt alone, I knew that my parents loved me. When you're as protective of someone as they were of me, that's real love. With twelve children, Momma and Daddy had very little time. Now that I'm older, I can see that having only one girl, with all those young boys running around, they didn't have any choice but to keep me separated. It wasn't only the six brothers; there were field workers at the farm every day.

Nanny Eve and the other ladies who did the cooking and cleaning were given strict orders to keep a close eye on me. Nanny Eve never missed a thing. She saw to it that I was kept on the sidelines. It was being on the sidelines that made me a good listener.

There weren't any toys for us in those days. After I was old enough to be trusted with a pair of scissors, Mother would give me her old Sears & Roebuck catalog. Soon, I figured out that I could create my own paper dolls. I collected a shoe box full of figures from the catalog. I'd ease myself under the long table in the kitchen to cut out then play with my paper dolls. As I played, I'd listen to Nanny Eve and the others hum songs or talk while they worked. Isolated under the table gave me a lonely feeling, but what Larry did to me was more like being a prisoner. I was truly alone until he came home to eat his dinner. We were always in bed by eight.

Over the next few weeks, he had another mood swing. At times, we'd actually have a conversation; other times he wouldn't talk to me, but he wasn't cruel and he didn't slap me again. During one of his talkative spells, he told me that he'd had another letter from the navy yard, this one much more insistent that he return to his old job. He treated it like a joke, remarking on how sorry he felt for them since he had no intention of ever going back. He ended with, "There's nothing anybody can do to make me do something I don't want to do." But he wasn't mad. I came to the conclusion that staying to myself had brought about a remarkable change in him. Evidently, I was learning to do things the way he wanted them done. There still wasn't any affection from him, but he was nicer. I was sure he would stay that way.

Wrong!

He was only leading up to another one of his episodes. He liked to play his little games with me and now he had another one in mind.

About four o'clock one afternoon in December, he left the garage two hours earlier than his usual quitting time. Thank goodness, I already had his supper cooked. I was standing in front of the stove when he eased up behind me. I was shocked when he put his arms around me to give me a light hug. He was in the happiest mood I'd ever seen him.

"Does Christmas make you feel this good?" I asked, smiling. "If it does, it'd be nice for it to come around more often."

He chuckled. That in itself was Christmas to my ears. I was so starved for any type of love or affection, just to hear him laugh and to be in a jolly mood, was heaven. I had been shut up in those two rooms for such a long time I felt I was going stir crazy.

"Go ahead and set the table," he said. "Put supper out so we can eat early."

"That's fine with me."

He further surprised me by asking, "Are you feeling better?"

"Matter of fact, I feel real good. Why do you ask?"

"Oh, nothing much. I just got a little Christmas surprise for you."

I could feel myself getting excited. "What?" I giggled, afraid to believe my ears.

"Hurry up and wash the dishes. When you get finished, I'll think about telling you what it is."

Like a small child eager to please, he hadn't any sooner made the request than the dishes were washed and put away. Once again, he came up behind me as I was putting the last of the dishes in the cabinet and put his arm around me.

"Hey," I said. "I kinda like this little game you're playing."

"You do, eh? Well now, if you'll hurry and get your best duds packed, I just might let you go to Walhalla with me."

"What? When? Now? Tonight?"

"Yes, tonight."

"You gotta be kidding. Oh, please, tell me you're not kidding!"

"No, I'm not kidding. If you'll shut up long enough to do what I'm telling you, we'll be out of here and on our way."

9

Going to Walhalla was the best news I'd had since we got to Jamestown. To be near my people and not be allowed to spend time with them had been painful as well as embarrassing. Yet none of them had ever visited me or tried to investigate the cause for me not seeing them. They knew I'd only been to my mother's that one time, back when I was sick. Weren't they curious? Didn't they wonder?

While finishing up the packing for our trip, it dawned on me that I should let Momma and Daddy know we were going to be gone for Christmas. I was sure they expected us to be with them.

"Larry, don't you think we should let my folks know that we'll be gone for Christmas? Momma always makes a big Christmas dinner for the whole family. They'll be expecting us."

"Aw, come on," he said. "Don't worry about a thing like that. They'll understand. Surely they know, since we've been right here under them all this time, that I want to go and see my family for Christmas. It's the last chance I'll have for a long time to go see my momma. Come on now, you know your folks won't mind." He couldn't wait to get in the car and get started. We hadn't gone very far before he began whistling a tune.

The night air was cool and damp. He had the heater on. Time passed slowly. I began turning and twisting, trying to be get comfortable. I had lost so much body weight while I was sick that my tail bone was cutting through my skin. Other than that, the trip was fairly pleasant considering it lasted nine hours. We pulled into the Barkley driveway just after two o'clock Christmas morning.

I felt giggly and excited. "Your folks will really think that Santa Claus has come this Christmas, slipping in on them like this."

Larry laughed. "Come on. Get out. Let's go wake 'em up."

"Oh gosh! I just remembered, we didn't bring them a single present!" I felt bad, but there just hadn't been money for anything. We barely had enough for gas to get there.

He tried to comfort me with, "Aw, nothing to worry about. I'll just tell them that they'll be getting a late Christmas present."

"What are you talking about? What kind of late Christmas present?"

"A baby. Have you forgot?"

No, I hadn't forgotten, but I wasn't expecting him to say something like that. He didn't talk much about the baby and I wasn't prepared for him to sound so happy about it.

"I can't think of anything that would make my momma any happier," he said, "than to know she's going to have a new grand baby. Ah, man, you should have seen her when Betty and Dot were born. She wanted a boy when she got Dot. The way it turned out, she got two granddaughters instead. Maybe we can give her a grandson."

I couldn't believe my ears, the way that he was carrying on. He never failed to amaze me with his mood swings.

Larry opened the screen door. We went in through the kitchen. Nobody ever locked their doors back in those days.

"Hey, hey, hey," Larry called out. "You'd better wake up! Santa Claus is here!"

Mrs. Barkley had heard us in the driveway and was already up, pulling a coat over her nightgown. The fire in the fireplace had gone out, the house had gotten pretty chilly. It was much colder in Walhalla, at the foothills of the mountains, than in Charleston.

Mr. Barkley hurried to start a new fire in the fireplace. We were all standing as close to the flames as we could get until the room warmed up. Everyone seemed happy to see us. Grandma, who had come for the holidays, got out of bed to join in the merriment. Her long salt-and-pepper hair hung to her waist; I thought she looked beautiful.

Behind her, Laura Mae said, "You guys don't care who you wake up on Christmas morning, do you?", but she was kidding. I could tell she was glad we were there.

After getting the fire going, Mr. Barkley went into the kitchen to start up the old wood-burning cook stove. Then he came back to announce he had put on a pot of coffee. Soon as the stove was hot enough to start cooking, Mrs. Barkley began fixing our Christmas breakfast.

It sure was nice to be away from the smell of kerosene. The scent of country ham in the frying pan, mixed with the odor of the wood-burning fire, was beginning to wake up an appetite in me. That was something I hadn't had for a very long time. Quick as the food was on the table, everyone gathered around, stuffing their faces. It was the first full meal I'd had since I had gotten in the family way. There was indeed a spirit of Christmas in the air. I thought about my mother, how I'd spent very little time with her since I was thirteen and not a lot of quality time before I was thirteen, Nanny Eve was more my constant companion. In my memories of Mother I see her reading to us from the Bible every night, though I also remember what a great story-teller she was.

Later on that morning, Mrs. Barkley said, "Come here, girl. Let me take a good look at you."

"What?"

"You've lost a lot of weight, haven't you?"

"Aw, come on, Momma, " Larry protested. "There's nothing for you to worry about. She's all right."

But she was concerned. "No, son, she's not all right. You don't lose that much weight without a reason."

"She just went and got herself in the family way, that's all."

His mother lifted one eyebrow. "What did you just say?"

"I said she just went and got herself in the family way, that's all."

"Larry, you said that she got herself in the family way."

"That's right, Momma. She did."

Mrs. Barkley had to laugh at that. "Are you telling me she

managed to do that all by herself, without any help from you?

Larry, I neglected to mention it before, it takes two to make babies. She couldn't possibly have done that all by herself." Then she said more seriously, "Whatever the reason for it happening, it's the best Christmas present I could hope for."

"Well, Momma, it looks as if you're going to get your Christmas present from us in July this year."

"That's great. Now I have something special to look forward to."

Was Larry really happy or was it just a pretense in front of his family? How long would this happiness over the baby last? My feelings were mixed.

There wasn't any Christmas tree or gifts wrapped in pretty paper though there was plenty of good country food, the kind that had been set-aside for special occasions like this one. The feast that we're accustomed to today wasn't available to us in those days. My mother-in-law had made it a very merry Christmas by baking a cake to celebrate Jesus' birth. Before it was served around mid-afternoon, we all held hands and sang "Happy Birthday, Jesus." She told us that this day wasn't about any of us, it was about the birth of our Lord.

It was the best Christmas day I'd had in a very long time.

I was more than grateful that Larry was on his best behavior. Most of all, I was glad that he was happy about the baby. I got the feeling that putting three hundred miles between him and the Charleston navy yard contributed to some of his joy. When his two brothers arrived later that day, he went so far as to brag that he was going to be a daddy.

My understanding before we left to go to Walhalla was that we'd only be there for Christmas and we'd spend New Year's Day with my parents. The day before New Year's Eve, however, he had another mood swing. He announced that we were moving to Salem, and that his father and his brother, George, were going to help us. We would be living in the house with his parents. George had come home for Christmas on a sixteen-day leave from the army before shipping out to Germany. From there, he would go straight to the front lines of the war zone.

The next morning the three men had an early breakfast and left immediately for Jamestown.

Once they were on their way, I went into the living room. Grandma was sitting in one of the rocking chairs, ready to tell one of her stories. Some were heart-wrenching, but nonetheless interesting. She told me how her husband had been killed after he got caught up on a huge belt in the cotton mill where he worked. This had left her a widow with several young children to bring up. It was difficult, she said, being a single mother. She told me that her son, Patrick, whom everyone called Uncle Pat, had thrown his hat in the political ring for the office of magistrate and had won the election. She was so proud of him, as was all the family yet she confessed to me that she just didn't feel right about him holding that office. That surprised me. "What is it about Uncle Pat being magistrate that you don't like?"

"Well," she said, "it's like this, that position makes him a judge. The Bible tells us not to judge lest we be judged. I just don't feel right about him sitting in judgment of others."

Grandma was in her late seventies. Despite the fact her hands shook a little, she would tell me stories while she kept her crochet needle moving.

"Now take Dora there," she said. Dora was my mother-in-law's given name. "Dora's my baby. She's the only one I have left that I still have to worry about. Now you take that there man of Dora's. He's something else to be reckoned with. Alonzo ..." Her voice sort of drifted off.

I asked if that was Mr. Barkley's first name and she said, "Yes. How Dora's been able to hold up under what she has all these years, I'll never understand. All the heartbreaking things that man has put her through, only the good Lord knows." Then she stopped and slowly shook her head back and forth. "A.P., that's who I'm talking about." At times she would call Larry's daddy Alonza, other times she referred to him as A.P. "It's not just what he's put Dora through, but my Lord, those children of hers, too."

"What kind of things, Grandma?"

"Hasn't Dora told you this?" She paused to answer her own question. "Well, I guess not. You haven't been here long enough. My, my, my, how awful it was, the way he's beaten those boys. The blood runs cold in my veins every time I stop to think about what he'd done to them. I'm here to tell you, Evelyn, Alonzo has a real mean streak in him. Yes, ma'am, a real bad, mean streak in him. Pat and me both worry about Dora and the children all the time. I'm telling you, that's one for you to be careful of."

The part about how he'd beat the boys struck a nerve in me. It was easy for me to comprehend the seriousness of what she was telling me. With the treatment I'd already suffered at the hands of my husband, my antennas was tuned in to her every word. "What boys was it that he beat, Grandma?"

"I'm talking about Albert, Larry, and George, all three of them. One time I was here when Alonzo said he found a hair in his razor. He lined those boys up, one in front of the other." She pointed to an old Singer sewing machine in the corner. "Look there. You see that there round leather belt on that sewing machine? Well, Alonzo took that very belt off of that very machine and beat those boys with it." She was choking back tears as she remembered the horrible things her grandchildren had endured. She paused long enough to wipe away her tears with her apron, then she continued with the rest of the story.

"There was blood puddled right there on the floor. We tried to stop him, Dora and me, but once he gets started, there's not any stopping that man. Alonzo has never made me believe he found hair in that razor. Even if he had, what damage could a hair have done? I still say he lied. It was just his excuse to beat those boys. A.P.'s mean, I tell you. He's a cruel, vicious man. Evelyn, there are times when it seems like he just has to have human flesh to beat on. That's one of the reasons why I insist Pat keep bringing me up here. I've always worried about Dora and the children. Only God himself knows what Alonzo just might try next. It really gets to me, but I can't stand to stay away very long at a time. Dora tells me that he does better when I'm here. My, my, my, all the pain and hurt it causes me every time I think about how he's treated Dora and those children over the years."

She pulled her crocheting closer. "I lost my train of thought. What was I telling you? Oh, yes. Oh my, what a time we had cleaning up the gashes on those little bodies!" I saw another tear slip down her cheek. "Alonzo wouldn't let us touch the boys. We knew him well enough to know that if we did try helping them, he wouldn't hesitate to beat us the same way he beat them. If not that, then he'd only get madder and he'd beat them harder. Thank God he didn't stick around too long after he wore himself out. He stayed gone, let's see, must have been at least four days. Dora and me, we decided that he went to spend some time with his other woman."

I felt my mouth drop.

"He must have treated his other woman all right," she said. "If he didn't, we never heard anything about it. I'll tell you one thing, just as he got out the door, I grabbed a wash pan and started washing those children. Dora got out the jar of chicken grease and we proceeded to clean them up. I still say that man will never stop until he kills somebody. He's evil. I think he's possessed with demons."

Chicken grease was all they had to use in those days. They'd boil a fat hen then let it set until the broth got cold. As the grease cooled it would rise to the top. They would skim it off and put it in a jar to be saved for just such an occasion. That was before we have salves like we do today.

Now that Grandma had related those stories to me, I was beginning to understand a bit more about what made Larry the way he was. At least I thought I was beginning to understand. Having grown up in an environment such as that would affect anyone. I was getting educated fast. I intended to stay as far away from my father-in-law as humanly possible. I never knew that a person like Alonzo Barkley existed. My father never beat any of us, well, except two of my brothers. He took a leather strap and set two of my older siblings backsides on fire. They were sixteen and seventeen years old and had been fist fighting each other. Daddy had twice warned them to stop. When they didn't mind him, my father was as good as his word. After that whipping, my brothers stayed best of friends for the rest of their life. He made them understand that he wasn't raising any Cain and Abels.

Four days after I heard Grandma's story, Larry, George, and their father returned, pulling an old homemade trailer behind the car with our few earthly possessions in it.

My mother-in-law greeted them with, "Welcome back. How'd your trip go?"

"Not too good," my father-in-law replied. "We had a tire blow out. Almost lost the trailer. I'll be happy to tell you about it later, but first we want something to eat. You girls get some food on the table. We're starving."

They were about halfway through their meal when George started laughing. Every time he looked at Larry, he burst out with fresh chuckles. This went on for a long time without any explanation. Finally my mother-in-law couldn't stand it any longer. She had to know the joke. "What's so funny, George?"

George was hysterical, trying to tell us, but he wasn't quite sure if he should.

Larry turned red-faced. "Shut up, George. I'll tell 'em." He cleared his throat and looked at me. "I went by Margie's to get your dress like you asked me to do." I had asked him to run by my sister's place and pick up a dress she had said she'd make for me. I'd given her the fabric and I told Larry that if she hadn't finished the outfit, or maybe hadn't even started it yet, to bring the material back and I'd do it myself.

Larry was saying, "She told me to tell you that she hadn't had time to make the dress for you, so I brought the material back."

When Larry said that, George started laughing even harder.

Mr. Barkley took up where Larry left off. "Your momma found out that Larry was stopping by Margie's before he came back here, so she was waiting for us. Evelyn, I've never seen a woman that raging mad in my entire life."

I had to smile. My mother never showed any mercy when someone disappointed her, and Larry had certainly disappointed her. I asked what she said to them.

Mr. Barkley said, "What she didn't say to Larry I don't think could have been thought of. I didn't know a woman could use so many words to tell a person what she thinks about them without one filthy expression coming out of her mouth."

Mrs. Barkley asked Larry, "Son, what'd you say to her?"

Mr. Barkley answered her question. "What could he say? He grinned and took it."

A couple of weeks after that, I received a letter from my mother. The sad and painful part of it was her tears that stained the letter.

She wrote in part, "Anything, I do mean anything, happens to you, or to that baby, Larry had better give his heart to God. I promise you on my mother's grave that there will be a day of reckoning for that young man."

I read the very long letter with tears running down my cheeks. Just to read her words cut deep within me. There wasn't any way for me to explain. How could I possibly confide in her exactly how things were with me? I couldn't tell her how much safer I felt being with my mother-in-law, even though Grandma had warned me about my father-in-law. I didn't see any way I could change things. The guilt that I was feeling was tremendous. The shame I felt having to live the way I was living is still indescribable. I felt guilty that I had let my parents down when they had been so proud of my work record; they had so much faith that I would go on to bigger and better things. Finding me in the family way, at death's door, I knew Momma felt that she had a reason for worrying. Without a doubt, she did save my life.

So there we were, married more than eight months, without any money in our pockets. What's even worse, neither of us had a job. We were both sitting on our duffs in his parents' home with not one cent of income to look forward to. The five of us were in a three-room, rundown farmhouse long past the stage of being condemned. The sale of vegetables from the garden and hen eggs was our only means of livelihood.

I waited more than a week before I could bring myself to answer Momma's letter. The pain in my heart felt like someone was twisting a knife. I told her how well Mrs. Barkley was treating me. I told her that Larry had been good to me since we'd been there. I didn't write anything that was negative.

Mother's letter had gotten Larry caught in another one of his lies. He had told me that he asked Lena to explain to my mother that we had gone to his parents' for Christmas and would be back to Shulerville no later than New Year's Eve; we would spend New Year's Day with them. Mother wrote that she had worried herself sick all through Christmas because nobody knew where we were. Then someone told her that they had seen Larry in Jamestown, loading our things into a trailer. Whoever that person was, had also talked with Larry because he'd told this person that he was coming to Margie's to pick up some material for me. "That's why I went to Margie's, to face the young man," Momma wrote. "When Lena and her family came for Christmas, I asked if she'd heard from you or Larry. I wanted to know if you were going to be with us for Christmas dinner. Lena told me that the two of you had gone to visit the Barkley's for Christmas. What made me so mad was that I knew you had no business taking that kind of trip in your condition."

A couple of weeks after we got settled in with the Barkley's, I started out to the porch to sit with Larry and his father. I heard them talking as I approached.

"I don't know how they found me this quick," Larry was saying.

Mr. Barkley asked him, "What'd the letter say exactly?"

I stopped without opening the screen door, to listen.

Larry kind of laughed. "Well, Daddy, they don't seem to be very happy with me. They was threatening me with what they were going to do to me if I didn't report back on my job."

It seems a letter from the navy yard had arrived while the men were in Jamestown. Larry never mentioned the letter to me and I never asked about it.

◘

Now that Grandma was back at Uncle Pat's, Mrs. Barkley designated her bed near the fireplace as our bedroom. One cold morning in mid-January, with Jack Frost everywhere, I woke to a *bip bip bip* sound. I wondered what on earth it could be. I looked out the window and saw five goats having more fun than a barrel of monkeys. They would jump on the fender of our car, then onto the hood, then on the top of the car, down on the trunk, and back on the ground. Over and over, around and around they went, in perfect unison, as if they were a fully trained act. The whole top of the car was ripped to pieces. 1936 Plymouths had about a four foot square inset on the top that was a type of canvas with some kind of tar-like substance over it. Age and weather had weakened it. The goats' feet went right through. They were fun to watch, but I had to wonder where money was coming from to replace the top of the car before rain set in.

A few mornings later, I awoke to a much different sound. This was more of a distressed sound, a definite sound of trouble. Jumping up from my bed to investigate, I ran into the kitchen trying to see what was happening. Everyone was there, looking out a window, toward the corral. I could hardly believe what my eyes were seeing. My father-in-law had the prettiest teams of mules I'd ever seen; he was beating one of them almost to death right in front of us. The poor thing was already down on its knees.

I ran out of the house with everyone yelling for me to come back. Larry had left early to take our car in to see about getting the roof fixed. The sky was threatening rain. My mother-in-law and Laura Mae were standing at the window, screaming at me. They feared for me to get near this raging man. Laura Mae had a nervous disorder that the doctors called St. Vitis Dance. When she got upset, she lost all control.

Once I reached the corral, Mr. Barkley looked up and saw me approaching. He immediately stopped beating the mule, and stared me straight in the eyes. He said in the most hateful voice I'd ever heard, "If I had a pitchfork, I'd finish her off." The mule looked as if she was dying.

To my right was a pitchfork leaning against the fence. I picked it up and threw it at him with every ounce of strength in me. He made a perfect catch, but the shocked expression on his face was something to see.

"Go ahead," I said. "She's almost dead anyway. Why not finish what you started?"

He stood holding the pitchfork, looking at me with fire in his eyes, for a good twenty seconds. Then he threw the pitchfork on the ground and stormed off. He didn't just walk away from the corral, he walked off the property. Last we saw of him, he was headed in the direction of Salem. It was four days before anyone heard from him again. When he returned, he came waltzing in as if he had only gone to the store to pick up a pound of coffee. Evidently that was the first time he had ever been challenged by a woman. I was pleased that I had been able to stop him. Mrs. Barkley said later that he wouldn't have stopped until he killed the mule, just as he once beat the family dog to death.

Larry returned from the garage with our car. By some miracle, they were able to mend the top. As he pulled into the yard, his mother called to him, "Larry, you need to come here and see if you can do anything to help get this poor mule back on its feet."

He took one look and didn't even ask what happened. He knew his father well enough to figure it out.

"Just be patient, Momma," he said. "I'll have to go see if I can get some of the neighbors to help me. If we can't get her on her feet, I might have to shoot her."

He gathered up three neighbor men and they managed to get the mule upright. It was interesting to see how they fashioned a type of sling out of burlap then fastened it over a couple of the crossbeams in the barn loft. Somehow, with a rope and pulley, they got her to a standing position. Amazingly, she survived the ordeal and eventually healed to the point that she lived a long, healthy life.

I wasn't able to sleep well for weeks, after witnessing what he did to that mule. His two mules were an important part of our livelihood. Without them there wouldn't be any farming come spring.

From that day on, I never had anything but hard feelings for my father-in-law. The first time I met him I'd gotten bad vibes, but now I detested him. It was incredible to me that he could beat a beautiful mule until it lay on its broadside crying like a baby. And to think he'd beaten the family dog to death, too, to say nothing of the beatings he'd given his children over the years. It made my blood boil. I no longer had to wonder why Larry was the way he was. Growing up with a man like that for a father, how could he possibly be anything other than what he was? I understood, too, why Larry spent hours staring into space. He had a lot to think about. A lot to try to understand.

I had no way of knowing it at the time, but things were destined to get much worse. A few days later, Louise came to visit. Her baby was due almost any day, so we had a lot in common.

I was making more frequent visits to the toilet since my baby was getting larger inside me and putting more and more pressure on my bladder. So, on this one day, I was on my way to the outhouse when Louise asked if I minded if she went along.

"Not at all," I said. "I'd be grateful for the company. I've been alone so much lately, it's nice to have someone to talk with."

Louise and I had bonded right away. There was an aura about her I couldn't help but like. Laura Mae decided to come along too. The three of us were at the little house behind the big house, doing our business and making small talk. I told them how much I liked Grandma and listening to her stories. I'd had very little time alone with my mother-in-law. I didn't mention it to them, but I'd noticed that she was most always up in the field at the top of the hill with Mr. Barkley. She'd be working in the house and he'd yell for her and she'd stop what she was doing to hurry to him. They'd be gone for long periods of time. There was something else I'd noticed, too. Laura Mae would kid around with Larry, but so far, I hadn't seen him engage in any conversation with Louise. I had the impression that he avoided his older sister. There was definitely something wrong between them. I decided not question her about it, but I sure was curious. I was also curious about the way their father treated his sons.

"Louise," I said, "Grandma told me how your daddy beat your three brothers once until the blood puddled on the floor."

"Once?" she scoffed. "Evelyn, did she say only once?"

"She told me about that one time."

"Well, it wasn't the only time, but, yes, that was the worst time. It was like he took pleasure in whipping them." She was silent for a time, then she said softly, "Did she tell you what he did to me?"

I shook my head.

"He, he, um...um," she stammered, fighting to get her words out. "He got me pregnant."

I gasped like the wind was knocked out of me. "Oh, my God! He *what*?

"He raped me and got me pregnant. It was just after my fourteenth birthday when my baby was born."

It was a few seconds before I could speak. "Wait a minute," I finally said, "Wait, wait, wait. You're telling me that your very own father got you pregnant? You had a baby from your own father?"

"That's exactly what I'm telling you."

"Good Lord, Louise. Come on now, a father would never do a thing like that, would he? Do they? Not to their very own daughters?"

"Mine did."

"But–where's the baby?"

"It died. We took it to the doctor in Walhalla. On our way home, it died in Momma's arms. Grandma was with us. It was two weeks old. We buried it up on the edge of the field, just to the right of the house. I'll take you up there and show you the grave, if you'd like to see it. They never let me see the baby, so I don't know if it was a girl or a boy. Grandma told me that it was terribly deformed."

I had never before heard such a thing. A father that would rape and get his very own blood daughter in a family way! My God, have mercy on all of us, what was the world coming to? A person such as that should be taken out and castrated like my father use to do pigs. A man that stoops that low is lower than a pig.

Louise said, "There's more. That's what Larry is mad at me about. It's why he won't talk to me."

"You're telling me that Larry won't speak to you because your father raped you and got you with child?"

"Well, he still don't know that Daddy was the one that got me pregnant. He's just mad because I got pregnant."

"Explain to me why Larry doesn't know it was your daddy."

"Well, Daddy told Larry that it was his best friend, Clark, that was responsible. Larry got furious and went hunting for Clark. He told us that he was going to kill him. It wasn't very long after that Larry left here to go to work in Charleston. Nobody has ever told him that the baby was Daddy's, not Clark's. Larry and Clark had been best friends since they were in grammar school. Now Larry hates him."

Payton Place seemed mild in comparison to this. My father-in-law had taken his beautiful daughter up in the woods, not more than a hundred yards from their house, and brutally raped her and got her pregnant.

Louise kept on talking. "I'm telling you the truth, if I have to die. If you want me to, I can show you the stick that Daddy was going to beat me with if I didn't let him have his way with me. I've seen him beat them boys with it. I'm still scared to death of him. Evelyn, my daddy was so mad when he told me to take my clothes off and I refused. He told me that he would beat me to death. You've only seen his good side and you've only heard a small portion of what he's capable of doing. Just you wait until he's around you longer. Pretty as you are, you won't be able to get away from him. Believe me, he'll get to you eventually. If you don't believe me, well, just you wait and see. I'm warning you, you'd better be careful around him once your baby gets here."

Laura Mae had just turned thirteen. If he'd gotten to her yet, nobody ever said, so I assumed that he hadn't. That moment I made a mental note to stay as far away from him in the future as possible. We went back to the house. I found Grandma sitting in her usual place. I went in and sat down in the rocking chair directly across from her.

Grandma took one glance at me and said, "My goodness, are you all right? Child, you're as white as a ghost."

I didn't know how to answer. I didn't know if I should, or should not, mention to her what Louise had confided in me. I felt the need to talk to her. I was afraid of Larry and now I was even more fearful of my father-in-law. Louise never told me not to repeat what she'd said. I just had to find out more about it.

"Grandma, Louise just told me that Mr. Barkley raped her and got her pregnant."

"Oh, yes, that's common knowledge around here."

"I don't understand how a father could do such a thing to his very own daughter. I just don't understand."

"Well, A.P. never would agree for Louise to date. She was only thirteen at the time. In fact, he had forbid her to date. He knew that Clark liked her, so he made arrangements for him to call on Louise. They'd sit out on the porch swing, but they weren't allowed to leave.

When Louise came up in the family way, Larry, of course, found out about it. Alonzo blamed Clark, just as he'd planned to do all along. Well, Larry got furious and he went hunting for Clark to kill him. To this day he thinks that Clark's the father of Louise's baby. I knew all the time that it wasn't Clark's baby. Clark never had a chance to get to Louise. I was here and I can vouch for the fact they were never alone. Clark's a nice boy. He comes from a good family. He valued his friendship with Larry too much to let something like that come between them. I knew it had to be A.P.'s child."

I sat in stone silence, listening, taking in each and every word she spoke to me. I knew it was the gospel truth.

Grandma continued on, saying whatever came to mind. "You don't want to tell Larry that A.P. got Louise in the family way. If you did, he'd probably wind up killing his daddy. It'd be terrible for him to go to jail for murdering his own father."

I couldn't help but think about the position they had placed Clark in. What if Larry went off the deep end and killed Clark who was completely innocent? If that didn't happen, then it seemed unfair that Clark should have to go through the rest of his life with the whole community looking down on him for something he didn't do. I couldn't get this earth-shaking news out of my mind.

A couple of hours later, at the supper table, I let it slip I knew that Louise had a baby out of wedlock. Everyone instantly stood up and left the table. Thank goodness Mr. Barkley wasn't there. Larry sat there just as still as if he were a corpse for about two minutes, holding his fork in his left hand. Then he slammed his fork down with a vengeance and proceeded to leave the table. He went to his car and roared away on two wheels. He didn't come back until way after midnight. I was beginning to understand little bit why he had called me bad names. He was thinking about his sister. He had lost trust in her and now he had no trust in me because of what had happened.

11

Louise had been married to Etley Dills for more than a year when we came to live with the Barkleys. Etley was a backwoodsman, but a very good, gentle, hard-working man with morals. He didn't have any formal education whatsoever. He couldn't read, but he could write his name. He didn't care for Mr. Barkley any more than I did and he didn't care too much for Larry, either.

Larry started being good to me from the time we moved in with his parents. Louise had her baby, a big, bouncing little girl. She named her Evelyn, after me. That gave Mrs. Barkley her third granddaughter, but still not a grandson.

One morning after breakfast, Mrs. Barkley said, "Larry, we need to dig up some of those Irish potatoes." She asked him to hitch the plow to the mule. It was getting late in the day, but she wanted at least a part of them harvested.

"Oh, good, Larry," I said. "If you'll plow them up, Laura Mae and me will pick them up behind you."

I was eight months pregnant and I knew it wouldn't be easy to bend over, but I was willing to give it a try. Laura Mae and me found a container to hold the potatoes and we went out into the field. Mr. Barkley was there, too, which was unusual. He wasn't ordinarily around when there was work to be done. Quick as Larry tilled the ground, Laura Mae and me started picking up the potatoes and placing them in the container. We both felt good that day. We were laughing and playing around like the seventeen-year-olds we were.

Larry called out to us to stop playing and get to work.

In unison we replied, "We are working!"

We kept on laughing and talking, but all the while we where picking up potatoes and putting them in the container. Again Larry yelled back to us, "I told both of you to quit your foolishness. Get back to work."

Again I told him, "Larry, we are working."

We stopped laughing, but continued on with our conversation, telling some neat little jokes while trying not to giggle. Larry was on the far end of the field when suddenly he yelled out to the mule to whoa. The mule stopped in its tracks. Larry screamed at us, "Dammit, if I have to come back there, I'm gonna take my belt off and I'm gonna wear both of you out with it."

Laura Mae spoke up. "Larry, she told you that we're working. What more do you want?"

That was the straw that broke the camel's back. I was now eight full months pregnant. There wasn't any way in hell I was going to stand there and let him beat me with his belt. I thought, *Enough is enough!* I stood up slowly and brushed my hands together to get the dirt off, and I told him, "It seems impossible to please you. Nothing I do, or have ever done, has pleased you so how about you pick up these potatoes yourself?"

I turned around and wobbled back in the house. That was the first flare of temper I'd shown since I'd known him. While my mouth sounded brave, inside I was scared of him. I wondered if the baby in my tummy was suffering from the same kind of terror I was feeling. I could feel my little one turning and twisting. Maybe it was trying to send me a message.

Once inside the house, I began to have second thoughts. I was apprehensive about what he was going to do once he came in. I wondered where Mrs. Barkley and Grandma had gone. I walked to the shelf that held two water buckets and a wash pan. I lifted the dipper from the bucket, poured some water into the pan and cupped my hands to splash a handful of the cool liquid on my face. Afterward, I went in and lay down across Laura Mae's bed and I started to cry. I'd felt so good earlier. Laura Mae and me were working and having such a nice time. I'd had about three weeks of not going through another trauma with Larry, and now this, I was thinking.

I heard the squeaking sound of the kitchen door. My heart jumped up in my throat. I had a great feeling of uncertainty. Then there were footsteps moving across the kitchen floorboards, coming my direction. I felt a flood of relief when I recognized the voices of Mrs. Barkley and Grandma. Maybe Larry would finish his work in the field before he came in, I thought. Just the idea of him beating me with his belt sent shivers up my body.

Lost in my thoughts, I suddenly realized from her tone that Mrs. Barkley wasn't very happy with her son at that moment. Evidently, she had seen, or heard, what happened. I could make out the topic of her conversation with Grandma, but I couldn't make out every word of it.

I didn't see Larry again until supper that night. I stayed in Mrs. Barkley's bedroom, too scared to leave. When everybody else was at the table, she insisted I come and eat my supper.

◘

It wasn't long after that we got word that Larry's brother, Albert, had a nervous breakdown on a German battlefield. He had been given a medical discharge from the army and he was back home. His wife Edith, the one Larry dated before she married Albert, was coming to visit the Barkley's more often all the sudden. Larry and Edith would sit out on the front porch having long conversations. They had been taking trips to Walhalla pretty frequently, but I never knew why. One time he came back laughing and having a great time. What was so funny, he told his folks, was the fact that on the drive to Walhalla, every time he took his foot off the gas pedal, for some reason the air vent on the old Plymouth would fly open sending wind straight up Edith's dress. He thought it was hilarious, the way Edith screamed when it happened. I didn't think it was all that funny.

One day, after Larry and Edith had left to go to Walhalla again, Mrs. Barkley and I were sitting in the living room. She had her crochet work in her lap, like always, and she started expressing her concern about the situation. Crocheting at a frantic pace, she said, "I knew the minute Larry moved back here, that this was going to happen. I knew Edith wouldn't leave him alone."

"What do you mean?"

"Can't you see what's going on?"

"No. I don't understand what you're telling me."

What Mrs. Barkley didn't realize was the relief that came over me while he was away. At least, while he was gone, I could relax. When he was around, I had to watch every word, every move I made. I had no qualms about Edith. I looked at it like she was doing me a favor. I didn't understand that my mother-in-law was trying to tell me there was more going on between the two of them than shopping. I had never heard of a married man having sex with his brother's wife or any woman except his wife.

My big concern right now was the baby due to arrive in just a few more days. There was no money for baby clothes and I hadn't seen a doctor except that one time when my mother took me, so I was surprised when Mrs. Barkley said out of the blue, "We're going to take you to the doctor."

"You know there isn't any money for that," I said.

"Well, there's a doctor up here at the D.A.R. School. Actually it's in Tomassee, about four or five miles from here. They have their own doctor there. It's a woman, a midwife, actually, but she's great. It won't cost you a thing. I'm going to see to it that Larry takes you tomorrow. It's getting too close to your time to take chances." As if detecting the fear I was feeling that suddenly sprang up inside me, she added, "Don't worry, Evelyn. I'm going with you. I won't let you go with him by yourself."

That night before going to bed, Mrs. Barkley said, "We're going to go see Mrs. Clifton in the morning. Try to be ready about nine."

When we arrived at the school, the midwife seemed excited to see my husband. She knew the family personally and had heard the good news about how Larry had enrolled in electric welding school, finishing the course in a record time of six weeks, then how he had gone on to work at the Charleston Navy Yard.

"Larry, how are you doing? How do you like working in the navy yard?" she asked him.

Larry dropped his head to study his shoes. He danced around the edge of her questions, not wanting to admit to her that he'd upped and quit. They did some small talk for a couple of minutes, then he confessed. With that, the midwife glanced at me. "Well, Larry," she said, "even if you did decide the navy yard wasn't where you were supposed to be, you sure didn't waste any time finding yourself a pretty wife while you were in Charleston."

"Yeah, and here she is pregnant. Well, uh, I guess you know now that I don't have any money." He was more interested in knowing how to get this baby here without him having to work to pay for it than he was about the navy yard.

"Well, if you're not working, you don't have any money. That's not a problem here. The county will pay for it."

There was a sigh of relief in the room. It came from me, not that I wanted a hand-out, far from it, I was more than willing to work for my living, but I was glad to know I was going to have a doctor help deliver my baby and wouldn't have to do it out in a field or something.

Mrs. Clifton continued. "You shouldn't have waited this long to bring Evelyn in to see me. She should have been having a checkup at least once a month. Now you listen to me, Larry, I want to see her every week. That's a must-do. If you aren't working, then getting her here shouldn't be a problem for you. She could go into labor any time." She handed him a few vitamins in an envelope. "You make sure she takes these. She's going to need all the strength she can get. You come get me when her contractions are five minutes apart."

I wasn't sure how that was going to happen. There wasn't a telephone within a five-mile radius of where we lived and it was at least five miles from where we lived to Mrs. Clifton's office.

This whole thing about the county taking care of us was a bit more than I could comprehend. My father and mother brought twelve children into this world without asking the county to pay. I felt like it was a sad state of affairs when two people, capable of holding down good jobs, simply decide to sit on their lazy butts and let the county pay their bills.

It was a Sunday night about three weeks later that we were sitting out on the porch when my back began to hurt something fierce. I tried not to let on. I went to bed without saying anything, but my back was throbbing. I turned and twisted, yet no matter what I tried, I couldn't get comfortable. About four o'clock in the morning I had a pain that drew me up into a knot. I didn't know then that I was having a contraction. It was at least thirty minutes before another one came. I tried to get Larry to wake up. I wanted to tell him that I thought I was going into labor. He'd just make a moaning sound and roll away from me.

At five, I heard Mr. Barkley in the kitchen, starting a fire in the cook stove. Mrs. Barkley always got up at the same time to dress, wash her face and hands, and start breakfast. I eased out of bed to put my dress on. Mrs. Barkley had the coffeepot in her hand. She turned to me just as another contraction hit and she almost dropped the percolator. Setting it down on the stove, she hurried to help me into a chair.

"How long's this been going on?" she asked.

"It's the third one. Just before the first one, I heard the clock on the mantle strike four."

"Well, if the contractions are that far apart, it's going to be a while." She sounded relieved.

By ten o'clock the hard pains were arriving every five minutes.

"Larry, it's time for you to go get Mrs. Clifton," his mother told him.

Larry never questioned his momma. It was easy to see that he adored her. He left and was gone maybe forty-five minutes. Ten minutes after he returned, Mrs. Clifton came racing up in the Jeep she had to drive in order to make it up and down those mountainous back roads there in the foothills. She jumped out with her little black doctor's bag in her hand.

I was sitting in a chair when she came in through the kitchen door. She sat down beside me to time my contractions. They were a few seconds under five minutes apart.

Mrs. Clifton called out, "Larry, where are you?"

"Right here."

"Oh. You were so quiet I didn't know you were in the room. Come here. This is what I want you to do. I'm going to take my Jeep back to the office and pick up my car. I want you to have Evelyn ready to go to Walhalla when I get back. I'll be driving her to the hospital myself."

That made Larry stutter. "B-but-but I thought you delivered babies at home."

"If you'll just hush up a minute and listen to what I'm about to tell you, you'll understand. I know from my examination when Evelyn was in my office that this baby is not in any way planning to cooperate with me. I want to time her contractions very carefully on the way to the hospital. I'll stay with her until after the baby's born. I want you to follow me and bring Dora with you."

She got me to the hospital and put me in bed then, after what seemed like an eternity, she had the doctor come in to examine me. The contractions were getting unbearable. Doctors had been drafted to serve their country. In fact, the war had left only one doctor to take care of the whole town of Walhalla. This was in the middle of a flu epidemic as well, so this one fellow was on the go day and night, around the clock.

Mrs. Clifton and Mrs. Barkley stayed beside me for several hours. Larry would come in and out from time to time. The midwife told him that he could wait outside with his cigarettes, adding, "But stay close. I want to know where you are at all times." She was one of those take charge people who spoke with authority. When she said something, you knew there was real meaning behind each word that came out of her mouth.

The contractions were now shy of three minutes apart. I couldn't tell from the expression on Mrs. Clifton's face if she was discouraged or frightened. When I'd ask her how much longer it would be, she didn't have an answer. My mother-in-law was by my bed, holding a constant vigil.

Mrs. Clifton told us, "It shouldn't be taking this long, it really shouldn't." She seemed nervous. She left and soon returned. "I have an emergency call from my office," she said. "I'm going to have to leave you for a while. I wanted so much to be able to stay here with you until the baby comes. If there's any way I can make it back, I will."

After she left, the doctor eventually got around to checking on me. He told my mother-in-law that I hadn't dilated enough; it was going to be a while longer. Then he walked out of the room. I didn't see him again until his nine o'clock rounds the next morning. The pain was almost more than anyone should have to bear. Once more, the doctor told me that I hadn't been in labor long enough. He didn't more than get those words out of his mouth when I reached up and grabbed his arm with a death grip ."How in the hell long does it take?" I screamed at him. After prying my hand loose from his arm, he left. My mother-in-law followed him to the door. I couldn't hear their conversation, but I did hear him tell a nurse to bring in a stretcher. It had now been fifty-nine hours since we'd left the Barkley house to come to the hospital.

Finally, they took me to the delivery room. In a matter of moments someone put chloroform over my nose. I was told to count backwards. Oh, to be out of the travail that I had suffered for much too long! The next thing I knew, I was back in my room. My mother-in-law was standing by my bed, looking down on me.

She said, "Hey, there. It's good to have you back. Guess what? We've got ourselves a big, healthy boy. He weighed in at eight pounds-two ounces." She had the grandson that she had so much wanted.

I was completely exhausted. I just wanted to sleep. How long had it been since I had been able to sleep without pain?

Just as I was dozing off, this wonderful woman who had not left my side, placed her hand gently on my arm. "I know you want to wake up long enough to see this fine boy," she said.

It had been a long pregnancy without any medical care. I silently prayed, "Oh, dear God, please let my baby be healthy!" When I took him in my arms to check him over, he was perfect in every way, with the exception of one minor flaw. When the doctor used forceps to pull him out of me, he had caught him beside his right eye and it was swollen shut.

Harvey made his entrance on July 10, 1944. Harvey was Larry's middle name. We got Harvey from the nurse's boyfriend.

I don't recall seeing Larry for two days after I gave birth, and I didn't have a clue where he was or what he had been up to. In those days, new mothers stayed in the hospital from nine to ten days. When Larry finally did show up, he had his mother with him. He followed a routine for the next several visits; he'd come with his momma, stay a few minutes, then leave and come back in time to take her home.

I began counting the days until I could get out of there. My back was raw from the heat caused by the rubber sheets they used in those days. Finally, it was time for the doctor to dismiss me.

"I want to wish you the best," he said, "but I have to admit I'm glad you got mad enough to curse me out. If you hadn't, I'm afraid that you or the baby probably wouldn't have made it. It's no excuse, but I was carrying the load of the whole town. Anyway, good luck. Take care of that baby. You have a fine little boy there."

When we got home I thought I sensed a bit of a rift between Larry and his mother. Later that afternoon curiosity got the best of me, so I asked her, "How about telling me what happened between you and your favorite son?"

Her look was a question in itself. I had taken her by surprise.

"It doesn't take a fortune teller to see there's something wrong between the two of you," I said. "Most of the time Larry can't do anything wrong in your eyes. Now, all of a sudden, you're not talking. Catch me up. What's been happening that I don't know about?"

She was slow to answer, and when she did, her voice quivered. "The problem is that Larry kept leaving the hospital. You know Mrs. Clifton told him to stay close, but he didn't. The night you delivered Harvey, he didn't get back home until after midnight. I couldn't even find him to tell him the baby had been born." She stopped to look at me. "Are you quite sure you want to hear this?"

"Yes, of course I do."

"Well, if it's going to come out, I'd rather you hear it from me than anyone else."

"What on earth could be so bad?"

"All the time you were in the hospital, he was with Edith. The night Harvey was born, they were at the late movie. God only knows what else they were up to. It just tears me up to think that while this baby was being born, Larry and Edith were in a picture show. His place was there with you."

"So that's what's been keeping him occupied?" "Evelyn, I am so sorry, " she whispered. "I'm ashamed for him. I tried to raise him better than that."

About then Larry came into the room. Evidently, he had overheard our conversation, but he didn't look ashamed. He sort of shrugged and started to turn around to leave.

"What's this your mother says about you and Edith having a good old time at the movies?" I asked.

He stopped in the doorway and turned back to me.

"Well," he said, without an ounce of guilt, "yes, we went the movies. What about it? How much help could I have been sitting there listening to you moan and groan? I couldn't help you have the baby. Momma was there with you. I'm sorry if you expected me to just sit there listening to you cry and whimper. That's all you've done the whole nine months!"

Mrs. Barkley was furious. It was the only time I ever saw her really lose her temper. "Boy, you'd better watch your mouth. What you did is unforgivable. You know what you did was wrong."

He dropped his head, but he didn't answer her. Then he walked out of the room.

12

After that little confrontation, he was on his best behavior again. I debated about what to do next. It was a toss-up as to which would be the best decision: should we move so that I'd have Larry to myself and take a chance on him kicking me around again, or should we stay where we were and let me take a chance on my father-in-law. The way he had been looking at me in the days right after I got back from the hospital, sent warnings flashing through my brain and cold chills up my spine. I wanted more than anything in the world to get away from this poverty-stricken community in the foothills. I wanted a home filled with peace and love. I wanted a life of kindness and understanding, and to work again. I wanted to have enough money to be able to provide a decent place for my baby to grow up.

My mother-in-law was the greatest. It broke my heart to see the mental hell she suffered every day of her life. What I'd gone through was minimal compared to what this good woman endured. She had survived hell on earth for more years than I cared to think about.

Larry didn't give me an answer when I asked him if we should stay where we were or get our own place. He just got in his car and left. When he returned, he told me that he'd found a place to rent. It was a big, old run-down house that, I came to realize, should have been condemned ages ago. However, it was only one mile from my mother-in-law.

When we moved in, I had to do the cooking, and heat water, on top of a two-burner wood stove. It was the middle of January, as cold as it ever gets in that part of the country. The house was so open we could see the chickens hovering underneath the floor, trying to stay warm. We could look through the outside walls and see the surroundings. There was no way to heat the place.

Despite all of that, Larry was very happy, primarily because he didn't have to work. We had fallen as low in poverty as it was possible to fall. We didn't have a penny between us, but it didn't seem to bother him. He could go to his mother and she would divide their last meal with us.

Once we got moved in, I asked him what he planned to do about work. "How do you expect us to live when neither of us have an income?" I wanted to know. "I'm going to farm, like Daddy. Other people make a living farming. I don't see any reason why we can't."

"Will you tell me how we're going to survive until this miracle farm appears? And by the way, what do you mean 'farm'? It takes animals, plows, fertilizers, hoes, seeds, lots of things to farm with. We don't have any of that. Anyway, farming starts in the spring and here it is winter. What are we supposed to do until spring? Besides that, you don't have anything to use to even put out a tomato plant."

He shrugged. "I'll use what Momma and Daddy have. They've been getting by all these years. I don't see any reason why we can't do it the same way."

"If you're going to use their equipment, what are they going to use? Larry, I don't know about you, but I expect more out of life than just getting by. My Bible reads that you have to earn your living by the sweat of your brow."

One night, a week or so later, I was awakened by a howling northeast wind. It was coming in through the spaces in our outside wall. It was so strong it almost blew the cover off our bed. Being so close to the mountains, the gale was sure to bring snow with it. I was afraid to sleep soundly, afraid that Harvey would kick off his covers, so I held him in my arms all night to keep him warm.

We woke up the next morning to find about four inches of snow on the floor inside the room, under the windows. It was as cold inside as it was outside. To my knowledge that was one of the biggest snows ever to hit the area. Larry measured it to twenty inches deep, with drifts as much as five feet. We decided to go back to my in-laws before it got any worse.

When we arrived, they had the fireplace going. We remained there, where we had food and firewood, for about a week before we went back to our place.

We didn't even have well water. I had to bring whatever we used for cooking and bathing up from a spring. Naturally, Larry figured that to be woman's work. I'd carry clothes to the spring to wash them and bring them back again just like the Indians use to do. On warm days, I'd make a comfortable place in the leaves for the baby, while I tended to the wash.

We were now living in complete isolation, rarely ever seeing another human being. It was seven miles to the nearest grocery store. Whatever outgoing personality I'd had was slowly fading away.

When Mr. Barkley started farming that spring, I noticed that Mrs. Barkley would take him food and water in the field twice each morning and three times at mid-afternoon. It was the same field Louise had pointed out to me as the place where her father had raped her. When my mother-in-law returned to the house, she almost always seemed to be disturbed. At times, it was evident that she had been crying. My heart went out to her.

I asked Grandma, "Why does Mrs. Barkley look so unhappy when she comes back from the field after taking Mr. Barkley his food?"

"Alonzo has to have sex every time she goes up there, and she hates it."

"Oh, my word! Did she tell you that?"

She nodded. "When Dora can't take care of him sexually, he leaves. He's usually gone three or four days at a time. Nobody knows where he goes. The children and Dora don't ask any questions. They just take care of the farming until he gets back."

Mr. Barkley's old momma hog had a litter of pigs. My father-in-law generously gave us one of them. I wasn't as grateful, though, as I was upset. We didn't have people food, let alone enough food to fatten a pig. I felt that if my husband had no intention of working enough to provide meals for himself or his baby or me, he sure wouldn't worry about a pig. I felt sorry for the little thing. My father-in-law expressed the need for us to fatten up the animal so we could have meat to carry us through the next winter months. I was pregnant again and I wanted to make sure the baby inside me would have proper nutrition. Nanny Eve had tried her best to instill in me patience and perseverance, but this situation had come down to what amounted to a live-or-starve-to-death predicament. I had to find a way out of this terrible spot we were in, but I didn't know how.

My father believed, and taught each of his children to believe, that work and prayer were the answers to life's problems, but we were about as close to starvation as we could get. Things were so bad that as soon as early spring arrived, we women were out scouring the countryside, hunting "poke salad" as it was known. The "salad" was just tall green weeds that I'd always been told, while I was growing up, was poison and couldn't be eaten. My mother-in-law cooked them with onions from her garden. She put it on the table with instructions to "eat it or starve".

They did have some corn stored in the barn, and they had a milk cow. There was also some pork meat stored in the smokehouse. My husband and I barely had clothes on our backs, and our only food was what his mother provided for us. To me this was inexcusable when Larry could have been working in the navy yard 24/7 had he chosen to do so. How could I have been so weak as to let myself get caught in a trap like this, I wondered? I made up my mind that God and I would find a way out of this mess. God had provided for Momma and Daddy's family of fourteen. I had enough faith to believe that He was going to show me a way out, but how remained to be seen.

I remembered a line from the Bible: "Ask and you shall receive." I thought, *Dear Lord, it's time I receive something more than this.* I wanted to live near a church, but I never heard any discussions about church. I knew God's presence was with me. I'd been taught that God never leaves us. I knew I didn't have to find a building to find God. I constantly prayed to Him to let me be able to provide a decent living for my babies. I asked God for milk, the kind of food needed to bring my next child into the world healthy. I wasn't asking for handouts, just a way to make it on our own. The only thing I had working for me was prayer.

I had been slack where God was concerned. I asked his forgiveness. My mother told me, "God never leaves us. We might walk away from God, but God never walks away from us."

I came to understand that the day Larry came into my life was the day I walked away from God's blessings. The devil had tempted me with that first movie and it was time to repent. With God's help I'd find a future for my children and for myself.

Thinking about that brought back to mind the time Nanny Eve was teaching me to sew together pieces of material to make quilt squares. When they didn't go together as neatly as I thought they should, I'd begin to lose patience and want to quit. That's when she'd say, "Now, now. Mr. Marion and Mrs. Elma has refused to bring up any quitters. You come here now; you sit your little self down until you make it fit. Child, where is your patience? All you got to do is think right. When you think right, then you can do it right. You get your mind set right, it will all come together for you. You just stop your fretting. Keep the faith and believe you can do it. If you believe with all that's in you to believe with, you can do anything, be anything you want to be. All things are possible when you truly believe in God."

I couldn't have been more than eight years old at the time, but I knew that Nanny Eve was right. I'd take my work apart and start from scratch. Not more than an hour later I'd display the beautiful piece of my handiwork.

"See, child!" she'd exclaim. "Eve told you. Mr. Marion and Mrs. Elma don't allow no quitters to live in this house. Why, you don't got no quitter's blood in your veins. Don't you tell me that word 'can't' again. There's no such thing as can't, 'cause I done gone buried can't in the fence corner."

I realized that I was going to have to apply that same logic to getting my life back in order. Some way, somehow, it had to be done, not only for my sake, but for the sake of my family. If the pieces didn't fit right, I'd just have to get my thinking right, so it would all come together eventually.

I had learned in no uncertain terms that I could never depend on my husband to make a move toward a job. Like his father, he would rather do without than work. Soon there would be two babies to provide for. I wanted to give them a better chance in life than I'd had. I wanted them to have more quality in their life. It doesn't matter how tough things get, we need to strive every day to better ourselves. Just because things don't go right the first time, we can't give up. Just because someone else wants things to be their way doesn't mean it's always the right way. Only compromise when you know you're wrong. I couldn't give up. I would have to keep praying. A strong person who has a strong drive about them can keep on keeping on.

My gut feeling was that even God wasn't happy with me living this sort of life. Sending me off to work at such an early age, it took a long time for me to understand that my parents did what they felt was in my best interest. I became a stronger person by being put in a position to accept responsibility. I understood in hindsight that my first mistake was in not finding a church after I got to Charleston. I didn't know how to go about it. There weren't any close to me that I knew about. I didn't even have a Bible.

Momma and Daddy believed that through my work I'd find a good man who would love and take care of me the way that Daddy had taken care of my mother all those years. Momma had worked side-by-side with my father. He took care of her by having Nanny Eve help with me, and three of the other older colored women take care of the house. They cooked meals for everyone. At noon each day, every worker, black and white, had a hot, home-cooked dinner.

I kept seeking a way back to a decent way of life. My mother told me many times how she had given me over to God the day she learned that she was in a family way. She reminded me of how I belong to God. I was beginning to feel the way Job in the Bible must have felt, with all my challenges and set-backs. I felt that God was allowing the devil to test me, just as the devil had been allowed to test Job. I had walked away from God, but I believed that God was getting me back on track.

It was time for me to make a plan and to put it in action. Uncle Pat would be the very person who could help. He was the only one I'd met who had the ability and the integrity that was needed. He reminded me of my father in so many ways. He was liked by everyone, and I knew that he liked me. I had faith in him, especially after Grandma told me that he was a preacher who gave it up to become a magistrate. Also, it was Uncle Pat who paid Larry's hospital bill when he had his hand shot off.

I had gotten myself into this mess by being cowardly and not standing up for myself. Mrs. Barkley made me feel braver, though. My husband still had his moments, but I felt that now that he was twenty-five years old, the time had come for him to mature and to take care of his family. He had forced me into this loveless marriage, and there still wasn't any romance. I doubted there ever would be, but it wasn't completely his fault. He hadn't grown up with parents who demonstrated love or affection for one another. I'd been more fortunate. Momma read from the Bible every day regardless of how tired she was, working the fields all day. Daddy prayed a short prayer three times a day, thanking God for his bountiful blessings. My husband never knew anything like that. He saw womanizing and physical abuse.

One thing was as sure as death and taxes, we were two people destined to have to live together until death do we part. Now another baby was on the way, I was determined to fight the good fight. Thoughts kept buzzing around about getting Uncle Pat's help. I'd have to approach him away from everyone else.

It finally happened on a Sunday morning. He was coming to take Grandma back home with him. I made sure I looked my best before he got there. My baby smelled clean and sweet as could be. I wanted to let Uncle Pat know that I had some class.

I knew that Larry had disappointed him; after all, he was the one who made it possible for Larry to get into the electric welding school and to land the job in the navy yard. I knew it hurt Uncle Pat to see Larry throw away such an opportunity.

Larry once told me how vocational rehabilitation had experimented with him. They had tried to fasten an artificial hand to his arm, but never did manage to get it to work. His arm kept getting infected, rejecting the artificial hand. It went on for a period of six months with him being in the hospital while doctors continued their experiments. He was one of the forerunners in experimentation to develop artificial limbs, such as those he and my brother wore. During that time, Uncle Pat would drive sixty miles to pick up his sister so that she could see her boy in rehab, then he'd take her back home and travel another eighty miles to return to his own home, an almost impossible feat to accomplish in one day and yet he did it, over and over again. Don't forget, we had no turnpikes or freeways back then and cars didn't get the speed they do now. Not once did Mr. Barkley visit his son in all that time.

Larry had been right-handed. Without it, he had a hard time feeding himself, and writing was out of the question. He once confided that he suffered a serious bout of depression during that period in his life. His ambition was to play guitar and learn to be a barber. So, at one time, before the accident, he had very high ambitions for himself.

But back to the Sunday morning Uncle Pat came to take Grandma home.

There wasn't any gas in the car and we didn't have ration stamps with which to get any until the first of the month. So I started out walking. I wanted to make sure I'd be at my in-laws' when Uncle Pat arrived.

Larry was in a good mood when he called out to me, "Hey, what's your hurry?"

He was a slow walker.

"The faster I walk, the sooner I'll get there with this heavy boy," I replied, shifting Harvey in my arms.

Larry kind of laughed. He seemed to be in one of his better moods. He loved his Uncle Pat and looked forward to seeing him. From about a dozen steps behind me, Larry called out, "If Harvey gets too heavy for you to carry, give him to me. I'll take him part way."

I didn't take a chance on him changing his mind. "Here he is," I said, turning abruptly. I handed the baby to him.

It was the first week in March and the weather was nice. Uncle Pat drove up in his Model-T Ford. He had a newer car at home, but this was his favorite toy and he loved to show it off. It was in mint condition. After Uncle Pat got out of the car, he stood beside the porch, under the chinaberry trees, talking to Larry and to my mother-in-law.

"My goodness, Pat," she finally said, "why don't you come in and sit down?"

"I will in a minute, Dora, but first I think I'll go over to the well. I want to draw up a cool bucket of that well water. It's so much better than that city stuff we get at our place."

Mr. Barkley had a dipper made from a gourd that hung on a nail on the well post. Uncle Pat was familiar with where the dipper was. I thought, *Now's my chance.*

13

"I'd like a drink of water myself, Uncle Pat," I said. "If you don't mind, I'll just walk along with you." I thought, *There is a God.* This was my chance, now or never. I prayed that nobody would follow us. I only needed a few moments alone with him. I began struggling to find the right words. *Dear Lord, please don't let me blow this opportunity!*

Uncle Pat asked me, "Well, Evelyn, tell me how you're liking this kind of life."

"Not very much. Not very much at all. That's why I came with you to get a drink of water."

"What do you mean?"

I confessed to him, "My parents brought me up to do better than this. Do you think there might be a way you could help? Larry needs to get a job so we can get out of here. I can't sit around doing nothing much longer. I want to get a job, too, just as soon as I can. I like to work."

"Wow, you caught me off-guard," he said. Then he looked as if he were in a deep study for a few seconds.

"I thought maybe, since you're the magistrate in Easley, you must have some clout to help him find a job. You're my only hope of getting him away from here."

"You know something? I just might be able to do that for you."

"Uncle Pat, there's just one more thing."

"What's that?"

"Will you make Larry think it was all your idea?"

"Sure. You just take it easy now. I'll get back to you as soon as I have time to see what I can do."

Two weeks later, Uncle Pat came back to visit. When no one else was looking, he gave me a wink, then he smiled real big. I was more than eager to hear the news.

Again he decided he wanted a drink of water from the well. After getting it, he walked back to the porch where the rest of the family was sitting around talking. "Dora," he said, "have you got any of your great biscuits left in the kitchen?"

Getting to her feet, she replied, "Sure. Come on, I'll get some for you. If there's not enough left over, I can make up a new batch right quick."

Everyone who knew Mrs. Barkley never questioned if there were homemade biscuits in the house. That was a fact that was understood by all of her friends and relatives. Somehow, her biscuits remained soft and tasty for hours after she made them.

At the word 'biscuits', everyone went in the house and proceeded to gather around the kitchen table. I wanted to make sure I didn't miss a word Uncle Pat had to say.

He sat there eating and taking a sip of coffee from time to time. He even told a joke or two, but he picked the perfect moment to tell Larry what he had to say.

"Larry, how you been making it these days with Evelyn in the family way again?"

"Just barely, Uncle Pat. I'm just barely getting by."

"Do you think you did the right thing in quitting the navy yard like you did?"

Larry dropped his head and looked at the floor. "Probably not."

"Well, son, the way I see it, you need to get a job so you can do more than just get by. There's no possibility of making something of yourself the way you've been going about it. You've got a pretty little wife, one that's willing to help you. With another baby on the way, don't you think it's time you accept some responsibility? You're old enough to understand that you need to try working toward a better life. There isn't any way you can do that living with your family. You do understand that you have to make a start somewhere, sometime, don't you? If you hate electric welding so much, there are other jobs out there. They don't pay as good, but you'll be able to put a roof over your head and some food on the table, as well as provide clothes for your family. That's more than you've been doing here."

"It wasn't my idea to have another baby."

"Well, son, it's like this. In case nobody told you, it isn't ideas that make babies, it's people like you and Evelyn that makes babies. Once you make them, it's up to you to be man enough to take care of them. If you're having a problem with making babies, then I suggest you find the cause."

Everyone laughed.

Uncle Pat continued, "I say this because you need to be more concerned about your family."

"Yes, sir, Uncle Pat. I know you're right."

"Larry, you can't just get married and sit around on your duff, letting other people take care of you. That's about all I have to say about it, but if you think you're interested, I'll talk to James. He owns a taxicab company in Easley. I'll see if he's in need of a driver. I think that would be a good job for you. I can't make you take it, but I hope you will. If you don't want to do it for yourself, you need to do it for your family's sake."

"Sure. Yeah, that sounds good to me. What can we do, though, about finding a place for us to live?"

"Well, Larry, I started this, but I'm not letting you get by that easy." Everyone laughed again when he surprised my husband with, "I bought the big house next door to me. I've remodeled it into four nice-sized apartments. One downstairs has just come empty. It rents for twelve dollars a month. I'd be happy to have you and Evelyn for my neighbors."

"Did James tell you how much he pays his drivers?"

"Twenty-seven dollars a week, plus tips."

Mrs. Barkley spoke up. "That's good money, son."

Larry said, "Uh, yes, Uncle Pat. If you can get the job for me, I'll take it. Now we've got that taken care of, I've got to see what can be done about my pig until butchering time. It's a pretty-good size now. We got a milk goat and rabbits I've been taken care of, too." The fact was, he wasn't taking care of them; his parents were.

Twenty-seven dollars a week was a far cry from the dollar an hour he refused while working in the navy yard. Had he worked the shift they asked him to work, he could have been making sixty or more dollars a week. However, twenty-seven sounded wonderful and I was glad he had a chance to once again be gainfully employed.

Mr. Barkley said, "Don't you worry, son. I'll see to it that everything's taken care of. I'll finish topping the hog out until butchering time then, when cold weather sets in, I'll butcher it for you and give you and Evelyn half the meat."

"Well," said Uncle Pat, "I guess that takes care of that. So now I guess I'd better get on back and make sure I can get you that job we've been sitting here talking about." He reached over, took hold of my arm, and gave it a little shake. "How about it, Evelyn? Think you're ready to move to Easley?"

"Yes, sir! Oh yes, sir!" I was much more excited than I dared to show.

"Larry," he said, turning back to my husband, "when you come to Easley, just go ahead and bring your things with you. Come by my office for the key to the apartment. If I've got time, I'll go with you myself and show you around the place."

Larry said, "You think the job's a pretty sure bet then, huh?"

"I feel ninety-nine per cent positive you'll get it."

"How do I go about giving you the rent?"

"You can pay it out of your first paycheck." Uncle Pat looked at me and winked again, before saying, "Evelyn will see to it that you get the rent paid, won't you?"

"Yes, sir. I sure will."

We moved to Easley the following week.

The apartment was in an old, colonial-style house. Our three rooms had previously been used for the master bedroom, formal dining room and kitchen. It was very roomy, with hot and cold running water. The bathroom was nice and private. Moving in there was the happiest I'd been since we got married.

Once we got settled, Larry would swing by every day for

lunch. He also seemed to be paying Harvey and me a bit more attention. I still had to wash all the clothes by hand, but it wasn't that big a deal. This was the 40's when only rich folks had a washing machine. I had a number three zinc tin tub, the same type I grew up bathing in. There was an old rub board to scrub clothes against to get them clean, quite an improvement over washing them at the spring. I also had enough room in the kitchen to set the tub near the sink. While the baby took his nap every day, I would wash up all the clothes that needed washing, then I'd take them out back and hang them up on the clothesline to dry.

Once some money started coming in, I found a used furniture store and bought an icebox for ten dollars. It didn't take long to get the apartment looking nice. Annie Mae, my neighbor across the hall, brought me material from the cotton mill where fabric was just ten cents a yard. I had a seamstress turn it into the most beautiful, frilly living room curtains you've ever seen.

One day when Larry came home for lunch, he decided to take Harvey with him in the taxi. I quickly dressed the baby in his little red overalls. Larry kept him until it was time to stop home to eat supper. Harvey had his pockets full of small change that the fares had given him during the afternoon. Next day when Larry got home for lunch, Harvey was ready to go again. It was so good to see how they were starting to bond.

My second baby was due sometime soon, but since I'd never been to a doctor, I wasn't sure of the exact date. When I'd asked Larry if I could go, his answer was always the same.

"Why do you want to go see a doctor? You're not sick. There's no need to go wasting that kind of money for nothing."

I finally gave up asking.

He was taking Harvey with him a day or two the first part of the week, when he wasn't too busy. It seems the baby had won the hearts of all the other cab drivers. Larry confessed, "The guys kind of get upset with me when I don't bring Harvey along."

It was a lot of help to me when Larry took the baby for part of the day. Now that I was so heavy, everything seemed so difficult. Ten days before I went into labor, he came by the apartment around supper time. He brought his brother Albert and Albert's wife Edith, plus their girls, Betty and Dot. I didn't hold any grudge against Edith for going to the movies with Larry while I was in the hospital having Harvey, but I wondered what Albert thought about it.

"I got a fare to North Carolina today," Larry said, "so I decided that, since I was going to be that close to where they lived, I'd go by and get them. They're going to stay with us until after the baby comes."

Albert thought maybe he could get a job with the cab company. He'd had a medical service discharge due to the nervous breakdown he'd had while serving in the war. One day when Harvey had gone with his father and Albert on the taxi run, and everyone else was gone, I went into a housecleaning frenzy. I scrubbed and cleaned until everything was spotless. Just as I finished, Uncle Pat knocked on my door. I invited him in.

"Aunt Pearl wants you to come out back and eat some watermelon with us," he said. "It's really good. I just brought it in from my farm today." Pearl was his wife.

"Give me a couple of minutes. I'll be right out."

I had a really fun time. After I finished with the melon, I got up to put the remains in the garbage can. There were two huge oak trees in the back yard with at least a fifty-foot limb span to them. I was a little careless and tripped over a root, falling to the ground. I was so embarrassed. I tried to get up as quickly as I could, but being as pregnant as I was, it wasn't easy. My knee had a small cut that was bleeding a bit, but I seemed to be fine otherwise. Uncle Pat and Aunt Pearl were concerned about me, like most older people back in those days when it came to a pregnant woman. They handled me like a piece of delicate china. I assured them that I was fine, excused myself, and went back to my apartment.

The following morning around four o'clock I awoke with my back hurting more than usual. I started having contractions twenty minutes apart. From my count, this baby was coming at least a month early, but I couldn't be sure. It was November. The fire had long gone out in the fireplace and it was cold. Larry hadn't gotten home from work until after midnight so he was dead to the world, asleep. Try as I may, I could not get him awake.

I got out of bed and knocked on the door where Albert, Edith, and the girls were sleeping. Finally, I called out to Albert.

"Evelyn," he said when he saw me, "what's wrong?"

"I think my baby's coming."

He started a fire in the fireplace then, eventually, we managed to get Larry awake.

"Do you know what doctor you want me to get?" Larry asked, dressing.

"I don't know any doctor. I suppose whoever you can find."

He left, but two hours later, he still hadn't returned with anybody.

I said to Edith, "What do you suppose is taking him so long to find a doctor? This baby's in no mood to wait."

"Well, don't look at me," Edith replied. "Don't even think I'm going to deliver that child. All I gotta say is Larry better get himself back here with a doctor quick."

A few minutes later we heard someone at the kitchen door. It was Larry with a Dr. Cutchins. They came in, the doctor went to the kitchen sink. He washed his hands, then put on a pair of rubber gloves. Afterward, he sat down on the edge of my bed and proceeded to examine me, causing my water to break. Thank goodness I had padded my bed in preparation of this event. I'd also boiled water and put it in jars to cool. Mrs. Barkley's sister, Aunt Sally, and one of her daughters, had eased themselves into the room without me realizing they were there.

Dr. Cutchins looked up at Aunt Sally. "Do you have any clothes ready?"

"Is Evelyn having this baby that quick?"

"Get some clothes ready," the doctor said.

At that moment I had another contraction and the baby arrived. Dr. Cutchins gave him a whack on the butt and the baby screamed at the top of his lungs.

"It's a fine boy," the doctor said.

◘

Time went by in a hurry. Seemed like before I knew it, Dean was five weeks old. The closer it got to Christmas, the more it rained. The next month, January, would turn out to be the worst rainy season in South Carolina's history. When the weather was good, it wasn't a problem to keep the clothes washed up and dried, but it was a real challenge getting them dried during the rainy season. This was well before disposable diapers. I thanked God for the fireplace.

Larry had said he was going to get a few days off for Christmas. He was thinking about taking me to visit my parents. All I'd heard from them in the past year and a half was just one letter. I'd written to Mother, but so far I hadn't heard back. My husband told me that if he didn't get to take us for Christmas, he'd take us later, when he could manage some time off. The job had made a remarkable difference in Larry. He wasn't loving or compassionate, but he also wasn't mean to me or to our little ones. One main reason was that Uncle Pat lived next door. Larry had a lot of respect for him, or at least the most he was capable of having for anyone.

I got the feeling that he wanted my mother to eat her words, now that he was working and we had a nice apartment and food on the table. He didn't know my momma. She didn't hold grudges. We were doing well and she would be happy for us.

The morning of Christmas Eve we woke up to a light snowfall, just enough to send cars slipping and sliding all over the place. It didn't snow a lot in Easley like it did closer to the mountains, but when it did come, nobody was ever prepared for it. By nightfall about four inches had accumulated. The cab company had the drivers park their cars until the weather broke. Larry had grown up around Walhalla and Salem; he knew how to drive over snow and ice, so getting around didn't bother him in the least. He still had his '36 Plymouth and it got good traction on slippery roads.

When he came in from work, he asked if I had enough things packed so we could leave right away to go to Shulerville.

"Yes," I assured him. "We're ready."

"Let's go ahead and get started before the weather gets any worse. The farther we go south, the better it should be."

I had put aside a couple of toys, a pillow, a blanket, and a quilt to make quite sure the little ones were kept warm. I was homesick for my parents. I wanted them to see their grandbabies.

"My goodness, Evelyn," Larry said, looking at the stack of things piled high and ready to be put in the car. "Are you carrying everything we've got with you?"

"I want to make sure they're comfortable. With all those blankets, we won't have to worry about them getting cold. Hopefully, they'll sleep through the whole trip."

Ever since we'd been in Easley, he had given me complete cooperation and today was no exception. He didn't argue the point about how many things to carry, but went ahead and loaded everything in the car. Pretty soon we were on our way.

When we had the big snow while we were in Salem with his folks, I didn't get the chance to ride through the beautiful countryside. This was the first time I'd ever gotten to see the snow-laden forest. It was heaven to be out of the apartment, enjoying the beauty around me. Looking out across the white wonderland gave me a feeling of tranquility and merriment, a wonderful feeling that this must indeed be Christmas. I was very much looking forward to the holiday and seeing my parents. Getting to spend a few days with them, for the first time in a long time, I had begun to feel like a real person again.

Larry had been bringing home his entire twenty-seven dollars a week, keeping only his tips for himself. He left the bill paying and money managing entirely up to me. I was absolutely sure that this was going to be the best Christmas ever. I was feeling pretty positive that, since things were definitely on an upswing, most of my old worries were behind me.

Larry was in a good mood. I felt good. He was showing me much, much more consideration than he had ever shown. I thought, with a slight smile, he is slowly turning into a real human being. My father had always told me that a good woman could be the making of a good man, but a manipulating, deceiving, conniving woman would destroy the best of them.

The trip was going great until just before we got to the town of Greenwood. The sun had gone down and the roads were getting slippery. We had gotten far enough south that snow had quit falling, but now we faced a light, misty rain that froze as fast as it touched down. The temperature had dropped drastically. Ice was freezing on the trees and power lines. The road had become a solid sheet of ice. By the time we got into Greenwood, ice was so heavy on the power lines that the electricity was off in town.

Two miles outside the city limits, our headlights began to dim. It was so dark by that time that we could hardly see five feet in front of us. The black asphalt highway wasn't helping any. Larry was real quiet, concentrating on the road. I kept watching the headlights as they got dimmer and then brighter again.

"Is there something wrong with the headlights," I finally asked, "or is it just my imagination?"

"I think you might be right. It looks to me like the regulator could be going out. I think we better turn off the heater. As cold as it is, you make sure the babies are covered up good. I thought you were crazy bringing that many quilts and blankets, but now I'm glad you did. I guess you were right, it's better to be safe than sorry."

"It's probably the mother hen in me," I said, but I was getting worried.

We went another four miles or so when we spotted a very tiny, but very dim, light. There wasn't any way to determine its source. It was so cold with the freezing rain coming down that the windshield wipers couldn't keep the view clear. By this time, the car was creeping along, not more than five miles an hour. The little country road had barely passing room if we should meet another car, though it seemed to me there wasn't anyone else crazy enough to be out in that kind of weather. We were getting closer to the light. Luck was on our side. It turned out to be a kerosene lantern inside a small country garage.

Larry pulled in and parked, then he turned to me. "It'll be the miracle of all miracles if we find a regulator here that'll fit this car."

Inside the garage were two middle-aged men huddled around a big, old wood-burning, potbellied stove. One of them greeted Larry as if they had known one another all their lives.

"Hey, man," he grinned, " what in the world are you doing out here in this kind of weather?"

Larry cleared his throat, as he did most times these days because of the cigarette smoking habit he acquired at age seven. It was already more than taking its toll on his lungs.

"We're on our way to Shulerville to spend Christmas with my wife's parents," he told the fellow. "She hasn't seen them in going on two years now."

The man seemed alarmed by the news. "Ah, man, please don't tell me you've got your wife in the car with you, out here in this mess."

"Yes, sir, I do. Got our two babies, too. My oldest is a few days past seventeen months, the youngest just turned six weeks old."

"Mister, you do know this is the coldest weather here in these parts that we've had in quite a few years? Anyway, good buddy, what seems to be the problem? I'll be glad to help you in any way I possibly can."

"Well, sir, I'm not a mechanic, but I think it's the regulator."

The garage man went about trying to get the hood of the car up. Ice had already started to form fairly heavy on the windshield in the few minutes since we stopped. He finally got the hood to stay up. With his flashlight, he began to locate the trouble.

"You were right. It's your regulator. There shore ain't no way to get another one tonight, not with this weather being what it is. I'm sorry I can't be of more help to you and your family." Then he began to mumble as if he was talking to himself. "Aw, jest you wait a jiffy. Lemme try something else here."

He tinkered under the hood, then he got real quiet, like he was thinking things over, and he tried something else under there. "Hey there, fellar," he said, stepping back, "why don't you turn on yer lights, see what happens now?"

I heard him so I immediately reached over and pulled the light switch. The headlights came on bright as ever.

This man was a real southern gentleman. "You know." he said, "you must have a Guardian Angel watching over you. Your regulator isn't fixed, but it's quite possible it might get you where you're going. By the way, how much further did you say you had to drive?"

Larry answered him. "I didn't say but it shouldn't be more than another hundred miles."

"Yep, you just might be lucky enough fer it to get you there. How about you come around here, let me show you what I just done to make this thing work, in case you have any more trouble with it; then you'll know what to do yourself to get her going again."

Larry had a quick lesson, then he thanked the man for his help and got in the car. We were afraid to run the heater very much for fear we would undo what the mechanic had done, so we let the heater run just long enough to take some of the chill out of the car then we'd turn it off again. After we had gone another fifty or so miles south, the temperature was some warmer. At least it was no longer freezing, though we still had rainy, misty, messy weather from there on into Shulerville.

When I opened the car door in front of my parents' house, I heard my mother say loudly, "Oh, my Lord! It's Evelyn and Larry!"

She had obviously jumped out of bed. It was a race for her and my father to see which one got to us first. Trying to get the gate open to the yard was always a chore when you had an armful. I was carrying as much blanket as I was baby, so I couldn't manage it. Larry's artificial arm was useless for opening the gate, especially with him trying to juggle Harvey on one hip.

When Momma reached us, she said, "My goodness gracious alive!" That was one of her favorite phrases when she got excited. "This sure enough is going to be a good Christmas. I'm so glad you could make it." Then she took a look at Harvey and cuddled him in her arms. We had really taken her by surprise, with it being three o'clock in the morning. She continued on, "My goodness, Harvey's grown up to be such a big boy." Then she turned to my father. "Daddy, you'd best hurry and get a good fire going in the fireplace. I want to see this new baby that Evelyn has here, but it's just too cold until you get that fire going."

The next morning, when I went into the kitchen, there was food everywhere.

I said to my mother, "You must have been cooking for days."

"Oh, I had some help. Mud came by on her way to the post office. She pitched in and helped me out."

Mud was a big, heavy-set African-American friend of the family. I never did know her real name. Mud was all I ever heard her called and she didn't take offense, so I guess she liked it.

Christmas Day all my family came in for dinner. By the time

my brothers, excepting the ones in the service, gathered along with everybody else, it was quite a crowd. It seemed that everybody was talking without anybody listening. It was a normal Christmas for the Fort-Shuler family.

As a child at Christmastime, my brothers and sisters always bought toys for their children. Daddy bought food, lots of food, but never did he ever buy one toy. There wasn't any money for toys. When you're a young child, you don't understand why everyone else but you gets Christmas presents. It caused a very deep hurt inside me. I would go out to the outhouse to cry. I tried not to let anyone know my feelings. I was supposed to understand that my mother and father never bought a gift for any of their other eleven children. In fact, I've never confessed my true feelings about it until now.

That Christmas there was a gift under the tree for my mother and father from all of their children, just like most other Christmases. This time, though, I had the joy of giving my babies something. This holiday would be much different for me. I was getting to spend the day with my family. This Christmas I wouldn't walk away from the crowd to go to the outdoor toilet to cry. Just the pleasure of seeing Harvey get his presents would be sufficient.

The time had come for the family to open their gifts. Much to my surprise there was a package for me. I couldn't believe it. Were my eyes seeing right? Was there actually a package under the tree for me? I was ecstatic! Who could possibly have gotten me a gift, I wondered? I immediately jerked the pretty wrapper off to find not one, but two long-sleeved, floor-length, flannel nightgowns. One was pink with floral designs, the other was the same exact style except blue in color. Both of them had beautiful lace-trimmed collars.

Larry came and put his arm around me. "Merry Christmas, Evelyn," he said. Tears of joy ran down my cheeks, I was so happy. For the first time in my life I received a Christmas present. Somehow, Larry had managed to buy those gowns for me and get them there without my knowledge. Oh, my, was I ever surprised! I was nineteen years old.

Mother was so pleased. "Evelyn, bring your present over here. Let me see what you got there. My goodness!" she exclaimed teasingly.

"Larry, you could have brought me one of those.

They'd sure be nice in this cold weather."

I was so excited I could hardly wait to sleep in one of them that night. No sooner had we gotten into bed before Larry snuggled up to my soft, fuzzy nightgown.

"You'd better watch out snuggling up to me like this," I teased. "You know that's what led up to me getting pregnant twice."

Each and every Christmas after that, there were two flannel nightgowns under the Christmas tree for me. It didn't matter what happened between us, he always remembered to buy those two nightgowns. That turned out to be a great Christmas for everyone.

14

Once we got the occasion over with, I was ready to go home. All my baby diapers were about used up. Larry had already taken the car to Mitchell's garage and had gotten it fixed. We made it back to Easley without any difficulty.

Larry stopped by the cab company before we went home. He wanted to let his boss know that he was back in town, ready to go to work. He hadn't more than got the car stopped when his brother Albert came whipping into the taxi parking lot in his cab, all excited about something.

"Hey, Larry! Daddy called today and told me to tell you just as soon as you and Evelyn got back, for you to come straight on to the house. He wants you to come and get the meat. While the weather was cold, he went ahead and butchered your hog."

"What do you mean, Daddy went ahead and butchered the hog?"

"He didn't know you were going to take Evelyn to Shulerville. If you don't come straight on there and get that meat pretty quick, it'll spoil."

Larry was not pleased to hear that, but he was left without a choice. "All right," he said, "In that case, I guess I better go."

It was late Friday. He was still off work until Monday morning. He was hoping that he'd get to work some overtime hours. Lord knows I wanted him to stay focused.

In those days there weren't any refrigerators or freezers in my world yet. Everyone had to depend on the weather to be able to home-cure meat. To cure the hams and shoulders, they had to be covered in a bed of salt and packed in a large box during hard, cold weather, usually during the month of January. Farmers tried to pick the coldest, driest time, so the meat wouldn't soak up as much of the salt, like it would in warmer, damp weather. If it wasn't cold enough in whatever part of the country a person happened to live in, the meat could spoil regardless of how much salt padded the ham. That's why it was such a shock for us to hear that Mr. Barkley would be foolish enough to go ahead and butcher with the weather being rainy.

I protested, "How can we possibly go straight on from here? I'm about out of clean diapers and it's still raining. I don't know how or when I'm going to be able to get all these dirty clothes washed and dried. I can only hang so many at a time around the fireplace."

"Don't worry about the diapers," Larry said. "We have to go through Walhalla. I'll stop and buy another dozen. That should take care of it until we get home. I know Momma's looking forward to seeing these boys."

When we got to Walhalla, true to his promise, Larry bought a dozen diapers. When we came to the road that went to Mr. Barkley's farm, he just kept on going.

" You missed the road, didn't you?" I asked, puzzled.

"No, no, I didn't." Then he kind of laughed, "Momma and Daddy moved. They had to be out of the place before the first of the year. The landlord has another tenant ready to move in, said he wasn't happy with the small amount of farming Daddy did this past year, least that's the way Albert told me."

He went about four miles, made a right turn onto a little narrow country road that looked more like a wagon trail. The car was slipping and sliding all over the place. We eventually got sight of the house.

"Oh, my Lord!" I exclaimed. "What a dump! I wonder how long it took your dad to find this place?"

It was off the road at least two miles. From the look of things, it had rained every day since we'd been gone. The dirt was soft and the car was dragging. We were lucky to make it that far without having gotten stuck. The Plymouth was throwing mud every-which-a-way, clear up to the house.

Once we got there, the rain started coming down more forcefully. Larry drove the car as near to the porch as he possibly could. We didn't want the babies to get wet or chilled. Dean had already started taking a cold from the change in the climate at Shulerville. Mrs. Barkley looked out of the window to see who it was, then she ran into the rain with open arms. She grabbed Harvey and pulled the blanket up over his head, making sure he didn't get wet. She had only seen the new baby once, when Albert brought her to see us a couple of days after Dean was born. Harvey definitely remembered her. He gave her a big bear hug. She was talking to him, trying to get him to call her Granny when Mr. Barkley reached out to get him.

Mrs. Barkley said to Harvey, "No, no. Don't push your grandfather away."

Larry laughed. "Daddy, I guess he told you who his favorite is."

Mrs. Barkley asked me, "Did you all have a good Christmas at your mother's?"

"Yes, we did," I said. "It was my best Christmas ever. Oh, I gotta show you the pretty gowns Larry bought me."

She seemed to be pleased. "That's great. I hope the weather wasn't as bad there as it's been here. It has rained practically day and night for an entire month."

After we got inside, the rain began coming down with so much force against the old rusty tin roof that it was almost deafening.

"I've heard the expression all my life about it raining cats and dogs, but if this isn't the perfect time for it, I don't think it'll ever happen, " I said. That drew a laugh from everyone.

Then I asked my husband, "Did you hear what your mother just told me, that it's been raining every day for a month?" I turned to Mrs. Barkley. "How'd you manage to get moved?"

"In the rain, of course," she replied with a wide smile.

"You moved all your things with the mule and wagon in the rain?"

"Yes, we sure did."

I looked at Mr. Barkley. "How'd you find this ungodly place? I heard about the boondocks, but this is really in the sticks!"

I didn't get an answer to that.

Larry's brother, George, had made it through his hitch in the Army. He and his spouse, Francis, were there to spend some time with Mr. and Mrs. Barkley. I guessed maybe he helped them get settled in.

The house was much smaller than the one they moved from, but also much more open and run-down. Those days, people were allowed to live in any kind of shack. I couldn't understand how he could move his dear, sweet wife into a dump like that. It was terrible. The living room was maybe twelve-foot square with an old-time tongue-and-groove ceiling. The kitchen had no ceiling at all; 2x4 studs were exposed. That night I lay in bed listening to the rain come down hard on the tin roof. Every time I woke up during the night, the rain was still pouring. It sounded like it was going to come straight through, into the house. It was depressing. There had been times when I would have loved to go to sleep to the sound of rain falling on a tin roof, but this wasn't one of those times. I had all those dirty clothes on my mind that needed to be washed and dried. I could think of little else than getting home and getting it done.

As I lay there, I breathed a prayer, thanking God for getting me away from that part of the country and into a comfortable home. One thing my mother-in-law never had was a convenient place to live. I hear people talk about roughing it when they're out camping. That's pretty much what her entire life was like, even while she was bringing up her five children. The kitchen was so small they could only get the wood-burning stove, plus the homemade table, in it. Mr. Barkley had made a bench to go with the table. It was jammed as close to the wall as possible. It gave me a very weird feeling just to be there.

Time marched on. It was getting on into late afternoon and it was still raining. The darkness of night was moving in. Larry was having a problem tearing himself away. I knew how much he loved his mother.

"It must be getting close to four o'clock, as dark as it is outside," I finally said.

Larry glanced out the window. "I think you're right. We better get loaded up while we still have a chance of getting back to the hard surface road before night."

"Are you sure we can make it there?" I asked Larry, but he didn't answer me.

Mrs. Barkley begged, "Oh, please, don't go yet. You don't have to go now, do you? Couldn't you stay on at least until tomorrow?"

"I'm afraid we have to go, Momma. You know I have to go to work in the morning. We sure do appreciate all the work you did canning sausage for us while we were away." Those days all meat, like sausage, had to be cooked and canned in jars to keep for when we needed it later.

She gave him a hug. "You're quite welcome, son. I'm always happy to help you out whenever I can. Are you sure you can't take one more day off?"

"No, Momma. I can't take a chance of losing my job. Besides that, Evelyn's got a lot of dirty clothes to get washed. We been gone from home now for almost a week. It takes a lot for two babies."

"Oh, please, Larry. You and Evelyn don't have to leave to go back right now."

It wasn't like her to keep insisting over and over like that even though I knew she loved the babies and she was always happy to have us around. She was so pleased when Uncle Pat got Larry the job, yet she kept trying to get us to stay. It was hard to say no. There was something different about her this time. We could see in her eyes that she was pleading with us. This wasn't her usual personality, though I realized that having to live in a place like that would be depressing for anyone.

Larry held strong and went ahead and got the car loaded. We honestly had to go home.

"Are you sure we can get outta here?" I asked Larry for the second time.

Mr. Barkley said, "Aw, stop your worrying. George and me will help you'ns get out to the main road."

George grabbed a shovel and placed it across the bumper of the car. If they needed to dig us out when we got stuck, they would have it. I figured that we would be lucky if the whole car didn't sink with the road being the mess it was.

Mrs. Barkley followed us onto the porch as we pulled away. I looked back after we had gone a short distance. She was standing, holding the screen open, watching us until we were out of sight.

Mr. Barkley and George followed along behind in case they were needed, and it turns out they sure were. The car would go maybe ten or so feet, then it would stall. Mr. Barkley and George would push until the car would go another few feet. It kept stalling in the thick, red, sticky mud, over and over again. They followed this process until eventually they got us onto the hard surface road.

Once we were headed toward Easley, I said to Larry, "We probably won't be able to get back into that God awful place until July."

Larry kind of laughed. "It'll most likely take that long for it to dry out. Daddy always seemed to find the worst places there was for us to live in. He'd work hard for a few weeks trying to fix it up, then he'd take that spell of going off to God only knows where. He couldn't care less if the crops were tended or not. That's why the landlords got rid of him before the following crop season. I don't think he's stayed at the same farm more than two years in a row his whole life. If he could find a place on a dead-end road, he'd move there every time. He knows how Uncle Pat feels about him. That's why her family has very little to do with Momma. They all have plenty and they're ashamed of the way she has to live."

That was the most conversation I'd heard from Larry since I'd known him.

"Wow," I said. "He sure picked a doozie to move her into this time. I don't know how she'll be able to live in a place like that. She'd have to be depressed. No wonder she wanted us to stay on, being stuck out there in all this rain. I know it's hard on her, but she has George and Francis there with her another few days anyway."

Larry shook his head. "She'll stay there and she won't complain. She must love him a lot to be able to put up with what she has."

We'd been so busy talking that time went quickly and we were home before we realized it. Harvey started pointing and saying, "Home, Mommy, home." When we got inside, Harvey ran for his toys. "Yes, Honey," I said, grateful to be in my pretty, little apartment. "I'm just as happy to be back as you are."

The next morning it was still raining. I made myself get out the old, tin tub and get busy washing all those dirty diapers and clothes. I hung as much as I could in front of the fireplace to dry. All morning long I washed clothes and watched the children play. For some reason, I couldn't stop thinking about how Mrs. Barkley had begged us to stay.

Larry didn't come home for lunch at twelve that day like he did most times. Albert stopped by to tell me that Larry had taken a fare to North Carolina. That was a taxi driver's dream, to get a good paying trip to North Carolina instead of running all over the city with twenty-five cent customers. The longer journeys usually involved a good tip. Albert told me to keep Larry's food warm, that he'd be by to eat when he got back, so I put his meal in the oven and got on with my laundry.

I'd been so busy that I didn't hear Larry come in at first. A glance at the clock told me it was three-fifteen. He was leaning against the kitchen sink and making a noise I'd never heard come from him before. It was like an animal with his leg caught in a trap. He was in fierce pain. Tears were streaming down his face. I remembered what Grandma had told me, as a child his father had never allowed him or the other children to cry. That accounted for the strange sound he was making; he wanted to sob out loud, but he didn't know how.

I ran to him. "Larry, what's wrong?" He looked at me like he was trying to answer me, but couldn't. I shook his arm. "Good Lord, tell me what's wrong! Tell me what happened!"

I still didn't get an answer from him. About then I saw out the window that another taxi had pulled into the driveway. Albert was driving, but when the door on the passenger side opened, Uncle Pat got out.

Something was drastically wrong. I became terror-stricken. When Uncle Pat and Albert came in, I kept begging them to tell me what was going on. Uncle Pat put one finger up to his lips and shook his head back and forth. I understood that he wanted me to be quiet, but I was going crazy with worry. I thought, *dear God in heaven, why won't somebody tell me what's wrong?*

Eventually, Uncle Pat put his hand on my arm. "Evelyn, just calm down."

"Why won't you tell me what happened?"

"Alonzo has shot Dora," he said simply.

I put my hands over my mouth, fighting to keep from screaming. "Oh, Dear God in Heaven, no! Will someone please tell me it's not so!" I thought I was going to be sick. "How bad is she hurt?"

By that time, Larry got himself to where he could speak. "I'm going up there." His voice sounded more like a croak.

"Wait," I said. "Let me go with you."

"No, you stay here. If Daddy's deliberately shot Mamma, I'm going to kill him when I get there!"

Uncle Pat said, "Larry, you wait up. I'm going with you."

After they left, Annie Mae, and a woman named Hallie from upstairs, came to help me get all the clothes washed, rinsed and hung up in the hallways to dry. I kept thinking that someone would eventually call Uncle Pat's house to let us know how bad she was hurt. Then I thought about that gosh-awful road to the Barkley house. How would they ever be able to get an ambulance to the house? I was sure they would never be able to accomplish that feat. By now it was after midnight and there still hadn't been any word.

The neighbors had, first one then the other, come by until pretty late, curious to know what was going on.

I prayed, "Dear God, please let my mother-in-law be all right!" I felt that if I didn't soon hear something I'd go out of my mind. There was no news until the next day at two o'clock when Larry came walking in the kitchen.

"How is she?" I asked, afraid to hear the answer.

He looked at me, then down at the floor, but not one word came out of his mouth.

I said, "Please tell me something! Can't you see I'm going out of my mind?"

"She's dead."

15

I swayed against the wall in stunned silence. I could feel the blood drain from my face. The room began to spin around me and my knees almost went out from under me. I was gasping when I managed to say, "You did tell me that she's dead? You did say that she was dead, didn't you?" Larry had a way of mumbling his words. I couldn't be sure if I'd heard him right or not.

"Yes, that's what I said. She's dead." He was silent for a few moments, then he said, "She died instantly, Evelyn. They didn't want me to see her. I made them let me."

"You made them let you see her? Who? Who did you make let you see her?" "The people, you know, the people, the ones that had the inquest."

"You're going too fast for me. There's already been an inquest?"

He spoke very brokenly, "Yes...the road...it was so bad...that...Daddy thought...it best...to go ahead...and have the inquest...before they moved Momma...out of the house, into the back of a pick-up truck. They had...to take her out...in the bed of a...pickup truck. Daddy sent George...he went and found enough neighbors...to come...hold an inquest. They ruled it...to be an accident." He repeated, "The inquest ruled...it to be an accident."

He was in a state of shock. He was repeating and stumbling over his words, evidently not understanding the real meaning of what he had just told me.

I took him by his arm. "Larry, listen to me. Did anyone tell you how it happened?"

"Daddy said...that the rain had let up some about mid-day. He decided to go rabbit hunting with George. Momma had gotten up early that morning and churned butter...then her and Francis had put a quilt...into the quilting frame...Momma was sitting there, across from Francis, Daddy said, when he reached up to take his shotgun down out of the gun rack...He almost dropped it. That's when the gun...went off...killed her. Evelyn...it almost blew...her entire head off. Her brains...is all splattered...all over the walls and the ceiling."

My head was spinning. The gun in the gun rack was pointed toward the left wall. That would be the opposite direction from where Larry was saying that Mrs. Barkley was sitting. If she was sitting directly across from Francis at the quilt frame, even if Mr. Barkley had dropped the gun, a bullet shouldn't have hit either one of them. The only way I could see the gun would have shot her head off is if he made a complete turn and aimed it straight between her eyes.

"Where was George when it happened?" I asked.

Larry rambled on. "Daddy said that George was outside... waiting for him to come back with the gun...so they could go hunting. Like he said... it had stopped raining for about a half an hour. You know how it is... when it rains like this. After a downpour, there are times it slacks off before the next downpour. That's when... he decided to go rabbit hunting. They'd been hanging around outside... watching the weather. Once there was a break...that's when Daddy decided he'd go inside to get the gun...When he reached for it.. that's when it happened."

"What did Francis say?"

"Well, she told me that she was sitting on the opposite side of the quilt, facing Momma. She had her back to the gun rack when the gun went off in her ear. It deafened her. She heard the gun when it went off...but she didn't see anything. When she looked up she said that Momma wasn't sitting at the quilting frame any more."

He went on to say that Francis told him that when Mrs. Barkley fell to the floor, it flattened her head. Mr. Barkley was standing directly behind Francis, facing my mother-in-law. Francis had been concentrating on her quilting. My God, I thought, sickened, *how gruesome for Larry to have to live with that for the rest of his life, seeing his mother that way.* What was worse than that, was the fact his own father had brutally murdered her in cold blood.

It was like every fiber in my body was crying out, "No! No! No! This hasn't happened!" I didn't care what that inquest said, it was not an accident. The ones who conducted an inquest didn't have the least clue what that man was about. He could charm rattles off a rattlesnake in public.

It didn't sound to me as if Mr. Barkley had been very upset over his wife's death. After all, only minutes after he shot her, he had the presence of mind to find enough people in the community to hold an inquest. It seemed to me, with something like that suddenly happening, he would have been more in a state of shock. It seemed to me that it was a well-thought-out plan. If the shock that Larry was experiencing would have made him incapable of hunting down people to hold an inquest, how come Mr. Barkley could do it? Larry still didn't have presence of mind to see that it had to be a cold-blooded murder.

While getting things together for us to take to what, in my way of thinking, was the scene of the crime, Larry said, "Make sure you carry enough things for the children. Take what all of us will be needing to wear to the funeral."

As quickly as I got our things packed, we left. I dreaded the thought of walking back in that house, under the circumstances. I had witnessed the dark side of Alonzo Barkley when he beat that poor mule almost to death. As my Mother would have said, his story was just too thin to wash.

After what seemed like an eternity, we reached the road that we'd had such a hard time traveling on not more than twenty-four hours before. Larry parked the car and left it on the side of the asphalt highway. One of the neighbors was waiting for us with his horse and buggy to take us on up to the house. It wasn't easy for the horse to pull us over the terrible road, which was even worse than the day before. A large, flatbed truck had been going in and out, cutting ruts much deeper than they had been.

When we eventually reached the house, cold chills permeated my entire body. I went in knowing that just a few short hours ago my mother-in-law had been killed in this room. The first thing I noticed was that the quilt frame was no longer in sight. It had been taken out of the living room. The bed had been put back the same as when we left the day before. There was a scattering of people standing around that I took to be neighbors.

George hugged his brother. He was heartbroken and appeared to still be in a state of shock. Afterwards, he put his arms around me as tears flowed down our cheeks.

I had to walk across the very spot where my beloved mother-in-law had lain dead. The fact that she had to remain on the floor until they could get enough men together to hold an inquest was unbelievable. That meant traveling around the community on horseback or by horse and buggy, the weather being what it was, to find folks willing to come back to the house.

I stared at the floor and visualized the darling Mrs. Barkley, the woman who had befriended me, shown me love and compassion, the woman who had turned my husband's life around. He was now holding a steady job. He hadn't mistreated me in almost three years. Heaven had truly received an angel, in my opnion. The hurt and the shock of losing her was tremendous.

It was quiet in the house as I crossed the living room and went into the kitchen. We began receiving condolences from well-wishers that came by. Then, all of a sudden, I heard Mr. Barkley as he broke out boo-hooing. I thought, *If he's doing that for my sympathy, he's certainly barking up the wrong tree.* He could save his little act; I didn't have any sympathy for him whatsoever. Just the sound of his voice made me want to throw up.

When I sat down at the kitchen table, someone poured me a strong cup of black coffee. I was never fond of coffee, especially after the smell made me so sick when I was pregnant with Harvey, but out of courtesy, I pretended to take a sip.

At a little after midnight, Mr. Barkley came out of the bedroom, and walked by the table where I was still sitting. He never spoke a word to anyone. He crossed the living room and went out the front door, into the yard. Just the sight of him made me even angrier than I had already been. I knew in my heart that I was going to have to be careful to not open my mouth or I'd insert my foot in it. That could be very dangerous. If I did set Larry off, with his hot temper, without a doubt we would have another family murder on our hands.

A few minutes later someone wanted to know where Mr. Barkley went. It was easy to see that the neighbors had all the sympathy in the world for him. He'd done his job well. He had put on his pitiful, poor-me look and had everyone convinced the whole thing was an accident. There was just one exception to those buying his story, and that happened to be me.

My memory went back to the time when I was a small child and a civil court case had been tried on my father's front porch. Daddy was a constable. Most of the court trials were held on our front porch. When that would happen, I had to be quiet. I would conveniently get me a comfortable seat out in the yard, but within hearing distance, and I'd sit there spellbound, taking in every word that was said.

A voice brought me back to the present, but it wasn't talking to me.

"Is Mr. Barkley all right?"

Someone answered that he was outside smoking a cigarette. I never knew whose voice it was. I had gotten up and walked around the table by the cook stove to try to see where Larry had gone. At that moment, Mr. Barkley came back through the front door. He sat down on the bed and proceeded to take off his shoes. He unbuckled one strap of his overalls, eased the other one down, and sat on the side of the bed in his long underwear. Then, like any other night, he lay down and pulled the covers up around him. In a matter of minutes, he was snoring loudly. This was the very same room that his wife was sitting in when he shot her and her head all but came completely off. He hadn't expressed any remorse, whatsoever. I simply couldn't comprehend what my eyes had just seen. How cold-blooded can this man possibly be, I wondered?

I felt like I was caught in a web. Just when my husband was beginning to come around to some degree of normalcy, this happened. I kept thinking to myself, *What in the name of God and all that is holy, could those people who held the inquest possibly have been thinking?*

What's worse, they were letting him get away with it. I wanted to scream out at them. I wanted to tell them, "People, you don't have the least idea what this evil person is capable of doing!" No sheriff or coroner was ever called. There was never any investigation. He played his role like a professional. He was never questioned by any law officer in any way. He was quite the charming actor through it all.

That was a very long night. When it was beginning to get light outside, some lady started a fire in the old, wood stove. Another one of the neighbors went about making breakfast. Mr. Barkley had slept through until his normal get-up time of five o'clock. When breakfast was ready, he sat down at the head of the table, ready to eat. As he walked past me, he shot darts into my eyes with his staring look. The freshly-shaped mound of homemade butter that was on the table, was churned by Mrs. Barkley only a couple of hours before he killed her. When she had patted it to fit the round dish, she left prints of her fingers in the butter. Mr. Barkley proceeded to place pats of it between his steaming, hot biscuits. This brash, shameless man made me sick to watch. He sat there eating his breakfast as if he'd killed a rabbit or a cockroach.

Once again he looked at me. "Look there," he said with his mouth half full. "She left her fingerprints in the butter."

These were the first words he'd spoken to me. I had to get out of the kitchen and get some fresh air. I went to the porch where several neighbors had gathered. There was still a steady rain falling. It couldn't have been a worse time to have to bury a loved one. Oh, how I wished the rain would stop. It kept on raining and raining. I quietly prayed, Dear God, how can we bury this good woman in this downpour? I was standing there so hurt and angry that it was hard for me to breathe. I continued to watch the rain come down while thoughts ran wildly through my mind. My father-in-law must have known I didn't like him, because, Lord knows, I had shunned him enough. Now, at this moment, I disliked him more than ever before.

From the way he'd been watching me, I couldn't help but believe he knew I wasn't convinced that her death was an accident. I also knew that I had placed myself in jeopardy by giving him such a notion. He hadn't hesitated in blowing my mother-in-law's head off.

What, in the name of all that's holy, would make him think twice about mine? If he once realized the need to get rid of me, he would find a way. I had been around him long enough to know that I would have to keep my distance.

I've always been a plainspoken person. I don't know how to be a hypocrite.

One thing for sure, he had taken from me the best friend I ever had, or ever will have again. I thought back to the time when Larry had returned from Jamestown, after he and George moved our things to Salem. George was kidding around with me while Larry and his father were out of hearing distance.

"Did Larry ever tell you about how Daddy can make people think he's drunk when he's completely sober?" he asked with a big smile on his face.

"No, no, he didn't. Is your dad that much of an actor?"

"He sure is." The thought made George chuckle. "You ought to get him to show you sometime."

"He must put on a pretty funny act."

"You have to see him do it. He's absolutely hysterical."

I stopped the memory, realizing it had come time for me to get the babies dressed to go to the funeral. My body was so numb that time didn't seem to have any meaning, then I remembered hearing someone say they found a preacher for the service. I'd been concerned about that because I never knew them to attend any church.

There were approximately thirty to forty people who had walked to the house then gathered to ride to the funeral. There were very few cars in that part of the country. Almost everyone there that day was a poor, share-cropper-farmer. Most of them were hard-working country people without any means of transportation. The nice gentleman who was also a woodcutter brought over his big, pulpwood truck and made arrangements for them to ride on the back of it. Without his truck there wouldn't have been any way to get from the house back to the road other than by horse and buggy, and there weren't enough buggies to accommodate the crowd. Rain was still coming down with a vengeance. It was quite a scene, all those people dressed in their Sunday best, standing in the pouring rain on the back of that huge, flatbed truck.

The first stop was the funeral home. Grandma, a bit more stooped than usual, and Aunt Sally appeared to be exhausted. The whole affair had more than taken its toll on them. I went over and put my arms around Grandma.

"I told you, didn't I?" she said. "I knew that man wasn't going to stop until he killed one of them. I did tell you that, didn't I?"

"Yes," I said softly. "You told me that several times."

It was a very sad funeral indeed with the casket closed, which was understandable under the circumstances. Grandma asked the funeral attendant if he would please open it to let her see her baby daughter one last time. He refused her in a very nice way. I'm sure he was thinking that at Grandma's age, she shouldn't look at her daughter the way she was. Nothing they could say or do, however, would change Grandma's mind. She was going to see inside that casket.

She stood patiently and quietly until the attendant left the room, then she took it upon herself to open the casket. She stood staring into it for a couple of minutes before she closed the lid back like she found it, and walked to where I was standing with some of the family. She looked me straight in the eyes and said, "I feel much better now. Alonzo might think he's got by with it but, Evelyn, just you remember what I'm telling you; he may have gotten by here on earth, but God will take care of him for an eternity. You just wait and watch and listen. Alonzo will confess this terrible thing that he's done before he dies. Nobody can do a thing like this and get by God. There's just one thing I'm praying for and that's that God will let me outlive him. I want to live long enough to know he confessed to killing my Dora in cold blood." Her entire body was trembling.

I took her hand. "Grandma, are you all right?"

"Yes, child, I feel much better now that I got to see they had her head wrapped in a white lace scarf. I got to touch her hands. I was wondering if she saw the gun in her face and threw her hands up, but they weren't shot. The lace was real nice around her head."

It was tragic to stand there and watch her. My heart went out to this great, lovely, old lady, a lady who worked in the cotton mill for ten cents an hour to raise her children after she was left a widow.

Something she said, and I don't know just what, made me think of the way Mrs. Barkley looked that Sunday when she begged us to not leave. Now, less than forty-eight hours later, we were here with her cold body.

It was still raining when we left the funeral home to go to the grave. We had to get all the people back onto the pulpwood truck that followed along in the short procession. On our way to the church for the funeral services, the rain had been coming down in force. Not more than a mile before we reached the cemetery, though, it was as if a miracle happened. The downpour stopped as suddenly as when you turn off the water faucet in your kitchen. A couple of minutes later, the sun came out sunny and bright and beautiful. It stayed out all during the funeral service and at the grave-side service as well.

We hadn't gone more than a mile or so after leaving the cemetery, when it began to rain again. There were many people that took notice of this unusual happening. Some of them expressed it as a phenomenon or an omen. My thought was that God, in His own way, was telling us that He had received this dear women home. She had to be much happier than she had ever been here on earth.

In the following days and weeks, Larry once again began to get antsy. He became unapproachable and uncommunicative. I tried everything that a woman could do to stop him from falling back into that same old abyss as before. I understood that he had lost the one real true person who had been so important in his entire life, the one person who had been there to try and heal his wounds. She had been, and would remain, his one and only great love.

As for Mr. Barkley, he didn't even have to make a trip to the courthouse. It seemed that he was going to get away with murdering his wife without paying any consequences at all. The inquest had been nothing short of a kangaroo court.

The next day, when I was rocking my baby, my memory went back to a time when I was nine years-old. Mother had been having quite a bit of trouble with her ears so she made arrangements to go into Charleston to see a specialist. Since Momma had been sick so much of late, she had been trying to teach me how to cook. While she was getting dressed to go into Charleston for a check-up, I had asked her,

"Momma, what do you want me to cook for Daddy and the boys' supper?"

"Well, Evelyn," she replied, "you can go out to the chicken coup and catch five of them biggest roosters, then fry them for supper. The men'll enjoy some fried chicken."

That was a matter of a different color to be reckoned with. In the first place, I didn't like the feel of a live chicken in my hands. To catch them and tie a string around their feet then cut their heads off, I just didn't think I could bring myself to do it. I wrestled with the thought of doing this until it was time to get started. I had to try to get it over with. To dip a dead chicken in boiling water and take the feathers off, wasn't a problem; that part I'd done before. But to cut their heads off was another situation entirely. However, that's what my momma told me to do, so there wasn't any way of getting around it. To not do what your parents told you to do in those days, would be like breaking one of the Ten Commandments.

I went to the quilt scrap container and tore me off some strips of material. I tore them about two feet in length, making sure they were long enough to bind the chicken's feet together with enough left to go over the clothesline. I eased up to the chicken coup and opened the door as quietly as I could. I didn't want them to get to fluttering all around, scaring the lot of them. I figured the sneak-up approach would be best. I had to be careful not to let any of them get by me and run loose in the yard.

My heart was pounding so hard it felt as if it wanted to fly out of my chest.

I was very soon to find myself in a staring contest. When I would reach down to catch one of the chickens, it would run over to the side of the building and stand in a corner, staring back at me. It would stretch its neck and make weird sounds. I would reach for another one. It would get away and run over to the side, squawking as if to make fun of me. Finally, I managed to grab one. Fast as you can blink an eye, the first one I caught pecked blood out of my arm. I threw the chicken to the floor quicker than I had managed to catch it. It ran over against the wall, once again staring at me. I said to the chicken, "Okay, so you pecked me, but you're not getting by me that easy. You can stare, but I'm going to get you."

I must say that was much easier to say than to do. It was quite a chore, but eventually I had my five chickens. After getting their feet tied, then fastened to the clothesline, they fluttered for a bit, then calmed down. I hung all five of them upside-down, about two feet apart, then I turned and stared at the long kitchen knife I was supposed to use to kill them. I looked at it for several moments, trying to get the nerve to pick it up and saw across their throats. I placed my hand around the neck of one of the chickens. It gave out a ghoulish squawk. I immediately released it, then quickly jumped back, watching as it flapped and fluttered its wings. All this time, it kept looking at me with accusing eyes. I thought, *Oh, dear Lord in heaven, I can't do this!*

A rooster was staring at me as if he knew I had murder in my heart. At that moment the last thing on earth I wanted to do was cut the heads off those chickens. After at least a half-dozen tries, I got up the courage to pull the knife across its throat. When I did, there was its head in my hand. The chicken began to splutter. I was standing there with hot blood all over my face and clothes, in a state of shock, not knowing what to do with its head. I felt as if I was holding a hot coal. I immediately gave it a swift sling across the yard.

With my heart pounding like a drum, I killed the second one. Every time I killed one, it seemed easier to kill the next. Then I remembered what Daddy once said to me when he was talking about killing hogs to butcher for meat, and hunting for deer. He had said it was much harder to kill the first one. He said after you killed the first one or two, it doesn't bother you too much to keep on killing.

I asked myself if it was possible for that to apply to people who kill people? Could that be why there are so many repeat offenders? My father-in-law had killed my mother-in-law. Would it be easier for him the next time, should the occasion arise? Would he consider killing anyone who tried to get in his way? Would he consider killing me? Like Grandma, I didn't have any doubt whatsoever that he had planned my mother-in-law's execution and had carried it out very carefully and successfully. To my way of thinking, only a dummy could think otherwise.

I was not at peace with myself knowing that a good woman like that, after years of abuse, got gunned down in cold blood. With what I went through to kill those chickens, I wondered how anyone could kill a human being. I tried to figure out how he had planned it. The first thing that came to my mind was the place that he moved to. There was a reason he got a place so remote, so hard to get to, I was sure.

16

Six months had gone by since Mrs. Barkley's murder, but I could not for the life of me put it out of my mind.

I'd bought a stroller so I could get the children out of the house for some sunshine and fresh air. Dean wasn't quite old enough to sit alone; I placed him in front of Harvey so he could hold his little brother steady. Uncle Pat had retired from the magistrate's office and had opened a nice produce stand, selling lots of his fresh vegetables and fruit straight from the farm. One afternoon, after Larry had come home to eat his lunch, I got the bright idea to talk to Uncle Pat. He was the only one who could help me over my grieving. It was as if I was obsessed with the death of my mother-in-law. Somehow, I needed to put it to rest. She had been a real safety net between Larry and me. Now I had two small children and my husband hadn't gone on a rampage since the day with the potatoes. I was afraid he was going to revert back to the monster he had been in the beginning or, what's worse, a demon like his father.

It was a beautiful, early spring day, ideal for taking the boys for a ride in their stroller. When I got to Uncle Pat's market, he only had two customers. He seemed pleased to see me. After the customers left, he came over and played some with the babies.

"What can I do for you to make your life more pleasant today?" he asked me. "I'm right when I say that something's bothering you, aren't I?"

"Yes, Uncle Pat. May ask you a question?"

"Go ahead. Anything."

"Can you truthfully tell me that your sister's death was an accident?"

He was stunned by my question. I had caught him off-guard and he was stalling.

"Don't tell me what you think I need to hear," I continued. "I just want you to be honest with me, tell me your true feelings. Uncle Pat, you were there when they held that so-called inquest. Come on, you know the law. I just want you to tell me your honest opinion about what happened that day."

"Well, Evelyn, I wouldn't be leveling with you if I told you that I think what happened was an accident, because it wasn't."

"Why, dear God in heaven and all the names that are holy, didn't you do something about it? That was your sister. You were a magistrate. Why? Please tell me why you didn't do something...send him to jail...or...or...something."

"This is the way I looked at it, and you may not understand or believe me. First off, you're a hundred-percent right. I want you to know that you've been right all along. The whole family knew Alonzo's background. They begged Dora not to marry him. We knew he was lazy and didn't want to work. There were rumors throughout the community that there was incest involved in his family. We didn't want that for her."

"What has that got to do with him killing her?"

"That day up there, when I looked at her lifeless body laying on the floor, and I looked at the wall with her brains spattered all over it, I thought about all the hard times as well as the abuse I knew she'd been through from day one of her marriage. There will never be any way for me to comprehend all the things he's put her though, but I'm going to be honest with you; I hate to put it into words, but you know, Evelyn, it was kind of a relief to me to know that she was at peace for the first time in years. Believe me, she's much better off now than when she was living with him. I knew in my heart that God would punish him. I couldn't see any advantage of putting him in jail."

He motioned toward the boys in the stroller. "Now, you tell me just how putting him in jail will help your kids and all the other grandchildren, growing up knowing their grandfather killed their grandmother in cold blood?"

I thanked him for his opinion and left to go home with an ache in my heart as well as a question on my mind: What was incest?

It was getting harder for me to get to the grocery store with the two babies. I had been taking them in the stroller like I did when I went to see Uncle Pat that day. Pushing two children wasn't all that bad, but to carry a bag of groceries and push the stroller at the same time, was a different matter. The ones they made back in those days weren't all that strong, at least mine wasn't. I won't say that it was impossible, because I managed to do it quite a few times, but I finally asked Larry if he could bring groceries home in the cab, if I went to the store and shopped first.

"You know my boss won't let me do that. The only way that I could do it would be to pay the taxi fare, but he'd still question me."

"My goodness, Larry, its only thirty-five cents. If your boss won't let you bring groceries home in your cab, how about if I pay one of the other drivers to bring us home with the groceries?"

"No, you just go on and manage like you been doing. We need to save that thirty-five cents."

◘

Ever since the death of his mother, Larry had been slowly slipping back into his old ways. I realized that he was still deeply depressed over her death, but it bothered me that he expected me to haul groceries home and take care of the babies with that flimsy stroller. I tried to put it out of my mind, but already I could see that he was going back to having no consideration for me compared to how he had for the past three years.

The next day I went to the market as usual. When I got back to our driveway, pushing the stroller with the two boys in it with one hand and carrying my bag of groceries in the other, Dean almost toppled out on his head. I dropped the sack, breaking half of the eggs. After a flare of temper, I glanced up and thought I must be one of the biggest fools on the planet. There was a perfectly good car parked in our driveway, the same 1936 Plymouth that Larry had when I first met him. It stayed there, day after day, without being moved. This had been going on ever since my husband took the job driving the taxi. I made up my mind that somehow, some way, I was going to learn to drive that car.

I said to my babies, "Boys, can you tell me why I'm being so stupid as to struggle like this when there's a perfectly good car in front of me? Am I not just as entitled to drive that car as your daddy? I know he's working long hours, but I work just as hard as he does. I think this foolishness is going to have to come to a halt, fellows. Our Poppa just has to teach me how to drive."

The boys didn't protest.

That night when Larry came home for his supper, I told him my story of how I dropped the groceries. He thought it was funny. To me it wasn't funny worth a damn. I decided to ask him then and there to teach me how to drive, but he protested that he didn't have time.

"You don't have time. So, don't you think you should maybe try and find the time? I have a good reason for wanting to drive, you know. These boys are getting bigger and heavier, and they're about more than I can handle by myself, not to mention trying to juggle groceries, too."

He thought for a minute. "All right then, if I get the time to teach you, I will, but I don't know when that will be."

I had a feeling he would never find the time.

His mother had now been gone for a little more than a year. He was becoming more introverted than ever. Nothing that I said or did seemed to get through to him. He was stopping by less and less for meals. Sometimes he would get home at two o'clock in the morning, sometimes it was even six a.m. before I saw him. His regular time to be off was midnight, but I just never knew when to expect him anymore. When I'd question him, he always said that he had a fare that needed to go to North Carolina. The money he brought home didn't reflect those kinds of trips.

This pattern continued for more than six months. I was still struggling with the boys and still fighting with the bag of groceries. According to Larry, if there wasn't time for him to eat, there sure wasn't time to teach me how to drive.

On one of the rare days that he came home for lunch, he asked me how much money I had managed to save.

"Seven hundred dollars. Why?"

"'Cause I found a three-room house with an acre of land out to the back of Arial Mill. It's four miles in the country. I made a deal with a guy to buy it. I know you and the boys are gonna like being out in the country again. The man's asking seven hundred dollars for it."

Amazing! I thought. *The exact penny that I've scrimped to save.*

Had I not been so naive, maybe things could have been different. We had a nice apartment less than a half mile from the taxi stand. We had running water and an inside toilet. I'd managed to make it to the grocery store by myself, and to let him do his job, and I'd been able to save a little money for our future. It was not my heart's desire to move four miles out in the country and give up everything we'd accomplished. As long as Uncle Pat was next door, I felt safe. Yet it was his being so close that made Larry feel inhibited. The last thing I suspected was another woman in his life.

We didn't discuss the subject of buying a house again until the papers were ready to be signed. That was when I found out a husband could buy a house without the wife's signature. Larry took time off work to move us.

The three little rooms he was so excited about, in my opinion, left a lot to be desired. All the place did was get him back to the way his father had always preferred to live. It did have electricity, but all we had that was electric were the lights.

Larry had spent our last dollar to get me isolated and away from everyone again. We couldn't use the icebox any longer since the ice truck didn't deliver that far out in the country. We had a well for water, which meant I had to draw it up with a bucket that was fastened to a rope. We were back to using a wood-burning stove. Guess who got to cut the wood that had to be cut before any cooking took place. We also had an outside toilet about five hundred yards from the house. The tongue-and-groove ceiling was smoked black. In fact, the entire house smelled like a used fireplace. I was right back to the kind of poverty we had moved away from. I was now four miles from the grocery store. I hadn't seen Uncle Pat, but I was certain he'd be awfully disappointed in us.

I should have realized how things were when I admitted to myself that he hadn't made love to me since Dean was born. The fact that he had stopped taking Harvey with him, plus all those late hours he was keeping, should have added up to a huge warning sign, but it didn't. Not at first. He never brought home any money at all any more. His reason was that I could no longer get to the store, so I didn't need any money.

The groceries he brought home were always the same: a twenty-five pound bag of self-rising flour and a box of lard. That was it, nothing more. Thank goodness I had some jellies that Mrs. Barkley and I had made. There were also cherry preserves that we made from the cherries we picked fresh from the tree on the farm. Like his father, Larry thought that all we needed were biscuits and jelly three times a day. At least his father had butter. My boys had no milk.

Red lipstick kept showing up on his white shirt collar along with the sickening smell of cheap perfume. I kept quiet, though, and didn't confront him about any of it, knowing he was still grieving over his mother. In trying not to get him upset, I was too dumb to see the forest for the trees. He knew he had me where he wanted me. He had once again taken control away from me. A short time later, he came home with a few buckets of paint.

"What's that for?" I asked.

"I'm going to paint the inside of the house when I get around to it."

I set the buckets aside with a strong suspicion they would be there for a long while. Harvey and Dean had fun sitting on them.

When I tried to comfort him or ask how he was feeling, he'd respond with, "Why do you want to know? You ain't no damn doctor."

It seemed to me that the time had come for him to start healing.

One day he left for work like usual, but in less than three hours he was back again. One of the other drivers had given him a lift in their taxi. Seeing him walk through the door at that hour of the day scared me. I was afraid that something else drastic had happened.

"What's wrong?" I asked. "Why'd you come home in a cab? Why aren't you working?"

He gave me that strange look of his. I was sure he didn't have any intention of answering any of my questions, but he surprised me with, "Well, Evelyn, if you must know, dammit, I quit."

"Oh, dear God! You quit your job?"

"Yes, dammit. I quit." Then he went off on a tangent. "You're about the most hard-headed, damned woman I have ever seen in my life. Why can't you listen, or is it that you don't understand English? When I say I quit, that means I quit, dammit."

"But why?"

" 'Cause I wanted to."

He took the money pouch he wore on his belt and threw it against the wall. I wanted so much to scream at him, but fear choked back any sound I might have made. He had worked at the cab company for almost three years and now, all of a sudden, he decided that we could live just like we did when we were in Salem. This time there was going to be a tremendous difference. This time he didn't have his mother to supply us with food.

The next day he got out the paint buckets and brushes and started painting the kitchen. After that, he sat around the house for six weeks. The four of us lived on biscuits and home-canned peaches the entire time.

"When are you going to look for another job?" I asked for the hundredth time.

His answer was the same as always, "What the hell are you worried about? We're doing all right."

"What do you mean, we're doing all right?"

"There you go again, just like in Charleston; all you ever think about is work, work, work. Don't you ever think about anything besides work?"

"I think it'd be nice if you decided to work enough to get these babies some milk and some other food they need."

Evidently, I must have touched a nerve. The next morning he got up and left. All he told me was that he was going to town. I hoped against hope that he was going to look for a job. While he was gone, there was a knock on the door. It was Uncle Pat.

"What a nice surprise," I said, letting him in. "What could possibly bring you out this way?"

"I come out here pretty often. My farm's just a little ways from here."

"I knew you had a farm, Uncle Pat, but no one ever told me where it was."

"Where's Larry?"

"He said he was going to town. Hopefully, he's looking for a job."

"Did he tell you why he quit the one he had?"

"The only reason he'd give was that he just wanted to."

"I talked to James today. He said that Larry got into a fight with one of the other drivers over his woman."

"His woman? What woman?"

"I won't call any names, but one of the drivers took Larry's woman away from him. That's why he got mad and quit. Evelyn, it seems to me that history is repeating itself. I thought you needed to know, because I sure would hate for you to have to go through what my sister went through." He looked at me with pity in his eyes. "You just might be headed down that same road."

"I'm so ashamed that Larry has let you down this way. You're the one person who helped me get out of the poverty we were in back in Salem. Now he's brought us back to that same kind of misery."

"It was my pleasure to help you. I have to admit, Larry worked longer than I ever thought he would."

A couple of hours after Uncle Pat had gone, Larry came back in a navy blue 1941 Plymouth.

"Where'd you get the car?" I wanted to know, but I was careful with my tone of voice. I had to keep it light.

"I bought it."

"Well, how in the world did you manage to buy it without any money? And what do we need with a second car?"

"I just wanted it. I got it financed for twenty-five dollars a week. I didn't need any cash to buy it with."

"How will you make payments when you don't have a job?"

He laughed a little bit before he answered me. "I guess you'd like to know that, too, now wouldn't you? You wanna know everything, don't you?"

I could see trouble coming my way again.

"Well," I said carefully, "it sure would help if I knew a little about what's going on. My main concern is keeping the wolf away from the door and some food in these children's mouths besides biscuits."

"If you have to know, I'm going in the morning to get a license, then I'm going to start my own taxi business. That's how I'm going to pay for it."

I didn't know how he thought he'd manage to accomplish a feat like that, but I was proud of the fact that he wanted to get something going toward making a living again.

While we were still checking out the new purchase, another taxicab drove up. It stopped and a man got out. Of all the people in the world I didn't want to see, it was my father-in-law. Just the sight of him made my heart pound with fear. What was he doing here, I wondered? My pulse was going so fast I thought it was going to throb out of my chest, and the butterflies in my stomach were having a field day. Larry didn't seem to be much happier to see his father than I was. Albert told me that Larry had completely ignored his father the last few times he'd come by the cab company to see them. In any case, Larry invited his father to come in the house. I went about making biscuits for our supper to try to calm down.

While I was cooking, I overheard Mr. Barkley say, "Larry, I went ahead and got rid of everything I had. I made up my mind that the best thing for me to do was to just come here and live with you and Evelyn. You know, son, that I don't know anything about cooking. When your momma was alive, she always kept things clean, and she had plenty of biscuits baked up for me."

I turned so sick at my stomach I was expecting to upchuck any second. I opened the back door and stepped onto the porch. By that time everything in me seemed to come up. I finally sat down, trying to get my stomach to quiet itself. I knew there was more to him being here than what he just told Larry.

Then I heard Mr. Barkley inside the house. "What's wrong with Evelyn? Is she in the family way again?"

"No," Larry said. "Not that I know of."

There wasn't any way this man was going to stay in my house with me and my two babies. I desperately tried to find a chance to tell Larry that I refused for him to stay with us. This was one time I was going to have my say; the man couldn't be here while Larry was at work and that was that.

I knew I'd have to very careful about how I handled the situation. I truly believed that Mr. Barkley was after me in more ways than one. It crossed my mind that he might even consider raping me as he'd done his own daughter. Or could it be that he intended to shut me up like he had shut-up my mother-in-law?

An hour later, he announced that he had to go to the outside toilet. Now was my chance to talk to Larry. Quickly, with my father-in-law out of hearing, I asked Larry, "Did you tell your daddy that he could live with us?"

Larry began clearing his throat. Without a doubt, his cigarettes were getting to him. He took his time in answering me. "Not yet," he finally said. "Why?"

"I plain refuse to stay here with him while you're away at work."

"What do you mean?"

"You tell me how it'll look with him staying here while you're gone all the time."

"I don't see what's wrong with it."

I was in a panic over two things Larry didn't know: his father had gotten his own daughter pregnant, and he had killed his wife. I knew that Mr. Barkley had succeeded in convincing Larry that her death was an accident.

"I don't trust him, Larry. I'm scared of him."

"All right," Larry said, nodding. "All right. If that's the way you want it to be. I'll tell him he can't stay here. I'll tell him that he's going to have to go stay with Albert and Edith."

Thank goodness that for once I got his attention, even though I could tell it had upset him.

The next morning Larry got up and got ready to go to town to get his taxi license to start his business. He told his father, "Dad, get your suitcase. I'm going to take you to stay with Albert."

He did like Larry told him. He got his suitcase and they left.

Larry got his license to start operating his own taxi service. Later, after he started working, he'd tell me about how busy he was or, when it was slow, he'd tell me about that, too. We had real conversations. I thought for a while that we were actually going to be all right. Then, with no warning, he started staying away more and more. And we almost never talked.

17

It was spring of 1947. I made up my mind that somehow I was going to go back to work. I didn't know how I was going to go about it, but I figured that between God and me, we'd find a way. I refused to keep on being forced to live such a primitive lifestyle. I knew that I was forced to live with him until death do us part, but some way, somehow, my children and I were going to have some food other than biscuits. My father had seen to it that I never went hungry, in much harder times than we were having. His only means of support was the farm, with very simple tools. During deer season he served as a hunting guide to men from the upper part of the state. Those days, if there was meat on the table the men hunted and fished to put it there.

Once again, I felt I become a gutless creature and I wondered if I could find the nerve to tell Larry just how fed up I was with all his stupid little games. He truly thought he had me believing I was the only woman in his life. He didn't have any idea that I would ever find out about his affairs. In truth, he didn't have a woman, he had *women*! If he wanted to live his life like that, then so be it. I was making plans of my own to go back to work, one way or another.

The first thing I did was to start looking for my Social Security card. I had somehow misplaced it, in fact, I'd given it up for lost. Somehow I had to find it. If I didn't, I wouldn't be able to apply for a job. Out of desperation, I looked at my two-year-old. "Harvey, baby, do you have any idea where Momma's billfold is?"

He calmly walked over to the bed, reached under it and dragged out a wooden box where I kept small pieces of material left over from sewing, hoping one day I could make another quilt out of them. Harvey reached in and pulled out my billfold. He handed it to me with a big smile on his precious face.

I ran and grabbed him up. "Aw, Baby! Momma will love you forever for finding my billfold for me!"

A couple of days later Larry decided to come home to change clothes. "Larry," I said. "I need to talk to you."

"Just what do you want to talk to me about?"

"About me going to work."

"Well now, what brought that on? I'm not taking good enough care of you?"

"I can't live like this any longer. I'm able and willing to work. The boys are big enough now that I can leave them with a good sitter." I could see he was getting upset. So be it. I was upset, too. "No way. That's just not right. A woman's place is at home taking care of the young'uns."

"I need you to drive me over to apply for a job."

Making his usual throat noises, he looked at me as if he was in a deep study. I breathed a silent prayer to please let him cooperate with me one more time. Finally, in a low, monotone, he said, "Might not be a bad idea at that for you to go back to work."

"It's a very good idea," I said, so relieved I was about to pass out. "There isn't any way that we'll ever be able to accomplish anything the way things are now. All of the progress we got accustomed to has already gone down the drain in one fell swoop. The way I see it, we can choose to live in poverty or we can get up off our duffs and be somebody. It's our decision to make, nobody can do it for us."

Larry calmly replied, "You know, Evelyn, I never really looked at it like that before." Again he cleared his throat. "One of the cab driver's I use to work with, his wife works at the tape mill. Her name's Virginia."

"You mean Hudson Narrow Fabrics?"

"Yeah, that's the one. Tell you what. I'll ask Ray if Virginia thinks she could help you get a job there. If she says yes, then I'll let you do it."

It wasn't much, but it was a step in the right direction. He seemed to be getting some motivation back since he started driving his own cab. Next morning, as quickly as I got his breakfast on the table, I asked him, "Did you ask Ray about his wife helping me get a job?"

He nodded. "Yep. He said Virginia will do what she can to help you." That left nothing more for me to do now, but to wait, hope, and pray.

The following Saturday he said that he'd come get the boys and me, and drop us off at the movies, which was the first time he'd done that, even when we lived not more than a half mile from the theater. He proved to be as good as his word. He picked us up, and the babies and I went to a double feature. The late show was over at midnight. Leaving with two tired little boys, I walked the short distance to the cab company and waited for Larry to come back from a fare, to take us home. When he got back there was someone else waiting for a taxi, so he took off again. This went on and on. There was a very pretty young woman standing close by. I thought maybe she was also waiting for a cab. Much to my surprise, she introduced herself to me as Ray's wife.

"Oh, goodness," I said. "You must be Virginia. It's nice to meet you! I'm Larry's wife, Evelyn."

"It's nice to meet you, too. I asked about a job for you today."

"Great. Thank you. What happened?"

"Ernie, my boss, told me that he'd let me know as soon as he can place you." *Wow,* I thought. "Do you think that might mean a definite yes? If it turns out to be a definite yes, it'll be music to my ears." "Yes, oh yes, I'm sure he'll hire you. He'll let me know when he has an opening."

"I really appreciate that, Virginia. You've made my day, or night, whichever it is here at midnight. I sure do want to go to work." Again I was thinking, *God really does work in mysterious ways, His miracle's to perform.*

Virginia invited the boys and me to her apartment to wait for Larry. He would be working until after the cabs had accommodated all the people needing a taxi. I was grateful for her offer, otherwise I would have been standing there until at least two o'clock in the morning with two babies before he'd ever have the chance to take us home, and there was no place to sit down. I knew I didn't dare leave with her, though, without getting permission.

"I'll have to ask Larry if it's all right," I said. "He needs to know where we are." When he pulled in to pick up his next fare, Virginia went to him and asked if we could go with her. He said it would be okay and that he would come by for us when he got off work. Then he left on another trip.

"Let's go," Virginia said. "I just live a couple of houses down the street."

"Are you sure you don't mind?"

"No, not at all. I'm more than happy to have you and the boys."

She took Harvey in her arms and we went directly to her apartment, which was only two buildings away from the taxi stand. Once we got there, she helped me make the babies comfortable, and in a matter of seconds they were sleeping soundly.

We went into the kitchen where everything was sparkling clean and neat. It was decorated so nicely that I stood in awe. It made my mind wander back to the apartment we had, next door to Uncle Pat. I knew I'd be ashamed to invite her to where we lived.

She asked me to be seated at the table then she insisted I have a sandwich with her. It was like I'd known her all my life. I began to question her about work, what she thought I might be doing when I got there. She explained that she was a weaver, which was the best paying job for women in the cotton mills.

"I feel sure Ernie will put you to weaving because of your height. The taller you are, the easier it is on you."

"How's that?"

"You have to reach a lot and if you're tall it's just easier."

The following Monday morning, after I'd gotten the boys fed and dressed, I went across the road and knocked on the door of my neighbor, Mrs. Aikens. I asked her if she knew where I could get a good babysitter, just in case I got the mill job. She referred me to a middle-aged lady who used to live with a family down the way from us. I thanked her and went home thinking that if I could get Larry to drive me over to see the woman, she might possibly agree to come and stay with us.

Just as I feared, he didn't come home for lunch that day. By the time he got in that night, I had his supper cooked and ready to go on the table. I kept telling myself to psyche him out, to make sure what kind of mood he was in before I opened my mouth. If he wasn't in one of his good moods, I was apt to blow it.

His mood was fine and he agreed to take me to talk with the lady whose name I learned was Dolly. She wanted the job taking care of my babies even when she understood she'd have to live-in. She named her wages, ten dollars a week plus board. That would be half of my pay for at least six weeks. Virginia said that after that amount of time, I'd be eligible for a raise.

I got the job.

Virginia and I became friends immediately. Now that I was back working, every time she saw Larry around the cab company, she would talk him into bringing the children and me to spend Saturday afternoons with her so we could go to the early, as well as the late, movie.

One Saturday night, several weeks later, after we got back to her apartment, Virginia suggested that we try to talk Larry and Ray into taking a trip through the North Carolina mountains the following weekend. Ray was going to be off work on Sunday and, since Larry had promoted himself to being his own boss, with no one telling him what to do, I thought it just might work. After all, he loved to drive and to be on the go.

"That sounds good to me," I said, "but Larry hasn't been taking Sundays off."

When he came to pick me and the boys up, he and Ray came through the door, one behind the other. Virginia greeted them with, "Hey, guys, what do you think about Evelyn and me cooking up a batch of food next Sunday and taking a trip across the North Carolina Mountains? We could go on up to the Cherokee Indian Reservation."

Both of them jumped on the idea like ducks on a June bug. We agreed that Virginia, myself and the boys would meet the following Saturday. After seeing only one movie, we'd do the grocery shopping and come back to Virginia and Ray's apartment to do the cooking.

With Virginia being the one to approach him, I knew Larry would have no problem with me buying our share of the food.

Virginia and I were happy that Ernie, our boss, had put me with her so that she could teach me how to weave. Later, after learning, I lucked out and stayed with her as her side weaver. We both worked fast and were highly productive. Of course, the more we turned out, the more money we had in our paycheck.

During that week, every chance Virginia and I got, we were making plans as to what dishes we were going to prepare for our trip. This would be my first time to go to those particular mountains. I'd heard about them all my life, though.

Things were going much better for Larry and me now that we had become friends with Virginia and Ray. Especially with the two men working on the same job, and Virginia and me on our same job. Once again I had high hopes.

Virginia had become my very first girlfriend ever, my best friend. I was surprised when Larry allowed me to have a friend. Never before had he let me talk to anyone beyond brief pleasantries.

Saturday afternoon we began to prepare for our trip to the mountains. First thing on the agenda was grocery shopping. Larry hadn't come to get me like he promised. The disappointment was about as traumatic as I could handle. I had the boys all dressed up in their new Roy Rogers outfits and we were sitting there, waiting.

I looked out in the yard. The old Plymouth was just sitting there, as if in mockery. I looked at the set of car keys hanging on a nail near the front door and I thought, *By dang, there's no time like the present.* Larry had let me try driving two or three times when we first got married. He had let me drive on the trolley tracks, up and down the old brick streets in Charleston, near Mrs. Clark's boarding house. He said that driving on the tracks would teach me to steer the car straight. I thought, *Heck, driving a car can't be all that hard. I've got as much good common sense as anyone else.*

I told the boys, "We're going to the movie. If you're ready, let's go." They gave me a look that you would have to see to believe.

"Don't worry, " I said. "Your momma's going to give it a try. This car is just as much mine as it is your daddy's. One way or another we're going to North Carolina tomorrow and what's more, we're going to cook up more food than you ever saw in your life."

I placed the children in the back seat of the car and told them to sit down and hold on. Then I placed my finger on the starter button. Amazingly, it started immediately. I took a look to check on my two- and-three year-olds, making sure they were still with me. I couldn't help but chuckle as I viewed their rigid little bodies. They were sitting there, big-eyed, not knowing what to expect next.

The car began spitting and sputtering from me not knowing how to give it the gas. I fumbled, scraping gears, trying to find the right one. The car would give a sudden jerk or two, then it would choke down. It took me four tries, but I finally got it going. By the time I reached the main highway, I had found the right gear and I was beginning to get the feel of the car. I drove it to Virginia's, picked her up and we went to Winn Dixie's, grocery shopping. After that, the four of us went to the seven o'clock movie.

From that day on, I drove the car to work and back, and any other place I needed to go. Five years after that, Virginia went with me to get my driver's license. I only missed one question. The most shocking part of the whole ordeal was that Larry never, ever mentioned anything about me driving the car. His reaction was the same as if I'd been driving all along.

When the seven o'clock movie was over, Virginia and the boys and I went back to her apartment to get started with our cooking. The more we cooked, the more we got excited about our trip. By the time we got everything cooked up we had a mountain of food, to say the least, and all we had to do was pack the picnic basket. There was southern fried chicken, potato salad, macaroni with cheese, the list went on and on. It looked more like we were preparing for a family reunion than a trip with a picnic along the way.

When Ray and Larry walked in the door, both of them were shocked and amazed. They had never before seen that much food in one house, at one time.

Larry gave us his biggest winning smile and said, "You've got it all done, already, have you?" He was talking to Virginia. It was three o'clock in the morning and, even though Larry had been driving the taxi since six .a.m., he suggested that if we were going to the mountains, we should leave no later than five, which was just two hours away.

Ray spoke up, "Hell, let's just pack up and get started, otherwise we'll lay around here and get sleepy. What do you say, guys? Wanna go? If we leave now, we can be up the mountains by the time it gets light."

This was the most excited I'd seen Larry since the trip we made to my parents house one Christmas.

We got the food, then the children, all packed up and we got started somewhere around four o'clock. Ray was right, by dawn we were in North Carolina. The scenery was breathtaking. It was early spring. The trees were bursting with lovely green tender buds, and the jonquils were in bloom in people's yards. The day broke bright and beautiful. The boys were excited about all the wonders they were seeing from the car windows.

Harvey would say, "Look, Mommy! The horsy! Look at the horsies, Momma! Look!"

Then I'd tell them, "Look! See the cows?"

Larry was driving, Ray was in the passenger seat. Virginia and the boys were in the back seat with me. Virginia would let Harvey stand next to her window. I was letting Dean stand next to mine. My, what a day of excitement for them! For all of us!

About ten o'clock we found a stream that seemed to frame the lower side of the mountain with its picturesque beauty. "Hey, Larry," Virginia said, "how about pulling over there? It's a perfect place to stop. What do you think? Let's go exploring."

Larry pulled over. The whole area was packed with breathtaking, unbelievable beauty. It was a real fantasyland with beautiful rocks lying around as if they were placed there just for us. There was one rock about three feet in diameter, but some were even larger. They were spread around at just the right height to sit on. There was one that was the perfect size to use for a table. The sound of water breaking over the rocks made the place just absolutely gorgeous.

Ray said, "Hey, how about bringing out some of that food?"

Indeed it was what most people those days only got to read about.

We brought out the food and spread a tablecloth over the large, flat rock. Even though it was only ten o'clock in the morning, that fried chicken was delicious. After we finished, we packed up the leftovers, but we had a problem pulling ourselves away from such a wonderful place.

We didn't stop again until we were in Cherokee. There was a celebration going on and Indians were out in headdresses of every vivid color of the rainbow. I was in as much awe and wonderment of the beauty surrounding us as my two small boys, if not more so. They had their pictures taken with one of the Indians, and after that, we went into some of the gift shops to buy souvenirs. I thought Larry would be ready to start back by five o'clock.

"I want some more of that fried chicken," he said, surprising me. " I can't speak for anyone else, but it sure would hit the spot with me." He grinned at Ray. "Think you could handle some more of that fried chicken?"

Just near the edge of the Indian reservation was another narrow creek, though somewhat wider than the one where we had stopped earlier. There were picnic tables under beautiful oak trees overlooking the creek. Again, it was a place of sheer beauty to picnic.

After we finished eating, we headed on up across the Smoky Mountains where every turn seemed to take us a bit higher. There was a sign that read "Clingman's Dome" that went off to our left. We were so high up, we were actually in the clouds. Everywhere around us, as far as we could see, was a misty fog. It was cold, which surprised me. We had left home without jackets, thinking it to be the good old summertime. Soon we reached the top of the Smoky Mountain ridge where, on a clear day, we could stand in one spot and see into three states: North Carolina, Tennessee and Georgia. We spent about thirty minutes just taking in the breathtaking scenery, then we jumped back in the car and turned on the heater to try to get warm.

Larry had an idea. "What's everyone think about going on into Gatlinberg, Tennessee?"

Ray quickly responded. "Why not? We've got plenty of food."

I'd never seen Larry so loose or having such a super-good time. Of course, I also never suspected that they had brought themselves some whiskey. They took a little drink every chance they got, when Virginia and I weren't looking.

The farther we went toward Gatlinburg, the slower the traffic seemed to get, until we came to a complete stop. We surmised there had been a bad wreck up ahead. When we got to where we could view the problem, much to our surprise, there were two small cub bears playing near the edge of the highway, looking as if they were posing for a Hollywood camera. Tourists were taking snapshots of the momma bear standing about ten feet away. She was assuring the safety of her two baby cubs. We didn't have a camera, but I still carry that picture in my mind.

It wasn't long until we were going through underground tunnels. Harvey and Dean didn't know what to make of them. They were amazed that we'd be driving along in the light, then it would get dark, and suddenly it was light again. They didn't seem to miss anything as that old 1941 Plymouth taxi wound its way around those mountains. Growing up in flat country, it was hard to believe there was a place like this in other parts of the world.

It was some time later before we reached Gatlinberg. We took in some of the sights, but it was getting late in the day. We had to go at least a hundred and fifty, maybe sixty, miles through those mountains to get back home. It was indeed a day that would hold a lot of great memories. Tomorrow would be another workday that I was very much looking forward to. I loved my job. I didn't want anything to happen to it. If I hadn't had that job, I wouldn't have been able to spend such a wonderful day with friends.

18

So far Dolly, my babysitter, had been doing a good job for me. The boys seemed to be taken good care of, but she was getting up in age. One day she decided that she didn't want to stay on any longer, so I told her to pack her things, that I would take her home. Afterward, I went to find Virginia to see if she knew about any other sitters.

"Why, yes," she said when I told her what I was facing. "There's a colored lady you may be able to get. I hear she's great with children. She used to be a midwife. Ray knows her real well and I think Larry does, too. They take her home in the taxi when she comes to town to buy groceries."

Some hope stirred within me as I breathed a prayer of thanks.

Virginia gave me directions to the lady's house, which wasn't hard to find. I knocked on her door and, when she answered, I introduced myself. I told her that I was desperately in need of someone to take care of my children while I worked.

"Yes, ma'am," she said, pleasantly. "Will you please step inside?"

I did so, but I was in a hurry. She introduced me to Ella Mae and Elvina, her beautiful high-school-age granddaughters that she had raised as her own. I told her that I worked second shift, but that I also worked a lot of overtime. In fact, most of the time now I worked two full shifts every day. "When I work two shifts," I explained, "I'll see you get paid double. I don't expect you to work two shifts for the price of one. After you get the children into bed at night, you can go to sleep until I get home, if you like."

"I have to come home to be with the girls once you get back from work," she said. "I have to make sure they get off to school on time. If you need to work two shifts, don't worry; Aunt Maggie will take care of the children for you. Them children will be all right with me."

"That'll be great. I need to get in all the overtime I can, for both our benefits."

"Miss, there may be times when I can't be there, because I'm a preacher woman. There will be some nights that I have to be at my church, but since you work evenings, that won't be a problem. I can send Ella Mae or Elvina in my place, that way you won't ever have to be worrying about a sitter."

Her name was Maggie Stevens and I was more than happy to find her. That day, when I started to leave to go to work, she noticed the boys coughing a bit and she said to me, "Miss, it sounds to me like those children need doctoring. If you don't care, I'll do some on them myself."

"Thanks. I'd be more than grateful to you."

She was such a sweet person, it was like finding my Nanny Eve all over again. Aunt Mag, as we called her, was a larger woman than Nanny Eve, but she sure made me think of Nanny Eve because of her kind and loving personality.

Larry still hadn't got home when I got back from work. I didn't have to stay overtime that night and Aunt Mag was awake when I got there. Just as I was getting ready to get the boys up to take her home, I heard Larry's car pull into the driveway. As soon as he was in the house, I told him I had to take Aunt Mag home and that I'd be right back. He didn't answer me, so I left. When I returned, Larry wanted to know if there was anything in the house to eat.

I said, "Sit tight. I'll go see if Aunt Mag cooked anything. If she didn't, I'll fix something as quick as I can."

I went into the kitchen. Aunt Mag had green beans, mashed potatoes, pork chops, biscuits and gravy on the back of the stove. She had also made some homemade, half-moon-shaped, fried-apple pies that were still warm.

I almost squealed, I was so excited. "Larry! Come quick!"

"What's wrong?"

"Just you come here. Nothing's wrong. Everything's right."

I had already put two place settings on the table and was laying the food out when Larry came into the kitchen. He was certainly surprised.

"Where'd all this come from?"

I gleefully said, "Aunt Mag cooked it."

"Sure looks good." He sounded sullen though.

He was almost through eating when I realized that something was bothering him. "What's the matter?" I asked. "Why do you want to know?" "You just look like you've got something on your mind." His temper flared. "Damn it, I thought you knew. I don't like niggers."

"What? What did you say?"

He repeated the statement.

I was shocked. I had grown up with colored people. They had been a part of my family, and family was all I'd ever known until I left for Charleston at thirteen.

"What are you talking about? She's not a nigger! She's a preacher and a midwife. She's a colored lady."

"Well, not in my book. She's a nigger."

I was dumbfounded. I'd had a wonderful black nanny. It dawned on me that Larry probably didn't realize that whatever stability I had, was because of Nanny Eve. My parents had taught their children to respect everyone, including colored people. I didn't dare to voice any more of my thoughts. I knew that if I did, he would make me give up my job. I shut up and left well enough alone while he sat there, without another word, and finished eating his meal.

The next day when I picked up Aunt Mag, I told her, "Aunt Mag, Dean gave me a real bad scare last night. He started coughing so much he almost lost his breath. I had to get him up to shake the breath back into him."

"Honey, those children has got the whooping cough."

By the end of the week, there was a remarkable difference in their health. Harvey was a big eater, but Dean was picky. Aunt Mag was telling me on a ride home how she had to play little games with Dean to get him to finish his meals. She also told me how she kept the boys spellbound with Bible stories. But then I found out she could neither read nor write. I had forgotten that back in her day colored people weren't allowed to go to school. I couldn't understand how she knew so much about the Bible. One night, as I was taking her home, my curiosity got the best of me.

"Aunt Mag, how do you know the Bible like you do when you can't read or write?"

I could hear her soft chuckle as she explained, "Aw, Miss Evelyn, that's easy; I just have the girls read it to me. Most of the time they only have to read it to me once and I remember it."

I was sure impressed.

After that first night, Larry didn't seem to have any more problems with her being there. She always had the children fed, bathed and in bed, and she always kept our supper warm on the back of the stove. It didn't take her long to get the boys through their bout with the whooping cough. She told me that she'd used her healing cloth and prayed over them. Aunt Mag was a true believer in God's powers.

Two months later, Larry came home in the middle of the day. Once more, he had quit working. My thoughts went back to Uncle Pat and the last time Larry quit his job. It had been because a woman had made him mad. I was so upset that I began to talk to Jesus. Now that he had his own business I thought sure he was going to be responsible. He caught me off-guard.

"What are you going to do now?" I asked.

"I'm moving to the country, by God."

My heart sank as I breathed another prayer, Oh, please, dear God in heaven, tell me I heard this man wrong!

I said to him, "What do you mean you're moving to the country? How can it get any more country than where we are right now?" I had heard my father say that some people couldn't handle prosperity; to my way of thinking, this husband of mine had to be one of them. This business of quitting was happening too often to suit me.

"You know what country I'm talking about. I'm talking about Shulerville."

"No, I didn't know that was the country you were talking about. You really expect me to give up my good job and move to Shulerville again with neither of us having a job, without any income whatsoever?"

"There you go again," he grumbled. I couldn't help but wonder if he ever had anything on his mind except how to get out of work. Like father, like son.

I'm thinking that "his woman" must have truly done a number on him this time. I didn't know who she was, but I prayed God's vengeance on whoever she might be. I had just read a scripture in the Bible about forgiveness, and now the words jumped out at me: "Don't hold hate in your heart; vengeance is mine, I will repay thus, saith the Lord." Not an easy thing to do, but I understood it was the right thing to do. The sin lay at the feet of my husband as well as his mistress. Loose women don't stop to think of the pain and suffering they cause wives and children. The last time he quit, we'd lived off of biscuits and peaches for over six weeks. Just to know that I had a Lord and Savior to distribute vengeance on behalf of my children and me, gave me some peace of mind.

Instead of getting into a word fight with Larry, a calmness came over me.

"You know," I said at last, "I've never gotten to the place where I could be comfortable with hunger. Working puts food on the table and a roof over our heads. My mother and father raised twelve of us and we never went without. My parents live in the same home they built the day they were married and they've never even thought about moving. My father worked six days a week on the farm, every week, and I never heard him once complain. When he wasn't working, he was hunting or fishing for food to go on the table. You just can't handle living a decent life, can you?"

I pushed the wrong button that time. "Shut your mouth," he snapped at me. "I mean now. You had best listen to me 'cause if you didn't hear me right, then by God you better clean your ears out. I just told you that I was moving to Shulerville to do some farming. I've made up my mind and, by God, that's what I'm going to do. Now, have you got it straight?"

It was like beating my head against a brick wall. That was his decision come Hell or high water, as the old folks used to say;

there wasn't any way of talking him out of it. He wanted to go to Shulerville, to get us into another one of his stinking sinkholes of poverty, like he had done in Jamestown. It had been the same way here in "his" seven-hundred-dollar house until I went to work in the mill. Only God had the answers. I also knew without a doubt that the devil himself had once again taken charge of my husband. I prayed, when Uncle Pat helped me to get him out of Salem, that Larry had put his father's ways behind him. So far that prayer had not yet been realized. My gut was telling me that things were going to get much worse before ever getting any better.

He sat around the house for two days. He would only make a grunting sound when the children or I tried to talk to him. Finally, on the third day, he got up and got dressed, then he left. After about three hours, he returned to tell me that he'd sold the house. I was beyond devastated. Oh, my God, was I ever devastated! I got so mad that I lost my temper for a few minutes and threw all the fear of him that I had ever experienced to the wind.

"All right, Larry, if you want to move to Shulerville, then you load up and you go, because I'm not going to give up my job. I'm making good money and I'm not going to move with you so we can live like a beggar."

At first he kind of smiled like he thought it was a big joke. Then he asked, "Just how the hell do you plan to go about doing that? I sold the house, remember? I have the money in my pocket. Where the hell do you think you're going to live?"

"I'll call Uncle Pat and see if he'll rent me another apartment."

"I have my job and, with Aunt Mag, I can make a good life for me and the children without you. You want to live in the country, then you go."

When I said that, it was as if I had slapped his face. He made a lunge for me. "Damn you, Evelyn, don't you come here talking that kind of bull crap to me! How the hell can you do that? You're my wife, damn you. You'll do what I tell you and that you had best not forget. You ever try pulling a damn trick like that on me, I'll hunt you down and blow your brains out."

"Will you do it just the way your father did it?" I was so distraught I forgot all about caution.

"I thought I made it crystal clear to you a long time back; by God, you belong to me! I own you and there's not any way you can change that!" He slapped me twice, finishing with a sucker punch to the stomach. Then he said, "Now, by God, you understand me; my Uncle Pat ain't going to rent to you now or ever again. Dammit, you better make up your mind that you're going to do what I tell you."

I knew he meant exactly what he said.

Now that he was mad, he began to rush his moving plans. I had to give my boss notice that I was leaving my job. Once I sat down in his office, I lost it. Tears began to flow. I cried my heart out.

He was an understanding man. He told me that he sure didn't want to lose me as an employee, and if I was ever to move back to Easley and needed a job, if there was an opening, it would be mine.

Soon we were back in Shulerville.

Larry had bought what was known as the David Shuler place. How he accomplished that without my knowing, I still don't have a clue. He couldn't write because he was born right-handed and that was the hand he'd lost in the gun accident. There were no telephones in Jamestown or Shulerville. All I can figure is that one of his lady friends did the paperwork for him.

David Shuler was one of my mother's nephews and had originally owned the place. My husband bought the house, with its small parcel of land, for four hundred dollars. It was a tiny home with four small rooms in an L shape. It had been painted when it was first built, white with green trim, now it was nearly to the point of collapse; the tin roof was about rusted out. As we drove into the yard with our few belongings, I thought of the house where my mother-in-law was killed. I'd thought that place was bad, but this one was worse.

I couldn't gather up much enthusiasm when I said to Larry, "Why is the left side of the house lower than the right side?"

"All of the floor joist have probably about gone out from under it."

"How in God's name can we live in a house that has half of the support gone out from under it? It's falling down!"

"Don't worry about it," he said. "It can be fixed."

Besides falling in, the place was filthy. Summers were very hot and humid, so the hogs had dug out cool pits under the house and the barn. Every room smelled like a pig pen. The whole place was infested with fleas, inside and out. Even after I cleaned and scalded the house with boiling water, they were still there. As fast as the wood floors dried out, the fleas once again took up occupancy. The place had once been fenced, but its use had long since been retired. The wire was about all down and what wasn't down, had big holes in it. I was ready to commit suicide. The only reason for me not to was my two boys.

Daily, I tried analyzing the situation. I understood that Larry was trying to break my spirit, there wasn't any doubt about that, but why did he want to? It was evident, just as I had heard my mother say many times, that he wanted to drag me down to his level. He wanted me to be content living in the lap of poverty. He loved it and wanted me to love it. The only time he ever appeared to be happy was when we were down to nothing. He knew that I had been content working and having my own place when he met me. He knew I strived every day to try and make a better life for all of us. He was determined he didn't want the lifestyle that I so desired for my children and for myself. One way or another, he was going to force me and our boys to be content with hot biscuits and jelly three times a day, three hundred and sixty-five days a year, for the rest of our lives. He forced me to move to this hell-hole, but he couldn't force me to like it. He wanted total domination, using each and every fete he could think of, to punish me. All of his abuse, along with his womanizing, only made me more determined to pull myself up to be somebody.

The more he punished me, the more I began to rebel against him. The more he punished me, the more determined I became to use my head to figure a way out. I had already accepted the fact that my way out would never be divorce. I was completely brainwashed into believing that I had to live with this man like the marriage vows had stated, "Behind Closed Doors".

Somehow, without any priming from me, Larry managed to get a job driving the school bus. He made seventy dollars a month, half of what I had brought home from the tape mill. With the mentality that he was using to do his thinking, this made him a great provider. Never mind that the cost of flour had just gone up and that a pound of margarine now cost all of ten cents.

During school hours, he and the other drivers would sit around shooting the bull until school let out and it was time to bring the children home. On weekends, he worked on getting the floor joist, that had rotted out from under the house, put back. The living room was so tilted that when we set the couch down, it slid across the room. I had to go under the floor with him, to help get the heavy joist put back in place. Why the whole structure didn't collapse on top of us, only God knows. There weren't any decent tools to work with, so it all had to be done by hand.

Besides being upset with our living conditions, every night when I went to bathe the boys, their little bodies were showing more evidence of flea bites. I was at the end of my rope. I went to see my mother to ask her how I could get rid of the pests. She gave me salt from the meat box and said to put it where I thought the fleas were breeding.

It seemed to me that the whole four acres was a breeding ground. Nevertheless, I sprinkled salt in the more obvious places. The flea bites had gotten so bad that I could hardly put my finger on the boys without touching a place where they hadn't been bitten. I knew that fleas carry germs; I feared that we were all going to come down with some kind of awful disease. One night when I went to put the children to bed, I had about all of the situation I could handle and I lost my cool. I threw a temper fit.

"You come here and look, for God's sake!" I screamed at Larry. "You come here! Look what you're putting these children through, living with fleas and rats!"

He casually looked, then turned and walked nonchalantly away, letting me know in no uncertain terms that he frankly didn't give a damn. His attitude infuriated me that much more. It was getting harder and harder to hold my temper. If this was what love and marriage had become, I'd had about all of wedded bliss I cared for. Whoever decided that a women had to live such a life, controlled by a demon-possessed man, should be placed in the electric chair, and at that moment I could have pulled the switch.

When I said as much, in a very loud and clear voice, he sort of chuckled. "Aw, stop worrying about it," he drawled. "They'll be all right."

Showing me how much pleasure he was getting out of watching me being so infuriated only infuriated me more. I lost all thought of the fact that the more I bucked him, the more severely he would punish me, but I didn't stop when I was ahead. The next thing I knew, he slapped me so hard I landed against the wall and crumbled to the floor. There I remained for several minutes. I was stunned. I cowered there, striving to get up enough strength to get back on my feet.

Suddenly, my husband squatted down in front of me. He put the hook that was on the end of his artificial arm to my nose and gently brushed it back and forth. He said in a soft voice, "Now you hear this: I hit you with my good hand that time, the next time it will be with this. Don't you think it's time for you to understand that you're going to do as you're told? You won't ever be telling me what you think of me. Do you suppose you can ever learn to keep your damn mouth shut?" As he waved his hook back and forth two inches from my nose, he added, "You just look cross-eyed at me, Evelyn, one more time, and I am going to knock the hell out of you with this!"

He lightly shook my arm to make sure he had my undivided attention. "You had best straighten up your act. Take a damn good look around, Evelyn. I'm telling you that you had better damn well remember what I'm telling you. It would be real easy for me to kill somebody with this; it's a legal weapon. You're my wife, you belong to me. You can't get it through your thick head that you're supposed to do what I tell you." And he slapped me again while I was still on the floor.

The boys were standing there, watching, scared out of their mind, tears rolling down their faces. They wanted to come to me, but Larry pointed his finger toward the living room. They had learned early on what that meant.

"Both of you, get in your corner until I tell you to come out."

It wasn't the first time he stood them in corners and they didn't waste any time getting there. Larry knew I was a mother hen when it comes to my children. He treated them the way he did as another form of punishment to hurt me, anything to make his point.

I knew in my heart that he wasn't finished with me yet. All he had to do all day long was sit around figuring another way to punish me for screaming at him. He was a slow thinker, but he never forgot anything. I was the opposite. I could think in a flash most times, except when he caught me off-guard, then fear would take over.

On the four acres of this miserable place that he had bought, were fence-to-fence stumps. After we had finished getting the entire floor joist replaced, he went out in the field and dug up some of them. Most of them were pine. The trees had been cut down a long time ago. This had given the main roots some time to rot, making it somewhat easier to dig them out. Sitting around, waiting for school to let out, Larry figured the perfect way to get all of the stumps dug up by the roots.

"Evelyn, come on out here with me for a few minutes," he said to me one Sunday afternoon. "I got something I want to show you." When we got outside, he stood looking over the field of stumps. "Do you see all those stumps out there?" He hesitated before continuing. "I want these stumps all dug out of here so I can plant this place come spring. You do understand what I'm saying? They have to be dug out, roots and all."

He began pointing out the ones he wanted dug up first.

"Now these that I've just pointed out to you, I expect you to have them dug up tomorrow when I get home off my school bus route. Listen, girl, listen to me good. You get them boys out here with you where you can see them 'cause this work better be done when I get home, or, by God, you'll wish you had."

The next day when Larry got home, I had them dug, every one that he had pointed out. I was so mad I felt as though I could've bulldozed all of them out with my fingernails. This went on day after day for a period of time. Even on rainy days, he insisted I keep up the good work.

"Don't you worry about a little bit of rain 'cause it ain't going to hurt you none. If anything, it'll just make it easier for you to dig them out."

Rain didn't make it any easier for me. What it did do was cause me and both of the boys to catch bad colds. I tried to keep the children on the porch, out of the downpour. They would stand and point toward me, crying and begging me to come inside. I'd stop long enough to feed them their lunch and try to put them down to take a nap. Then, during the time they were asleep, I'd work real hard.

I knew I couldn't quit until God answered my prayer and sent me a way out of this predicament. I fully understood that if I lost patience, Larry would kill all three of us without any hesitation. His threat always was to kill, not just me, but what he referred as my "damn young'uns". Every time we heard about a man taking his family out and executing them, my husband appeared to be thrilled. I had to keep my thinking hat on and stay a step ahead of him if I planned on my children and me surviving. I had to keep my mind's eye on Jesus, if I was to survive. Grandma and Mrs. Barkley had made me aware of what Larry, just like his father before him, was capable of accomplishing. For our own safety, I would do good to keep all of this in mind.

One month later, my sister, Margie, and her husband, Henry, had a fight. He was an alcoholic which, according to my family, gave her every right to leave him. He and Larry were as different as day and night. Larry wasn't an alcoholic. In fact he didn't drink at all that I knew of, with the exception of the day we explored the mountains.

Margie had been staying across the road with my sister, Susie. Something happened there and she came to stay with us, which turned out to be the miracle I had so fervently prayed for.

I knew Larry would never show his dark side in front of her. After she had been there a short time, her husband came looking for her. He wanted her to come back home, which was his normal pattern each time he sobered up.

I had to come up with a plan.

It was time for me to plant a small seed in her mind so it could begin to grow. I would have to do it without her ever suspecting the torment Larry had been putting me through. One way or another,

I had to get away from there. Slowly, I began to put my plan into action.

19

"Margie," I confided to her one day, "I hate this place. I absolutely hate it here. If you really want to get Henry off your back, why don't you talk to Larry and see if you can talk him into moving all of us back to Easley? You can move with us, get a job, and I can get my job back. Think about it. Let's do what we can to get away from here."

I detected a glimmer of light in her eyes.

"Do you think Larry would do that?"

"I believe he will for you, but I don't think he would for me. He likes it here, but you know school's going to be out in another a week. Larry will be out of a job. We won't have any money coming in at all until school starts back."

I knew Margie didn't have a dime to her name.

"If you can talk him into moving," I went on, "his last seventy-dollar paycheck will be enough to get us all to Easley."

Money was never Larry's worry. If he had it, if he didn't, he didn't give a tinker's damn. People catered to him because he had lost a limb, thinking he had lost it in the war. He was taken out of school after the fourth grade to help on the farm because of his father's laziness. According to Grandma, when his daddy took a notion to be gone for however long his heart desired, Mrs. Barkley would have to keep the young children home to help her with the gardening and farming. That was the way he had grown up, with an obedient mother and abusive father. It is kind of like my daddy said: it's impossible to teach old dogs new tricks. I have never figured out why a person who grew up like that couldn't somehow find a way to rise above it instead of living a monkey-see-monkey-do life. It was as if he was supposed to do the same things to others that his father had done to him. Larry had every chance to tighten up his old boot strings and make a good life for himself, as well as his family. Lord knows, Uncle Pat gave it his best shot not once, but twice; the navy yard job and the job with the taxi company.

The following Sunday I got the boys ready for Sunday school. Margie told me that she didn't feel like going to church. I knew her main reason was that she suspected her husband would be there, arguing for her to come back home with him. She didn't want to take a chance he might get her cornered there. Her staying home with Larry alone would give her the perfect chance she needed to approach him about our Easley plan.

While we were sitting at the dinner table after church, Larry informed me that he had decided to move back to Easley. He wanted to help my sister get away so she could find a job to make a living for her and her children. While I happily packed up to get out of there, I was giving God the thanks for blessing us with yet another miracle.

All of the stumps were never dug up and the spring planting of his dreams seemed to fade from his mind.

When we got back to Easley, Larry found a nice, four-room house and rented it. Evidently he had stashed away some cash he never let me know about. The seven of us -Larry, me, the two boys, Margie and two of her children, shared the tiny place. I got my job back at the mill. Margie got a part-time job sewing. Larry absolutely refused to go back to driving a taxi.

I was so happy to be back in Easley and getting work at the mill, that I had no intention of rocking his little boat. What I needed to do now was to do my thing and let him do his, then sit back and watch nature take its course. I know now that's the coward's way. I'd let him turn me into a coward. Well, I may have been a coward, but I was a coward with spirit. He hadn't been able to break that, try as he may.

Virginia got a legal separation from Ray once his drinking got the best of him. Like Larry, he no longer worked anywhere. She was working first shift and I'd been put on the second one, so I only got to see her during shift changes. I found Aunt Mag again, then threw myself on her mercy. I put in every overtime hour the mill would allow. My children and my work were all I had or seemly ever would have. I intended to do what I had to do to see that my boys didn't grow up in an environment such as my husband had. Larry had once again chosen not to work. So be it. Making the living was much easier than digging pine stumps out of a field during a rain storm to satisfy his sick ego.

We hadn't been back in Easley long when my brother, Carl, and Stephen, a cousin of my mother's, came to town to do some carpenter work. They wanted to stay with us and said they would pay me twenty-five dollars a week room and board. They didn't know how long their jobs would last, but it meant some extra financial help for, us so I agreed to let them move in. It also meant that we now had nine people living in a two-bedroom house. Between Aunt Mag and myself there were beds to be turned down in the evening and beds to be put up for the day every morning. Larry expected to be waited on hand and foot, demanding more attention than the children.

One Sunday, after Carl and Stephen came to stay with us, I told my brother that I needed to talk to him a minute.

"Sure. What's on your mind, Sis?"

"I need help. Do you think that maybe Larry can go to work with you and Stephen?"

I saw that I'd struck a nerve, "Sis, you know as well as I do that Larry can't do with one arm what we do."

"I know that, but don't carpenters need to have helpers?"

Carl didn't know which way to go with that question. "Well, yes," he said, reluctantly. I knew he didn't like Larry. He thought it over for a minute, then he said, "Sure. Okay. If it'll help you out, I'll talk to Stephen and see what he thinks we can do."

I didn't tell him, but my true motive was simply to get Larry out of the house. I didn't trust him to be alone with the children. He didn't need to work to bring in money; I was taking care of us and meeting all the bills.

Carl told me, "If we do hire him, you understand we can't pay him a lot."

"He's not making anything sitting here on his duff."

He talked to Stephen and they decided to take him to work with them. I appreciated what they were doing, but they had to promise that Larry would never know his job was a favor to me, or that I had asked Carl and Stephen to hire him.

They subcontracted finish carpenter work wherever they could find it and moved quickly from one house they were working on, to the next. Sometimes it meant working in the next town, whatever it took for them to stay busy. When a job took them to Aiken, South Carolina, I knew it was much too far to drive there and back, and that they'd have to make camp in one of the houses they were working on. They took cots and blankets and came home only on the weekends. While I worried they might not want to take Larry with them, since they were working out of town, I was more worried that he wouldn't go even if they needed him. God smiled on us. The men asked him to go and he went.

Time sped by. They finished up the out-of-town job, then they came back to work. This meant them being home every night. It also meant, even though I didn't get back from work until midnight, that I had to be up at five in the morning to cook their breakfast and pack lunches for them.

Harvey had turned six in July. I enrolled him in first grade since there wasn't any kindergarten back then. Legally, a child couldn't go to school until they turned six.

Things seemed to be going great for Stephen and Carl with the construction business. They managed to keep Larry on the job, working regular. Stephen had been trying to save up enough money to buy a car. He finally reached his goal and got a brand new 1950 Ford. He was a very proud owner. He kept it so clean that I laughingly warned that he was going to wash off all the paint.

One morning, after getting the men off to their job, I went into the bedroom to wake Harvey and get him ready for school. When I gently touched his shoulder and called his name, he didn't answer me as fast as usual. He was laying with his back to me. When he turned to me and looked into my eyes, I could see a tear slide down his cheek. There was pain in his eyes.

I asked him, "What's wrong, baby?" When he didn't answer, I asked again, "Harvey, what's wrong?"

I could see that he wanted to tell me something, but it seemed he couldn't quite bring himself to do it. Instead, he very slowly pushed the covers away, wincing in pain. My worst nightmare had become a reality. Larry had severely beaten the child. I was devastated. I once told Larry that if he ever beat a child of mine the way his father had beaten him, I'd be forced to kill him. God, forgive me, I committed murder in my heart that morning. But God does work in mysterious ways. I had gotten Larry off to work and out of the house before I saw this little tortured body. Time and prayer usually takes care of every thing in our life and this was no exception. I thanked the good Lord that I had gotten the men off to work already. That gave me time to get myself together before I approached Larry.

My boys loved Roy Rogers and were caught up, as kids were back then, in the whole wild west cowboy craze. I had bought them almost every cowboy outfit on the market, along with matching leather belts with fancy metal tips. It was one of those belts that Larry had used to beat this six-year-old. Both of his legs, front and back, all over his buttocks, every lick where Larry had hit him, had broken skin and made indentations deep in his flesh. Blood had dried on the bed sheet so that it stuck to him. With trembling hands, I quickly got out the baby oil to try to get the sheet loose from his body without causing him more pain.

If ever history repeats itself, this was truly one of those times. The picture vividly appeared in my mind again of the story Grandma had told me about how Mr. Barkley had beaten his three boys, how he didn't stop until their blood made a puddle on the floor, how they had to get out the jar of cold chicken grease to try to soothe the deep gashes in the little boys' flesh. Now the story repeated itself. The difference this time was that this was my child.

The image of that poor mule that Mr. Barkley had beaten almost to death came to mind. I was shaking, and tears streamed down my face. How dare Larry be so brutal! Was this going to end the same way it ended with his mother, I wondered, with my brains all over the walls and ceiling?

Harvey reached up and put his little hand on my face. "Don't cry, Momma," he managed to say. "Please don't cry. Momma, when you cry, I can't stop crying."

"Honey, I'm going to be all right when you're all right."

After trying furiously to calm myself down, I asked him, "Harvey, why did your daddy beat you like this? Please, I want you to tell me why he did this awful thing to you."

His little voice was jerking as he confessed, "I did wrong. Daddy said that it was my fault...I had it coming to me. I marked on the window of Uncle Stephen's car with a yellow crayon. Daddy said that if I told you, he would beat me again, next time harder. He made me promise not to tell you. Momma, you won't let him know that I told you, will you? Promise you won't let Daddy know I told you."

"Harvey, you know you shouldn't write on things with crayons, especially on Uncle Stephen's car. You know how crazy your Uncle Stephen is about his new car."

His lips trembled. "Yes, ma'am. I know. I promise I won't do it again."

I tried to calmly explain to him that it wasn't his fault, that his father was an idiot, but I had to express it in different words.

"Yes, you were wrong to write on Uncle Stephen's car window with a crayon, but what your father has done to you is unforgivable. He had no right to do this. Nobody deserves to be beat like this. Your daddy better not ever dare try a trick like this again."

That was the first time I'd ever said anything negative about their father to one of the boys. I hadn't a doubt that Harvey was right; if Larry found out the child told, it was anyone's guess what he would do.

I cleaned my baby up as best I could, then put some salve and bandages on him. I felt unbearable pain for him. Tears were still streaming down my face when Dean woke up, wanting to know why I was crying.

I had to keep Harvey out of school until his little body healed.

This was the price I had to pay for getting involved with Larry in the first place. Was this the kind of guilt I would have to live with for the rest of my life?

Aunt Mag walked to work most of the time since she lived close by. When I heard the front door open and close, I realized it was time for me to go to work. I told her what happened, what I had done to try to help the flesh to heal. She was the only one I could confide in.

"Honey, " she said, "you stop your worrying now. Maggie's here. She'll take care of it. Just you get yourself together, go on to your work. Leave all of it in Maggie and God's hands. Stop your fretting now. Go, go. The Bible says, 'Vengeance is mine, thus saith the Lord.' Aunt Mag is going to pray. God will heal this child."

"Aunt Mag, do you know why Larry decided to send you home early yesterday?"

"All he told me, Miss Evelyn, was I could go home because he would be here with the boys. Mr. Carl and Mr. Stephen took me home on their way to see their girlfriends."

I knew how Larry's mind worked. It was evident that he had purposely sent Aunt Mag home so he could do his dirty work. Whatever he had built up in his sick mind, he had to get it out, just like his father before him. Granted, Harvey had used a yellow crayon to make a small mark on the side window in Stephen's car. When a sick mind is searching for an excuse, something that minute works. It was then I understood why Grandma was so determined to educate me about her son-in-law, so I could better understand why Larry was the way he was. Just as it was with Mr. Barkley, once Larry committed a brutal act, it seemed to vent his anger and he could be quiet and content for a few days, sometimes even weeks, afterward.

After discussing this with Aunt Mag, I got dressed and went on to work. When I got home that night, everybody was asleep. I managed to slip my tired, aching body in bed next to Larry. It wasn't easy, even being dog tired. I almost never got to sleep just knowing I was there beside the evil person who had brutally beat my child.

Five o'clock came early. As I went about my usual routine of cooking breakfast and packing lunches, I was fighting not to show any emotion–because I had promised Harvey. I knew that if I said even one word, as mad as I was, I would be like my mother; I wouldn't know when to shut up. I managed to hold my temper until they had finished eating. As they picked up their lunches and started to walk out the door, I heard myself say, "Wait up a minute, Larry. I want to ask you something. I want you to tell me why you beat Harvey." I just couldn't hold it back any longer.

"What are you talking about? I whipped him, I didn't beat him. I didn't hurt him. Have you lost your mind?"

"I want to know why you did it."

"I whipped him 'cause he wrote on the window of Stephen's car with a crayon. Why are you all worked up? I had to correct him, didn't I?"

"Correct him is one thing. To literally beat him with that cowboy belt with a metal tip on the end of it, is quite a different matter."

Before saying anything more, he checked to see that Carl and Stephen were in the car waiting for him. "Aw, you best just shut your mouth," he said. "Like I told you, I didn't hurt him. When are you going to understand these boys have to be made to mind me? Every little thing with them, you have to make a big deal out of it."

"I'm going to tell you one thing, Larry; it had better never happen again. I told you before I was ever pregnant that if you ever beat a child of mine like your father beat you and your brothers, that I'd kill you. I just might do that very thing."

"He's six years old. He knew better than to do a thing like that. I can't figure out where you got that from, that I beat him with a belt that had a metal tip on it. I'm telling you there wasn't any metal on the belt I whipped him with."

"Larry, I told you once, now I am telling you again, if you ever break the skin on either one of my boys again, before God, you had best prepare to die."

He started laughing.

"You can stand there and laugh, but I promise you, I will kill you."

Larry reared back with his stupid grin. "Can you tell me just how you think you can kill me?"

"You have to go to sleep sometime."

Several weeks went by before Harvey was able to go back to school. One night, after I got home from work, Larry announced that we were moving.

"Oh, really?" I said. "Where?"

"I found a five-room house on East First Avenue."

"What about school?"

"It's only two or three houses from East End School. In fact, we'll be on the same side of the street as the school."

It's a shock to admit, but it turned out to be a good move for us. We had much more room. Margie found an apartment and moved out on her own. Dean especially liked the new place. I never figured out how Dean knew the time, but he always knew when to go walk his brother home from school. "Mother," he'd say, "I'm going to walk Harvey home." Since he didn't have to cross the street, I didn't worry about them.

Once more, Carl, Stephen, and Larry were working out of town and getting back only on weekends. Things seemed to be going in a somewhat peaceful manner again. Like always, though, when things appear to be too good to be true, I had learned from experience that it was time for me to be on my p's and q's, as my mother would say; it was a sure sign that all the hell was about to break loose. I could feel it. Larry's demeanor was off. I knew he was getting ready to take pleasure in making our life miserable. The children even sensed it. The minute he walked through the door, it was like we were suddenly on eggshells. God forbid the little ones should make any noise.

When a big carpenter job was to take them to Virginia for two weeks, Stephen wanted me to quit my job and go with them, to cook their meals and take care of them. Carl helped convince me to go. He and Stephen had contracted some houses in a city where the state line is in the center of a street. One side of it is Bristol, Virginia, the other side is Bristol, Tennessee. One side charged sales tax, the other side didn't, at least at that time it didn't.

I asked my boss for a two-week leave and he granted it. This was going to be a vacation-work kind of a deal. I wanted to make it as much fun for the boys as I could. We took their little camp stove with its portable oven and packed up some of my pots and pans. Stephen and Carl were paying Larry a pretty fair salary. I felt comfortable with taking two weeks off. My main concern was that if I didn't go, Larry would use the excuse to quit work again.

It was the beginning of summer. The weather was beautiful. Everything was working out in everyone's favor. After getting there, and getting things set up in one of the houses the men were working on, Harvey and Dean went out exploring their new territory. It wasn't long until they came running back, asking for a pan.

"What on earth do you want a pan for?" I asked them.

"Oh, Momma," Harvey beamed. "Dean and I found lots and lots of big, juicy blackberries. We want to pick some so you can make us a pie. You'll make us a pie, if we pick them, won't you?"

"I will if I can, that is if I can get this little camp stove to cooperate."

I gave them a pan. Gleefully, they started out toward where they had found the berries. I yelled out to them to hold up and wait a minute. It seemed that, on second thought, I had best go with them.

"Why?" they wanted to know.

"Because snakes have been known to frequent under blackberry bushes."

Dean asked, "Why do snakes get under blackberry bushes?"

"Because they like to eat blackberries just like you do," I told him.

It didn't take them long to pick enough blackberries for a pie. After that, they were ready to move on to bigger and better things. That was quite an adventure for them.

When the two weeks were up, we went back home. Larry told me that he was going to buy us a mobile home to live in during their upcoming job in Newport News. It was scheduled to last for three years. Once again, I would have to quit my job. I gave the mill two weeks notice.

20

"Larry bought an eight-by-thirty-six-foot trailer. After traveling all night, we got into Warwick, Virginia around one o'clock the next afternoon. We found a large mobile home park a mile from the James River Bridge and rented a space. We thought there would be someone to help get the water and sewage connected, but we learned that it was our responsibility, not the park's. I knew nothing about doing work like that and I was sure Larry didn't have a clue, either.

He had managed to get the trailer backed onto the designated concrete slab when a nice gentleman introduced himself as Mr. Kline and offered to help. He, his wife and their two sons had been living in the mobile park for a couple of years. He assured us that we were going to love the place. Having hooked up his own water and sewer, he was able to help us get ours done in pretty short order. The trailer was small, no doubt about it, but it was new and quite a treat for me to have something that pretty and clean to live in.

Everyone actually seemed to be happy. The boys loved their new school, but there always seemed to be a downside; ours was that the three-year job turned out to last for only one month. Larry had gone in debt for the next four years with the promise of a long-term job. Carl and Stephen packed up their tools and went back to South Carolina. Somehow, buying that small mobile home seemed to give Larry some incentive. With the payment hanging over his head, he looked for work and found a job doing drywall.

While the boys were in school, I went with him every day to the job to help out. Larry would cut sheet rock to fit a space on the wall, then he'd go measure another sheet to cut. I'd pick up the first piece and place it where it was suppose to go, then nail it to the studs. It paid much more than what both of us had made on our other jobs.

Now that Larry had decided to do subcontracting work himself, we found that work was plentiful. I came to realize that Carl and Stephen's decision to leave was based on the fact they were sick and tired of Larry. I felt sure that he had tried to control them on their jobs. And, too, there was Larry's attitude of not wanting anyone to tell him what to do. I'm sure that didn't sit well with my brother and his friend.

Every job that we went on, we always ran into the same big, muscular guy from West Virginia doing the plumbing. He seemed to be a nice enough man, but I could feel his eyes watching me. It wasn't like he was trying to put the make on me or anything like that, he let me know that he didn't agree with a woman doing man's work.

One day he asked Larry, "Mister, doesn't it bother you for your wife to be lifting that heavy sheet rock? If I had a wife like that, she wouldn't be doing that kind of heavy work."

Larry said, "I know where you're coming from, but this is the best we can do. I can't hang sheet rock by myself."

Larry knew how to play his little pity parties. That artificial arm did it every time.

"Well," the plumber said, "take it from me, if you care anything about your wife at all, you'll find a man to help you. If you keep on letting her lift the way she's been doing, you're going to break her health down."

Larry didn't seem to like his advice. Truth is, he was enjoying putting me through this. Had that man not have been as big as a football player, Larry would have gone off on a jealous tangent. Like when we went to a restaurant and three times a man looked at me from across the room. He didn't flirt, he just looked. Larry marched himself across the place and challenged him with a belligerent, "Just what the hell are you looking at?" After that I refused to go to another restaurant with him. Now, listening to this big man's man of a plumber, I couldn't help but smile knowing Larry had finally met someone he was scared to go up against. My next thought was, *There is a God.*

Two days later, Larry had me write a letter to Gordon, one of my sister Margie's sons. We had nicknamed him Red as a child because of his thick, red hair. Larry wanted me to ask Red about coming to New Port News and working with him. I wrote, "Red, if you do decide to come, don't worry about living arrangements. You can stay with us."

No doubt, the big plumber from West Virginia had intimidated Larry.

It wasn't but a few days later that I received an answer from Red who said he would arrive in a few days. We were all looking forward to him being with us. Little did I know how much he would forever change our lives.

Red and the boys were on the James River every afternoon after he got off work, playing on his new boat. He had them water skiing before I knew it. I told Red that I wanted him to teach me how to water ski. Being a big clown, he teased me for a few weeks until one day I decided to go shopping for a bathing suit. Larry had just started letting me wear shorts, so I wasn't sure how he was going to take to me wearing a bathing suit. I was twenty-six years old and I wanted very much to learn how to water ski.

When Red bought his boat, it came with a small motor, which was fine since he had only fishing on his mind. Now that he had taught the boys to water ski, he decided to buy another motor the same size as the first one. That gave the boat twin motors with twice the power. There wasn't a problem getting the boys up with the single motor, but he had to increase power to get an adult up on skis.

The middle of May that year I had to go in the hospital for some female surgery caused by exactly the kind of thing the plumber had warned my husband about. Afterward I just laid around, taking it easy, trying to get my strength back. I was feeling better and decided it was time to get up and go shopping for that bathing suit I'd been wanting.

I had met a Japanese woman named Mitori Eastman who lived

across the street from us. Her husband was in the army, stationed at Fort Eustice, though he'd been shipped out to do an eighteen-month hitch in Greenland. Mitori didn't have a car or a way of getting to the bank to deposit her check and pay her bills, so one day there was a knock at my door, and there she stood.

"I come to...ask you to...please drive...to bank to pay...electric bill. If you...take me, I be happy...pay you." Her English was quite broken.

"I'll be happy to take you," I told her. "I don't expect any pay. I've been looking forward to doing some shopping myself. I put it off to keep from going alone."

The boys were in school. Larry and Red were on a job, even though things had slowed down and they were only working part-time. Since they were doing subcontract labor, we were still getting the bills paid. It was now July. The weather was hot and muggy, unbelievably humid. Few people in those days had air conditioning.

I combed my hair and grabbed my purse, then I hurriedly scratched out a note, just in case the guys got home before I returned. We went to her bank, then we went shopping. We found a store that happened to have live models. My eye caught a medium-blue, Rose-Marie, one-piece suit, trimmed with tiny white pearls. It cost a staggering fifty dollars. That was a lot of money in those days, but I really wanted that swimsuit. I wanted it some kind of bad. I always had to be a penny-pincher. I didn't have much choice other than to be thrifty, but this was more temptation than I could handle.

Back then nobody was allowed to try on bathing suits before buying one. That was a time when syphilis was rampant everywhere. We had to pick a size and pray it fit when we got home. You couldn't return it once it had been purchased. There had actually been a law passed to prohibit anybody from trying on any type of undergarments in stores. I thought, *my Lord, what if I spend that kind of money, then I get home and it doesn't fit?*

I didn't worry too much about Larry as far as the money was concerned. I was more concerned about whether or not he'd let me wear it once I paid that much money for it. Mitori found a bathing suit she liked, too, and bought it. That give me the nerve to go ahead and buy mine. After we got into the car to go home, she asked,

"Do...like... Japanese...food?"

Working in restaurants, I knew how to conduct myself, even though I admit, I had no idea what to expect in a Japanese restaurant. It was so good to be able to sit down in a nice place like that with someone I could enjoy my meal with.

My new Japanese friend I nicknamed Mike, introduced me to my first Japanese food that day and I still love it. After finishing our meal, we took our bathing suits home. I asked Mike to come over to my place so we could model them. No sooner had we gotten into them and was admiring ourselves in the mirror, than we heard a car in the driveway.

Mike had taken a liking to Larry from the beginning, like most all women did. He was a charmer when he wanted to be. She called him "My Mr. Barkley" instead of plain "Mr. Barkley." There was never anything between them, but he was a person she admired as her friend. The thing about an abusive personality is that they are always nicer to outsiders than they are to their immediate family.

Larry and Red came inside. We could hear their voices in the living room. Red yelled out, "Hey, you in there! What're you two up to?"

"Yeah! What are you girls doing in there?" It was Larry.

Mike called back, "You be pleased...when...you see...my Mr. Barkley...you will...be pleased."

"Hey, hey now! If Larry is going to be pleased, let me in there!" Red kidded.

Mike broke up laughing. "Eblyn...sure look..pletty, my Mr. Barkley."

"Come on, Mike," Red said. "We know Evelyn can't look that good."

"Hey, Red..you wait...when you see Eblyn..she be real...knock you dead looks."

We heard Larry clearing his throat. "I think it's time you let us take a peek."

I told Mike, "You go first."

"Oh...no...Eblyn...you...must go now."

We were giggling and having more fun than I knew existed, even though in the back of my mind was the fear of how Larry was going to react when I came walking out in a bathing suit. Mike being so excited about it made me feel somewhat better. I knew my husband's feeling of not wanting anyone to ever suspect he had his dark side. After the bedroom door closed that night, would be when the truth would surface. I pushed away such thoughts and playfully shoved Mike out the door, ahead of me. Both Red and Larry let out loud wolf whistles. Mike reached back and caught my hand, pulling me out in front of them. I was watching for Larry's expression.

Mike pointed at me. "Look...don't Eblyn...look beautiful?"

Red said, "Got to admit it, Auntie., you do look good! Come on, Larry, it does kinda hurt to let her hear us say it, but she's looking good."

They laughed again. Larry didn't seem to care about my having the bathing suit, one way or the other. With Red providing a boat, and both of us women wearing bathing suits, everything seemed fine. Mike and Red brought out the best in Larry.

After this, we all started spending a lot of time at James River where it was clean and much more private than the beach. The water was only five or six feet deep for quite a way out. This was before ski belts and jackets; we had none of the safety features we find on the market these days. With the water shallow, it was safer for skiing. That place became our summer paradise.

One night, Red said to me, "Auntie, why don't you cook up a batch of food and take it to James River? Larry and I have to be on the job at five in the morning because of the heat. We'll finish up by one latest. We can pick up the boat after work and go straight to the river and have our dinner there, maybe stay until it cools down enough that we can sleep when we get home."

Anything Red wanted to do, Larry went along with it, so I knew it would be all right.

Mike and another one of my neighbors went along. Counting Dean and Harvey and me, that made six of us. Everyone was ready to eat when we got to the river. By one o'clock we were all famished. The men arrived hungry and the picnic was a huge success.

Afterward, Red looked at me with a little twinkle in his eye and said, "All right, Auntie, today's the day you had best put up or shut up. I'm giving you one hour to let your food settle, then I'm ready to see you stand up on that set of water skis. You've been pestering me to teach you how to water ski, so this is it."

The year was 1953. Water skiing was just being introduced in my part of the country. After Red towed the boys around for a while on the skis, he pulled the boat up beside me.

"Well," he said, "the time has come for you to show me what you do."

I put on my skis, feeling good about myself. I had on my new bathing suit and my new swim cap. When I was ready, Red threw me the rope. He took off with me hanging on with all my strength–but not for long! Down I went. Over and over, Red tried to get me up. The boys had had no problem, they were light enough that the skis would float them to the surface, but I didn't have strength enough to pull myself to a standing position.

Once or twice I almost made it, but then I'd fall back into the water. I kept trying until I wore myself out. Every day after that we were at the James River and every day Red had the patience to work with me. He sure missed his calling; he should have gone professional with his comedy.

About three weeks into the summer, I finally stood up on the skis. I went a good two hundred yards when suddenly my right ski hit a wake and down I went. I fell so hard it knocked the breath out of me. When my senses returned, I stood up in waist-deep water. That's when I realized, to my horror, that my bathing suit strap had broken. I was naked from the waist up! I shook my fist at him. The first time I finally made it upright and he dare pull a trick like that! Everyone on the beach was applauding.

Red was laughing so hard he could barely control himself, though he wouldn't come anywhere near me with that boat for several minutes. He went around and around in circles for a long time before he came back. He was definitely having fun at my expense.

It was one of the best summers I'd ever had, and it ended much too soon.

It was almost two years later, when one morning Dean called to me in such a weak voice I knew something was wrong. He was nine years old at the time.

I stood looking at him, trying to figure out what was wrong, when he said, "Mother, I can't get up."

He was so full of fun, that I thought he must be teasing me, so I said, "Oh, sure you can."

Fear gripped me as I took him by his hands and picked him up and tried to stand him on his feet. His knees buckled under him.

The mobile homes were parked close enough together that I could step to the door and call to Billie Kleine, who lived next door. I asked her to come over. She had three children of her own. The minute she set eyes on Dean, she said, "Evelyn, you need to get him to a doctor right away."

The doctor I called said to bring him right in. I got him there as fast as I could. The doctor said, "I can't be sure until I can run some tests, but this has every possibility of being polio."

I knew that polio was contagious. I'd heard stories about it. I remembered that the beloved president when I was a teen, Franklin D. Roosevelt, was paralyzed by the dreaded disease. Dean was admitted to the Riverside Hospital. The first thing they did was place him in quarantine. Three days later, it was lifted. It wasn't polio Dean had, it was rheumatic fever. He was in the hospital for nine weeks and bedridden for another six months. Because Red was with us, Larry didn't give me a hard time and I was able to concentrate on my son.

It was during this period that we received the news Mr. Barkley had died of a heart attack. When we went back for the funeral, Grandma gave me a big hug at the door and whispered in my ear, "I knew that God would answer my prayer and let me outlive Alonzo."

A short time later, we got another call. This one was much more disturbing. Edith, Albert's wife, has died very suddenly, and quite mysteriously. Albert said at her funeral that Edith hadn't been feeling well. She went to the outdoor toilet and, on her way back, slipped and fell, hitting her head on a rock. She had died instantly.

There was no reason to doubt the story and no one did. Except me. I'm still not sure that's the truth, the whole truth, and nothing but the truth. I had begun to question everything because nothing seemed to be as it appeared. Edith had played around with my husband, of that I was quite sure, and I had my suspicions about other things, too. If I had suspicions, maybe Albert had his own as well. I'm not making any judgments, or pointing a finger, I'm just saying that my mother-in-law had been brutally murdered by her husband and he'd gotten away with it. My husband had laid a cruel hand on both me and Harvey, and I had no one to turn to who would care or do anything about it. And now Edith simply fell down, bumped her head and died. Really? How could I be sure? It seems we no more than get through one bump in the road of life, when there's yet another bump to face.

When I took Dean for his check-up, he was looking good. His temperature had been normal for some time. After the doctor got through looking him over, he informed me that the rheumatic fever was gone, but that he'd found two situations that would require more medical attention. The first was a hernia on Dean's right side, the second was a matter of circumcision. Neither of the boys had been circumcised. The doctor found that rather astounding and proceeded to educate me on the necessity of such an operation. He concluded with, "I suppose the next thing you're going to tell me, is that your husband hasn't been circumcised either."

"Yes," I replied. "I can truthfully tell you that. I can also tell you that one is out of the question for any kind of operation."

The doctor seemed disturbed by my announcement. "I want you to understand that this is why you stay so full of infection. That's why you've had the female surgery you've had. A man can't keep himself clean when he hasn't been circumcised."

So the boys got circumcised and their daddy didn't.

◘

I made up my mind to find a waitress job to make extra money with construction work being so iffy. The boys were now in the fifth and sixth grades, and since they played mostly with Billie Kleine's son, Jimmy, I didn't mind asking if she could watch them until I got home from work.

Luck was on my side. I went to work the same night I went out job hunting. With the two of us employed again, all of our bills were getting paid on time. But my good luck was tempered by my husband's old ways.

One night when I'd been on the job for about a week, I glanced out the café window and there was Larry parked across the street, watching me. Visions of him in Charleston flashed through my mind. Fear gripped me as I thought, *Dear God, is he going to start that all over again? Why isn't he content to stay home with Red?*

The next night, it was the same thing. Jealousy was once more eating at him. After this many years, I recognize it as possession and control. I remembered something Mother told me one time about jealousy. She told a picture story of a dog guarding a bone. The dog didn't particularly want the bone, but it was sure going to see that no other dog got it. Sick minds apply this same logic to their relationships. How many times have we heard about stalking? In the old days I heard it referred to as a man "bird-dogging" his woman. We didn't hear much about husbands killing their wives years ago, but let me enlighten you, it's been going on since the beginning of time. When you hear a man, or a women, say, "If I can't have you, then no one else can either", you had better watch out. That's a major red flag. It isn't love, it isn't caring; it's possession, control and ownership.

I have asked myself many times how a person can hurt someone they love. So much of that answer depends on how a person was raised. Even through all that my husband did to me, I felt his pain and his anger toward his father. I can't truthfully say I loved him. I never had a chance to learn to love him; every time I thought I could, he'd find a new punishment for me and it would kill whatever tenderness had been building up in me. But I can honestly say that I wanted to help him. I never once deliberately mistreated him. Once I started working with, and trying to help, women in abusive relationships, I heard so many of them say, "I take his abuse because I love him." That's puzzling to me. I promise you that not one slap or sucker-punch that I received from Larry created love in my heart for him. I did feel for him, because no child should have to grow up in the kind of situation his father had created in their home, but I handled it wrong. I let myself become his comfort blanket, his caretaker. Today they call it being co-dependent. No such term, or way of thinking, existed back then.

21

"October 1956, almost four years to the day that we arrived in Warwick, Virginia, I put the last money order in the mail to pay off the note on the mobile home. All construction work had come to a screeching halt. Once Larry brought me that news, I was thinking now that's he out of debt, it's time for him to pull another stunt of some kind. He had already made the decision to move back to South Carolina. I thought about getting my job back at Hudson Narrow Fabrics, but I had two strikes against me. First, Larry was getting edgy again and that always led to trouble, and second, Red was leaving us to go into real estate.

Larry insisted that I go on ahead of him and, stay with my sister Margie in Easley, to line up a job for myself. He said that he would bring the trailer two weeks later. "There's no telling how long I'm going to be out of work," he remarked, and I thought, *You'll be out of work just as long as you can milk it.*

I begin packing what the boys and I would need until he came with the mobile home. Before I left, I made a point of reminding him to buy travel insurance on the trailer. It only cost fifteen dollars and it would cover him while he was in transit. Sure enough, on his way to South Carolina, the trailer jack-knifed and lay broadside on the side of the road. Everything that could break inside, broke. He eventually managed to patch it up so that it was livable, but on our own dime. He hadn't bought the insurance.

Once again we were back where we started. There are not words to express the butterflies in my stomach. My whole being was churning with disgust as I watched him park that raggedy piece of mess that used to be our home, on the street in front of my sister's house. It didn't matter how hard I pushed or tried, I never had a decent place to live for very long. The little trailer so far had been the best, but all I had left of it was a mangled shack. He had managed to bring me back down to nothing.

All my dishes were broken, plus most of our clothes ruined by leaking kerosene. Margie had him move the trailer to her backyard, so we wouldn't have to pay space rent. I got a job in a shirt factory, the hardest work with the least pay I ever had. Nevertheless, Larry had it made. Our only bill was electricity. Margie didn't charge us for water.

We had just gotten both boys over measles when we got a phone call from a nurse in a Seneca hospital telling us that we needed to get to Louise's house next Saturday morning. She hadn't asked us, she told us, which meant it had to be something bad. Larry's sister had seven children at home, two of which she had delivered herself.

With some prodding, I got Larry to agree to go. As much as he loved getting in the car and driving, this was the sister who had a baby out of wedlock, and he was still holding a grudge. I don't know what he would have done if he'd known the child was fathered by his own daddy.

We got up early Saturday morning and went to check out the problem. I hadn't seen Louise in about six months, so the boys and I were looking forward to the visit. When we got to her house, she was struggling to get the floor swept. It didn't require a detective's license to see that it was taking every ounce of energy she had just to stand on her feet, let alone use that broom.

I tried to appear casual. "Hey, girl," I said. "What's wrong with you?" She looked like death warmed over.

Forcing a smile, she replied, "I just came home from the hospital yesterday."

"Why were you there?"

She hesitated before answering. "The doctor thinks he may have to operate. What it amounts to is that I have a boil on my liver."

I took the broom out of her hands, told her you go sit down or lay down, whatever would make her feel better, and to let me do what needed to be done in the house. I started straightening up and cooking for everyone. Then we spent the rest of the afternoon in conversation and I never did get her to lie down.

Just after I got home from work on Tuesday, the telephone rang in my sister's house. It was the nurse calling for Larry. It was a call we had been expecting, so I wasn't surprised to hear that the doctor wanted us to be at the hospital by eight-thirty the next morning. Louise was scheduled for surgery at nine. We got there an hour early.

She was in surgery just a little over two hours. The doctor was almost overcome with emotion when he blurted out to us, "It's cancer. Her liver was so eaten up with it that I had to scrape it out of her."

"What are you telling us?" I asked

"She has five to six weeks at most."

He had just stated her life sentence. It seemed the family was dropping like flies.

There wasn't any money to hire a private nurse. After the first two weeks the head nurse came to me and confided that Louise had called for me every minute that I was away from her bedside. The further it went, the more she seemed to cling to me. Louise had gone to work in a garment factory about three months before she had gotten sick. Being pregnant most her adult life, it was the first job she'd ever held outside her home. Margie said that she would watch Dean and Harvey for me so I could stay at the hospital with Louise. Over and over she would tell me how much she loved me, how thankful she was to have me for a sister-in-law.

I had to quit my job. I was staying with her day and night. Larry would stay with us one night and Albert would stay the next. The morphine they gave her for pain was making her crazy. There were times when I would have to go home to bathe and change clothes, but I would get back as quickly as possible.

One day when I returned, I could hear Louise screaming my name from the minute I entered the building. The head nurse approached me before I reached Louise's room. She said, "Mrs. Barkley, this is getting to be unbearable for the entire staff. She's has been screaming for you like this from the moment you left the hospital. You're the only person that can keep her quiet. Lord knows, we've tried everything we can think of. The minute you walk in the room, she settles down. I'd like to make you a proposition. If you'll pack a suitcase with things you need, and bring them to the hospital, we'll provide a place for you to bathe. Since she's in a semi-private room, you can use the other bed for your own, unless we have an emergency, of course. It's much easier on all of us to have you here." I promised her that I would bring a bag with me the next day when I returned.

It was absolutely a replay of the movie, "Terms of Endearment". There were only a few days left before Christmas and, to my knowledge, there wasn't a dime of hospital insurance or income of any kind for Louise and her family. I began to worry about her children's Christmas, as well as Christmas for my own boys.

When news spread about this destitute family, the community came together to see that Louise's children received holiday gifts. Well-wishers dropped by the hospital, most of them with presents. It was evident the end was near for her.

At times Louise would look at the assortment of gifts and her eyes would get misty. Other times she wanted me to put a doll or a stuffed animal on the bed beside her. Just after Christmas, she began talking about how much she missed her mother.

"Louise," I said one day, " if I ask you something, will you promise not to be upset?"

"You know you can ask me anything you want to ask."

"Do you believe that your father planned the execution of your mother?"

"Sis," she replied, "you didn't really have to ask me that, did you? Yes, I believe Daddy planned Momma's murder, and I think I know why." She was getting weaker. She had to rest a moment or two between sentences.

"If you'd rather not--"

"No. I've wanted to talk to you about this for a long time."

"What are you trying to tell me?"

"Daddy...I'm talking about Daddy before he died. He would get down on the floor and he'd say, look here, look at me, everybody; this is the way she was laying on the floor."

Cold chills ran up and down my body, but I listened as she went on.

"Every time he got drunk, he'd get down on the floor and say that over and over again."

"Did you see him do that?"

"He came to stay with us, remember? He didn't have any place else to go after Larry wouldn't let him stay with you. Evelyn, I was still scared of him. Etley didn't like him staying with us at all. He told Daddy that if he ever touched me again and he found out about it, he was going to blow his brains out. But Daddy never bothered me."

Once Louise start talking, she kept rambling on. She didn't seem to get too upset, so I didn't try to stop her.

"Daddy stayed with us until he found..." she hesitated "...that woman he married."

"What do you mean, 'that' woman? She was a nice lady, wasn't she?"

"Well, yes, she was. She didn't have anything to do with what Daddy had done."

Louise became very tired, so she stopped talking and rested for a while. I thought she was drifting off to sleep. Suddenly, she opened her eyes. It was like she regained her strength. "Yes, Evelyn!"

"Yes, what?"

"Yes, I know what Daddy did!"

Again, she was quiet. She appeared to be in a deep study.

"You do know that Daddy has always messed around with other women, don't you?" she asked.

"Yes, I've heard that. Tell me what you know about it."

Her words seemed to be getting slower. I could see that she was losing consciousness. "You know...after Larry and you moved to Easley...Momma got down real sick for a good long time...She sent for me to come over to...her place...she needed me to...come wash some... clothes for her. Next morning...I got up early...Etley went with me... to draw well water...also...start a fire around the...wash pot. Evelyn, before I went out...to the wash bench...Momma handed me some clothes...wrapped in newspaper. She told me...whatever I did...not to touch them...So I...loosened the...newspaper from around them... before I let them drop..into the...hot water. It surprised me to see that...she only had her panties wrapped...up like that. Once I got... them into the...water...I quickly let the paper they was wrapped in... drop into the fire that was around the wash pot...and I let it burn."

She looked at me with pleading eyes.

"Evelyn, I believe that Daddy...gave Momma syphilis. I think that's what was wrong with her." She rested for another second before she said, "Why else...would she wrap panties up...like that...and tell me not to...touch them?"

I couldn't handle much more of this conversation. I felt forced to try and get her on another subject, but she wasn't through yet.

"I believe...Daddy killed Momma to...keep Larry and...the rest of the family from knowing...that he had given her...syphilis. Daddy was...afraid of Larry. He was...scared of...Uncle Pat, too..and even Grandma. He sure...didn't want them to...know about it."

Every word that she told me made perfect sense. This was the time in our history that syphilis was in epidemic proportions. The health department had been showing movies about the disease across the country, to try to educate people on how to save themselves from the crippling disease. Larry and I had gone to see the movie a short time before moving back to South Carolina. Some of the scenes were so graphic, they had nurses on duty to work with the audience. Folks at the drive-in movie where we saw it got sick watching it. Some even passed out, it was so gross.

"How about you try and get some rest now?" I suggested. I caught myself talking slow like her. She had tired herself out. It wasn't too long before she drifted off to sleep. She knew she was dying. She had demanded the doctor be honest with her, so he had told her the truth as gentle as he could.

Louise stirred and then asked me, without opening her eyes, "Will you take care of Gail for me after I am gone?" Gail was her youngest, she had just turned two. I promised her that I would. She was concerned about all seven of her children, but she also knew how much I'd always wanted a little girl. During the time we lived in

Virginia, my doctor found that I had the first stages of cancer of the uterus. He removed a fourth of my womb and also a tumor. He also told me that I couldn't have another child.

Louise was drifting in and out of consciousness. She motioned me to come closer. When I did, she took my hand. "Sis, you know you're going to get that little girl you wanted for so long." Then she smiled as if she had a secret.

I tried to get Larry to come to terms with Louise, even though he knew it was only a matter of time until she would be gone. I went so far as to tell him the story that Louise had so long ago confided to me that day in the outside toilet. He listened, but he didn't show any emotion. This concerned me greatly. I didn't want her to die without them getting things mended between them. Louise never showed any sign of malice toward Larry, ever. She loved him and didn't hesitate to do anything for him that she could. Larry, though, was like a bull elephant when he got it in for a person, there wasn't any letting go. As long as I had been in the family, I couldn't remember ever hearing the two of them engage in conversation. Louise always spoke to him, but he rarely acknowledged her.

Right at the last, while she was still clinging to life, Larry sat in a chair next to her bed, watching her intently. The one good thing I can say about him is that he had been faithful, never missing a shift to sit with her. He tried to make her as comfortable as possible during those last days. I watched him as he sat there, never taking his eyes off her, for long periods at a time. I prayed that he would give in and talk to her. I felt that he needed to let her know he had forgiven her. After all, he knew now that it was his father who had gotten Louise pregnant. That is, if he believed what I told him.

Louise kept wanting water. She was so parched, but the nurses were afraid she would choke, and refused to give her any. Finally, Larry went to her bedside, picked up a drinking straw and placed it in a glass of ice water. He eased himself up close beside her bed, then he said, "Louise, do you hear me?"

She nodded faintly.

"Louise, I'm going to give you some water with this straw. I want you to listen to what I'm going to tell you."

She managed to nod again.

"Now, if you don't fight me, I'll see to it you get all the water you want. If you do like I tell you, you won't strangle."

She hung onto every word that he was saying to her. She did as he wanted her to do and cooperated about taking water from the straw. I got the feeling that it amounted to an unspoken understanding between them.

The last few minutes of her life, Larry stood by her side, holding her hand.

I was sitting on the side of the other bed, looking on and then, suddenly, I fainted. The next thing I remember, a nurse was tending to me.

When her doctor walked Louise's body to the hearse, I heard him say to the driver, "This is one of my patients I hate like hell for you to get."

After the funeral, there were seven young children to be taken care of. Also, I had to get back into the swing of things. Money had to come in from somewhere. Fortunately, our wrecked mobile home was paid for. The electric bill and groceries were our biggest worries. I went back to work in the shirt factory. On weekends I would cook or do whatever else I could to make Louise's children's life, as well as Etley's, as pleasant as I could. I had taken Gail, the two-year-old, and John Henry, the four-year-old, home with me. The rest were riding the bus out and back to school every day. Etley had to start getting ready for planting season. He was a good, hard-working man, but he wasn't capable of working the farm and taking care of the two youngest children while the five older ones were in school. I now had me a little girl and a little boy that I loved dearly.

22

"Six weeks after Louise died, I started waking up feeling nauseous. I told myself that it was just the stress of everything I was going through. Although I had been calling around every place that I thought might give him work, Larry wasn't interested in finding a job. He would tell me, "Evelyn, you know there ain't nobody going to hire me." Then he'd hold up his artificial limb to remind me how handicapped he was. Every time he did that, I would think of my brother Stanley and how he never missed a day's work. Despite the fact Larry had worked steady with Carl and Stephen and Red for about six years, all the sudden he once again deemed himself helpless.

For some very unknown reason, he cultivated a compulsion for sex. Now that I was feeling nauseous, he wanted to have even more, and hotter, sex. During those sessions, he would say, "Don't you think it's time that we had that little girl?"

I began to ask myself things like, "Why, all of a sudden, has this man who has always been against having children talking about having another one?" He had done an about-face even though he knew I couldn't have any more babies. Of course he liked that kind of challenge. If someone told him that he couldn't do something, he'd give it his all to disprove them. Then, too, I was his only choice at the time. He had been busy with Louise and most likely lost contact with his other women.

As time went by, I had to give in to my nausea. I stayed home from work and went to see Dr. Jamison. He, of course, was aware that I couldn't be pregnant, but nevertheless, he ran the standard rabbit test on me and said he'd have his nurse call me with the results when they came in.

When I got home, Larry jokingly had the nerve to tell me, "It's a sorry wife that can't take care of one man. You didn't need to go to a doctor. I could have told you that you're pregnant and saved us the money."

"You know I can't get pregnant," I reminded him.

"So, what'd the doctor do?"

"He ran a rabbit test anyway."

"Well, now, he should have saved the rabbit. I'm telling you you're pregnant."

"If you're so smart you know I'm pregnant, you should have gone to school to be a doctor."

Not more than two hours went by before the nurse called me. "Evelyn, " she said, "guess what? Your rabbit died!"

Now I had an eleven, a ten, a five, and a two-year-old to look after, plus I was pregnant. All that, along with a husband who wouldn't even consider looking for a job. I started badgering him about trying to find work. He could have gone back to driving a taxi at any time, but it was out of the question.

"My Bible tells us, 'If we don't work, neither will we eat'. It also tells us to earn our living by the sweat of our brow," I reminded him.

He replied, "Well now, in that case, don't you think you need to think about these past years while you laid around on the beach suntanning and water skiing instead of working? Every day Red and I were on the job, slaving away. Now, Little Miss Workaholic, can you tell me just how, in your way of thinking, it's all right for you to not work, but it isn't all right for me not to work?"

I didn't give up on finding him a job. I heard through the grapevine that a man named John Hunter was a floor finisher, as well as tile contractor, so I looked him up in the phone book and called his house. When his wife answered the telephone, I said, "Does your husband need any help on his jobs?"

"John does most of the work himself, but right now he does need a helper."

I proceeded to tell her about Larry.

"You'll have to have your husband talk directly to John himself," she said.

I thought I'd better prepare her for the worst. "I need to explain before your husband meets him, that Larry got his right hand shot off in an accident and he wears an artificial arm. He's been doing construction work in Virginia for four years, though, and we've just moved back here. That's why he doesn't have employment yet."

Mrs. Hunter seemed perplexed. "I don't know if he'll be able to do this kind of work with only one hand."

"But you don't know that he can't. How can you truthfully know that unless you give him a chance?"

She didn't sound pleased about what I had just told her, yet I hung up feeling very hopeful. I couldn't wait to tell Larry about my call. I could see a spark of determination in his eyes. I knew I'd pushed the right button. He had that I'll-show-her look on his face. I closed my eyes and whispered, *Thank you, God, for another miracle.*

He went to see Mr. Hunter and he got the job.

◘

Dr. Jamison told me to stay in bed for ten days. In his words, "When I say ten days, I mean stay in bed ten days, not nine, if you want to carry this baby to full term."

It was a very long, hot summer closed up in an eight-foot-wide, wrecked home without even an electric fan. When I wasn't in bed, I hunted a tree, then put a fold-out chair under it during the warmest part of the day. Most of this time my sister, Margie, took care of our cooking.

Four nights after my last checkup, I had my first contraction. Twenty minutes later, another one. After the third one, I woke Larry up.

"If your pains are only twenty minutes apart, we'd better wait awhile, " he said, and turned over to go back to sleep.

"We can wait a while longer," I said, "but I think I'm safe in saying we had best go ahead and call Dr. Jamison." Greenville

General Hospital was about fourteen miles away.

Dr. Jamison was waiting for us when we arrived. After getting checked in, the nurses got me into bed. The doctor came in, examined me and said, "Hang in there; it won't be long now."

It was shift change time for the nurses. I'll never know what possessed the woman who was in charge of me to squeeze my legs together and ram her fingers up my vagina. It hurt so much that, out of reflex, I hit her so hard she landed in the windowsill. Dr. Jamison came running in when he heard the commotion. I was madder than any old wet hen. Dr. Jamison wanted to know what happened, so I told him, "That nurse better not put her hands on me again!"

I had gotten so mad that it speeded up my labor. I was taken straight to the delivery room where my baby girl weighed in at seven pounds, ten ounces on October 18, 1957, the day the first Russian Sputnik was put into orbit.

Dr. Jamison was proud of the fact he had seen me through such an ordeal, that he had delivered a normal, healthy, beautiful baby against all odds. Someone said to me, "This is indeed a miracle sent from God." We named her Bev.

Time went by fast and soon Christmas was less than a week away. There was a parcel of land across the street from Margie's place that hadn't been put on the market, yet somehow Larry found out about it. Three days before Christmas, Mr. Hunter made the down payment on two lots as my husband's Christmas bonus. Larry went ahead and made the other payments. After the holidays, he had a septic tank put in. Mid-March, he decided to go back to the same mobile home dealer who sold him the eight-wide. Even though it had been wrecked, he was able to get a good trade-in on a larger one.

I found a sitter and went to work for Saco Lowell, one of the newer businesses that had recently located about four miles from where we lived, on the Greenville Highway. The company made parts for cotton mill machinery. Once again, Larry and I both had jobs. Now that Gail was old enough to go to school with the other children, Etley wanted her back home. John Henry went, too. Etley wanted to keep them together as much as possible. All of his children were boarding at the D.A.R. School where they had room and board. They went home on weekends, holidays, and during the summer. I understood Etley's point of view, but I had become so attached to Gail and John Henry that I missed them more than I can express.

On weekends I'd take my boys and Bev in the station wagon, and go to Etley's. The children were certain that Bev was their new toy. They were so excited every time they got to see her. The second they spotted the station wagon they came running to get her. Every time I was there, I'd cook up a batch of food for them. During the summer, we'd can vegetables in glass jars. I was thrilled that taking care of all those vegetables had become a lot easier. Chest style freezers had just come on the market, and Etley bought one. Almost two months after Louise died, the garment factory where she had worked sent him a letter wanting to know why he hadn't applied for her life insurance. It ended up paying for her hospital and funeral bills with enough left over to buy the freezer.

He had planted lots of vegetables and had yielded a bumper crop that year. When he offered to pay me for all I'd done with the children, and in other ways, I told him that I didn't want cash, but that I'd be grateful if he'd plant enough vegetables to provide for both our families. It was definitely a win-win situation.

One day Larry came in from work with the left side of his face swollen. From the looks of it, someone had hit him mighty hard.

"What happened to you?" I wanted to know.

He began to laugh, like it was funny.

I took a closer look at him. "Somebody hit you?"

He continued to grin, though I didn't see anything funny about it. Finally, he told me the whole story. One of John Hunter's customers had called to complain about black spots in the hardwood floor that John and Larry had recently finished. John had sent Larry to the house to troubleshoot and find out why the customer was unhappy. He, too, wanted to know why the hardwood floors had developed dark spots on them.

"While I was in the living room looking over the floor," Larry told me, "I saw a small dog stick its head out from behind the couch. I knew the minute I saw it that it had urinated on the floor. That was the cause of the dark spots. When I told the man the source of the discoloration, he hit me. Well, I left, but before I could get to the truck, I heard a pistol shot. Then I heard another shot and a bullet whizzed by my ear."

Now, this was one of the most far-fetched stories he'd ever come up with. I didn't believe a man would shoot somebody for telling them that their dog was the cause of their floor problems. Knowing the way Larry liked women, it's always been my guess that the man walked in and caught his wife someplace she shouldn't have been with my husband. I truly feel the biggest black spot was the fact that Larry had been up to his old tricks.

In August of 1959 I was working quite a bit of overtime at Saco Lowell. We needed the extra money so we could add a porch, and a larger bedroom for the boys, to our mobile home. I was working in an area open to an alley where a front-end loader kept running up and down, delivering and picking up goods. I had a roll of chain in my hands that weighed about ten pounds and looked something like what you find on a bicycle. My job was to cut it into certain lengths. Workers had to go back and forth across the alley, but I was concerned about a particular driver who was awfully reckless. It often crossed my mind that one day he was going to hurt somebody.

I was starting to lay out the roll of chain so I could measure and dismantle it, when the front-end loader came sailing down the alley. I jumped back to keep him from hitting me. When I did, I heard, then felt, a pop in my lower back.

I went to my supervisor, Mr. Driscoll, and told him, "The fool that's driving that front-end loader came barreling down the alley; it was all I could do to jump out of his way. I don't know what happened, but I twisted my back and it hurts like everything."

He told me to report to the company nurse.

"I don't think I need to do that, but I thought you should know. Somebody's going to get hurt if he doesn't slow down."

Mr. Driscoll insisted I go to the nurse and make out a report, according to company policy. I did as he said.

The next day I was too sore to go to work. It was later that the pain began to increase from my hip to my ankle. I didn't miss any more work because of it, however about three months after the incident I woke up with no feeling in my legs. I was paralyzed from the waist down. I lay in bed with fear gripping me. After a few hours, feeling began to come back into my legs and I decided to get up and go see the doctor.

Dr. Jamison examined me, then told me that he was going to admit me to the hospital for tests. "But first I want you to go to Saco Lowell," he said, "to get this straight with their insurance company."

I assured him I had medical coverage.

"I know you do, but getting hurt on the job, your health insurance won't pay. You need to make sure your workmen's compensation will cover it before they'll admit you into the hospital."

I made an appointment with Saco Lowell to tell them what Dr. Jamison told me.

There was a different nurse on duty than the one I'd reported to on the night of the accident. This nurse gave me a suspicious look, then said, "If you got hurt on the job, why didn't you report it?"

I told her that, indeed, I had.

"You have a young baby, don't you?"

"Yes, I do."

"You could've hurt your back getting your baby out of the crib, couldn't you?"

"Well, yes, I could have, but I didn't."

"How do you know you didn't?"

"My baby doesn't have a crib. Look, all I'm asking is the insurance company to do is pay my hospital bill. I got hurt on the job, I went to the company nurse, and she made a record of it."

Not only did she turn away from me and refuse to listen further, neither she nor the insurance company would hear what Dr. Jamison had to say about the matter. The physician had no choice but to admit me to the hospital for tests, anyway. When he did that, Saco Lowell sent company doctors to evaluate me. They determined that I needed to be put in traction for twenty-eight days.

My neighbor down the street was watching Bev while the boys made out as best they could. In the meantime, I was going nearly out of my mind with worry. When the doctors released me from the hospital, I was in worse shape than when I had gone in. They wouldn't let me go back to work but, according to the front office, I hadn't been fired. This went on for days, with the company doctors giving me the run-around.

Dr. Jamison sent me to an orthopedic surgeon who also turned out to favor the company. I was told to get an attorney. The first thing the attorney said was that I needed to get rid of the company doctors. He recommended a Dr. Brady who ended up sending me back to the hospital for additional tests, which resulted in the discovery of two ruptured discs that needed to be removed, and one that had to be repaired. Meanwhile, workmen's comp still refused to pay up.

Weeks turned into months. I was getting desperate. My body was twisted from the constant pain. I asked Dr. Brady to take another look.

Larry took off work that day to drive me to the doctor's office. There was a lavatory in the examination room where I was waiting. When Dr. Brady walked in, I was in there, heaving my insides out. I felt sick unto death. One look at me and the doctor scheduled me for surgery, insurance or no insurance.

My January eleventh birthday present was news that in two days I'd have to have both sides of my body operated on at once.

On January 13, 1960, I went under the knife. Dr. Brady made an incision about twelve inches long on one side of my backbone. Then he went under the skin and cut the same length on the other side of it. I remember going into the operating room, but the next memory is that of a long, dark tunnel. I was trying to climb up and find a way out. I was climbing, climbing, climbing. I saw people lined up side-by-side along what looked to be a hospital corridor. They were well-dressed and respectfully quiet.

My first thought was that I was dead. If I wasn't yet dead, then everyone must be waiting around, expecting me to die. Then I thought, *The Death Angel must be close by.* I continued to climb out of that dark tunnel, trying to find a light. In looking back, I feel that I was fighting *not* to go to the light, because of my constant worry about my children. That's all I remember until Dr. Brady looked down at me and said, "Welcome back. I'm having you fitted with a back brace first thing in the morning, then I'm putting you in an ambulance to go home. I've never had a patient get so depressed over being in a hospital."

I thought, You probably never had a patient as worried as I am about her husband mistreating her children while she's away. To be honest, there's no telling what I said aloud during the six days that I was unconscious.

Dr. Brady was as good as his word. The next day, he had me fitted with a back brace, called an ambulance and sent me home. The surgery left me paralyzed from the waist down.

It was a cold, blustery, winter day. Flu season was in full bloom. At home, I was placed on a narrow roll-away bed with a thin mattress. I asked Larry, "Didn't Dr. Brady tell you to get a hospital bed?"

"He just told me to get you a bed, he didn't say what kind. I'm sorry if it isn't good enough for you."

"It's too soft. I'll wind up back in surgery. I'm sure he thought you understood to get a hospital bed."

"Well, just where the hell do you think I'm going to get a hospital bed in this town?"

"The funeral home, for God's sake. Everybody knows they have them for rent. Will you please call and have them deliver a hospital bed as soon as possible?"

He made the call. It took less than an hour to have it delivered to the house.

After I got settled in, Dean couldn't wait to go to get his baby sister so we could see her. The pain of having to be away from my children was bad enough, but I had been gone from Bev for so long, and I'd lost so much weight, that she didn't know me. She was only a little over two. For the longest time, Bev remained scared of me. I was heartbroken.

When I was taken back for my check-up, the doctor said quite bluntly, "Evelyn, I have to be honest with you, I can't foresee any way that you will ever walk again."

I thought, *He's not talking to me. I've got children. I've got a baby. She's my miracle baby! I've got to walk. There's not any way that I'm not ever going to walk again.*

My mind raged on, refusing to accept the doctor's verdict. I knew in my heart that God had given me my little miracle girl and that He would send me a miracle to walk so that I could take care of her. And what about the boys? They needed me, too. No, I wouldn't give up and I wouldn't give in. God was my doctor. The Great Physician. He had a medication more powerful than all the other medicines combined.

From that day on, every waking moment, I would try to move a toe or a muscle. The boys were in school, Larry was at work. I'd had to send my precious Bev to a neighbor lady who was more than happy to take her in. How I wished Momma was younger and lived closer, but that wasn't the reality. She and Daddy were in no condition to come to my rescue. And then, too, it was some relief to know that Bev was in loving hands; I was never positive that Larry wouldn't one day do to her what he'd done to little Harvey. I couldn't run the risk of that happening and me not able to do anything about it.

I was home alone most of the time. I wasn't at death's door any longer, but I couldn't get out of bed. I spent long, painful hours counting tiles on our bedroom ceiling and praying, praying, praying. I told myself, I've got to walk again, I will walk again. I love God, God loves me. I was believing in God. I knew that my parents were asking for Him to intervene. I read the Book of Job in the Bible, read how Job had suffered, yet God healed him. I knew He could, and would, do the same for me.

A little more than seven months later, I took the ambulance, as usual, to my next appointment with Dr. Brady. This time, though, I walked into the doctor's office. When he looked up and realized it was me, it was as if he saw a ghost.

"Well," he said when he could find his voice, "just when did this miracle take place?"

I couldn't help but smile as I told him.

"I awoke one morning and, all of a sudden, I realized I had some feeling in my right big toe. I asked myself if it was my imagination. I was awake, so I couldn't have been dreaming. That got my hopes up even higher. I made up my mind not to tell anyone just yet. I had to be sure. Over and over I asked myself if it was true or was I just doing some wishful thinking. The feeling was so subtle at first that I had to question myself. I didn't doubt God's ability to heal me, not in the least, but I had to be sure. It was because of the fact that I believed so strong, with all my heart and mind and soul, knowing beyond a shadow of a doubt God was going to make me to walk again, that the next day I could sense a bit more feeling in my right big toe, not a lot, but more than the day before. Then I knew for sure that I hadn't dreamed it.

"One week later there was more sensation in my left big toe. The feeling was beginning to come back. It was real. I cried tears of joy. God gave me my miracle."

"Well," Dr. Brady laughed, "if your intention was to surprise me, you certainly succeeded. Do you recall me telling you after you regained consciousness, that I had gone to church the night before you came around, and I'd lit a candle and said a prayer for you?"

I remembered.

Once home again, I intended to keep on doing what I had been doing. I knew it would only be a matter of time before all of my strength would return. I was thankful to the good doctor for seeing me through. I was even more thankful to God for sending him to me.

23

Cold, foggy, rainy weather set in. It was almost Christmas again. Construction work has never been good during winter months. I lay in bed worrying about how much work Larry was going to get during the bad weather. I always was a natural-born worrywart. I knew there wasn't much food in the house. I had been sending first one and then the other of the boys to the country store down the road from us. Dean knew Mr. Harris, the proprietor, much better than I knew him, but he appeared to be one of the finest men who ever lived. He never once refused me credit.

I called Mr. Harris and I told him that I was trying to get my lawyer to settle my insurance claim. Saco Lowell was still fighting me tooth and nail. I didn't have any idea how much longer it would take, and couldn't understand the holdup. I promised Harris that I would pay every dime I owed when the lawyer came up with some money for me.

One month after that call, we were down to one five-dollar bill. I was too embarrassed to ask for any more credit. I was slowly healing, but I was getting more impatient. The wolf was at the door, as my mother use to say. My boys would soon be home from school and there was no food in the house. I prayed, "Dear God, where are You?"

Even though feeling had returned to my legs, I could only stand up for short periods. Harvey and Dean were doing what little cooking was being done. I had always managed to keep my family fed, even during what I thought were the roughest of times, but here we were, on the verge of starving. I remembered there was a twenty-two caliber rifle in the closet. If I could just make it to that closet and get that rifle, I could end this living nightmare. It would be easier to kill myself than to bear the shame of not providing for my family. I was becoming as obsessed with the thought of ending it all as I had been with the thought of being able to walk again. I slid out of bed and got myself into a standing position and that's when I realized that each day seemed to be getting somewhat easier for me. About that time, there was a knock on the door. I called out, "The door's open. Come in."

It was two ladies from Saco Lowell. Although I remembered the face of one of them, I didn't know her name. I don't think I'd ever heard it. She was the one who took upon herself to explain their mission.

"I work in the same department that you worked in," she said, a little embarrassed. "I wasn't there while you were employed with us; I'm sort of new." She fidgeted a bit, then went on. "We heard that you're paralyzed, so the department decided to do what we can to help you."

I was surprised, to say the least. "It's been over a year since I left," I said.

"Well, all the people that worked with you feel bad about the way the company's treated you. If it won't hurt your feelings, we went in together and made up a pounding that we'd like to give you." A "pounding" is what people in that part of the country called it when folks got together to donate groceries to others who were experiencing hard times. The other lady went out to their car and started bringing in boxes and bags of groceries. There were so many they filled the table. The cabinets got filled and there were even bags of food on the floor. I was indeed grateful.

In trying to thank her, I couldn't hold back tears. My sister Margie and I had gotten together food and clothes for needy families quite a few times, but this was the first time I truly understood the passage in the Bible that reads, "It is more blessed to give than to receive".

That day I once again cried, thanking God for His blessing. He spoke to me in a wonderful way that afternoon. Getting some food back in the house certainly gave me peace of mind. God had sent His earth angels to perform His miracle.

A little more than a month after that, the attorney settled my claim. At that time in South Carolina, ten thousand dollars was all that anyone got, even wives whose husbands were killed on the job, yet my lawyer got me sixty-five hundred dollars. After paying the hospital and the doctors, I had enough left to pay Mr. Harris over eight hundred dollars that was owed for groceries. I'm sure he felt blessed that day, too!

My strength was slowly but surely picking up. My thinking was clearer. I decided it was time to let the boys in on my secret. I got up and worked my way into the back brace I was still forced to wear, and was in the kitchen when the boys got home from school. It was the first time they had seen me out of bed, standing on my feet, since the whole ordeal began. I will never forget the expression on their faces. It was the happiest I'd seen them in a very long time.

"Why don't you go get Bev and bring her home now?" I said to Dean.

He went racing out the door. In only a minute or two, he was back, but without his little sister. He was so upset he was nearly in tears. When I asked him what happened and where Bev was, he stammered, "Maude won't let me have her."

"Why won't she let you have her?"

He hesitated, then told me, "This has been going on for a while now. I've been going to Maude's to play with Bev in the afternoons on days when I didn't have to work after school, but Maude always said that Bev was asleep and I couldn't see her. I didn't want to tell you because I knew you'd be worried."

Maude was in her late seventies. She was the loving neighbor who had been keeping Bev for me for well over a year, so I understood that she felt the same way I felt when I had to give up Gail and John Henry. She was also taking care of her aged father who was in his nineties. Maude had told me that she had an adopted daughter, but that she couldn't have any children of her own. This she confided to me long before my accident.

She let me know that she'd had her share of bad luck. The adopted daughter, Suzanne, had suffered a fatal stroke when she was only in her early thirties. Hearing that made me trust Maude completely. She, too, had known heartache. She'd be extra good to Bev because of it, I was sure.

I had tried to do what I could to show her that our family cared. She didn't have any transportation, so Harvey, who had just gotten his license, drove her to the store and to see her mother seven miles away. We didn't allow Harvey to drive too much, but this was for a good cause. Maude led me to believe that she wanted to return the favor by taking care of Bev for me, free of charge As much as I missed my baby, the one worry I didn't have during the time I was flat on my back, was whether or not Bev was being well cared for.

After Dean came back without my little girl, I saw Larry go out the door without saying a word. We watched him as he went to Maude's house. I didn't want him to have a temper fit and hurt Maude's feelings. In a matter of minutes he came back, holding Bev by the hand. No sooner did they get in the trailer than the phone rang. I answered it. Maude, on the other end of the line, was about as mad as a person could be.

After my hello, she screamed, "If I ever see you or Larry again, even out in your yard, I'm going to shoot both of you."

"My Lord, Maude," I said, "what's wrong? What brought this on?"

"I don't ever want to see Bev, you, or any of your family again. Larry come got her. Now, damn you, you can keep her."

"Wait a minute. I don't intend to just take her away from you altogether. You're welcome to see her any time you want to see her."

"If I can't have her, I don't want to ever see her again."

"If it's money you want, tell me and I'll do what I can."

"I don't want your money. I want you to give me Bev."

I didn't know anything more to say to her except, "I'm truly sorry, Maude, if that's the way you feel. You won't ever know how much I appreciate all you've done for her but there's no way on God's green earth I can give you my baby. The good Lord knows I'm more than willing to share her with you, but I can't give her to you."

Again, she said, "If I can't have her, I don't ever want to see her again."

Maude never shot us, but she would never have anything more to do with any of us after that.

I couldn't believe she could be so cruel. Bev would cry and point toward Maude's house. She wanted her "Pee Paw". Maude's aged father had spent many hours playing with Bev, and he had become her Pee Paw. How could I ever explain it all to a two-year-old?

During the last few months that I was bedridden, a Baptist preacher named Trotter, dropped by for a visit. Several members of his church lived on our street. One of his followers told him about my being paralyzed. I mentioned to him about Maude and how depressed I'd been because of the misunderstanding.

Preacher Trotter shrugged and shook his head. "The lady wouldn't let me in her door because I'm a preacher. I don't think I'd want a woman like that taking care of my daughter. The best advice I can give you is to pray for her."

After I regained enough strength, I got myself and my family dressed and we visited Reverend Trotter's mission. One Sunday, when the altar call was given, Larry shocked me by going forward. Suddenly, he was a born-again Christian. I couldn't have been happier. I truly thought that now we would finally have a marriage of wedded bliss, just like my parents. Mr. Hunter had run out of work and Larry didn't have a job again. We were back to having no income, though he could have worked for the taxi company as a driver any time he wanted to, but he refused.

Not long after the church experience, Larry handed me a piece of paper with a name and an address on it. He asked if I'd write the man whose name I can't recall and order an eight-inch commercial sander and a seven-inch edger, along with all the cables he'd need to finish hardwood floors. I had no idea what he had in mind, but I knew we didn't have money to pay for equipment like that. When I questioned him, he said, "Just write the letter. There'll be a way."

I thought, *Well, I asked God to heal me and He did. Now that Larry has accepted Jesus in his heart, he's as entitled to his miracle as I was.* So, I wrote the letter for him. In all fairness, Larry had managed to pay for the two lots Mr. Hunter had put a down payment on for him, and he'd paid for our mobile home, plus his own taxi business.

Before we had any response, I was able to get work doing alternations for a department store. I had to bring my own sewing machine, iron and ironing board, but still the hours were good and the pay was decent.

One day soon after I mailed that letter I'd written for Larry, a station wagon pulled into our driveway and stopped. A well-dressed man in a business suit got out and came to the door. When he knocked, he introduced himself as a salesman here to deliver the sanding machine and other items that Larry had ordered. I knew we didn't have a cent in the house, but then I hadn't ordered the things, my husband had, so I invited him in. After a few uncomfortable minutes, I finally said, "Sir, the only way I know to tell you this, is plain and simple. We don't have any money. I had very serious back surgery and we're broke, but I'm going to get to do some alteration work over the weekend."

The man didn't falter, nor did his expression change when he said to Larry, "Do you have credit established?"

Larry told him that we had never asked for credit.

The salesman wasn't discouraged. "What you're saying is that you've never been turned down for any credit, is that right?"

"Yes, sir."

Then the salesman asked, "Have you ever had credit through a bank?"

"Uh, yes, sir. I did buy a car through the bank here in Easley."

"I certainly appreciate your honesty. I'd like to help you folks out if I possibly can."

He looked at his watch. "The bank won't be closed for another hour. What do you say we take a ride and see what we can come up with?"

I could see the excitement in my husband's eyes. "Sounds good to me."

Immediately, they left to go to the bank where they talked to a loan officer who heard the situation then said, "If you had a cash down payment, Mr. Barkley, we could do business. I'm more than willing to let you have two-thirds of what you need, if that will help you."

When they came back and told me, I thought, *If we can come up with that much money, it will indeed be a miracle.* My heart went out to Larry, as well as to the salesman. Larry hadn't gotten the equipment he had his heart set on, and the salesman had made a two hundred-mile trip without the success of a sale.

The next morning, Larry said to me, "Evelyn, you know I'm not going to be able to get a job. With those machines I can own my own business. It's the only way I can think of to make a decent living for us. I need you to tell me what to do."

I told him to accept the two-thirds of the money needed from the bank. He could owe the salesman and pay the balance on the equipment in monthly installments with another monthly payment going to the bank loan.

I said to him, "I don't know how much I'll be able to help you, but I'll do all I can."

After our conversation, he left with the salesman to go to the bank to get the money. Now Larry had his miracle, too. The next miracle that he needed was to find some houses that needed their hardwood floors sanded and finished.

We went to prayer meeting the following Wednesday night. With my husband being a born-again Christian, he was so full of the spirit he could hardly contain himself. He was also excited about his fancy new machines. They were the latest models on the market. He was eager to tell Preacher Trotter about them after prayer meeting that night.

We got home from church, had a late night snack then, just before going to bed, the telephone rang. A man asked to speak to Mr. Barkley. I handed the receiver to Larry. His listened for a bit, spoke very little, and when he hung up, his face was lit up like I'd never seen it before. He kind of danced around a bit before telling me, "I just got my first floor finishing job. I go to work in the morning. That was a building contractor. He not only has one house for me to do, but he has two new houses ready to be sanded and finished as soon as I can get them done. If he likes the job I do for him, he's going to send me all his work."

God was really smiling on my husband since he'd invited Jesus to live in his heart.

That was the beginning. The work poured in. The boys, at fifteen and sixteen, were old enough to help him. Dean also found a part-time job working at a television repair shop, mainly after school and on Saturdays. He wanted to be there rather than work with his father and did all he could to keep a distance between them.

Harvey, being more the outdoor type, liked working with Larry. I took on the job of driving him to meet his father wherever they were working. Before long I became their gopher; it was go-fer this, go-fer that. But I thanked God every day that I was able to help out that much, especially now that work was coming in faster than Larry could get it done. I knew him well enough to know that while he was motivated, I had to put forth every effort I could to keep him that way.

I couldn't have been more proud of him than I was at that time. It was the most determined effort he had put forth in all the years we'd been married. Customers were ecstatic. Hearing them rave about the fact he could do such wonderful work with only one good hand was music to my ears.

My husband was on the job every morning by eight. All of his payments were made on time. His prices were reasonable. He was making the best money he'd ever made in his life. I really felt that he was the happiest he'd ever been. Much of his earlier attitudes and beliefs had come from preachers preaching half-truths. They ranted on about hell fire and damnation. If a man saw a woman's ankle, she was doomed. There wasn't any way out, according to some of the preachers, these women were going to "split hell wide open", to put it in their words. When a child was born out of wedlock, it was preached that God would never forgive the evil mother. If a woman wore make-up, she was doomed to hell. The Bible tells us that a little wine is good for the stomach's sake, yet how many times have I heard preachers say that if you drink wine, you'll surely burn in hell?

I understood more of why my siblings started walking away from church. In those days there was no preaching about restoration. You sinned, you would surely go to hell. People who had been forced into divorce had no choice, they were hell bound for sure. It had gotten so strict that many people were afraid to go near the church building, let alone walk inside.

People who read and know the Bible can figure it out for themselves, but people with the kind of mind the devil gets into, become destructive like my husband had in the past. I truly believed, even during those days, that God would surely one day bring these so-called preachers to accountability for their false teachings.

The one thing that stuck in my husband's mind was "once married always married". I, too, was taught, even by my wonderful father, just as he'd been taught by his father, that this was the Truth, the absolute Truth. What I never understood was that for some reason, when a man divorced, God would forgive him (according to one preacher in particular that I heard talk), but for women, there was no redemption. I can't help but wonder if these so-called Godly men realize the damage and hurt they've caused with their messages. I don't profess to be the sharpest knife in the drawer, but people want to hear about the love of Jesus. They want to hear that God loves them and that they can be forgiven. They want to know that with faith comes hope.

My husband had become motivated at most every level. He was working hard, he was good to his family, and he was ready to go to church for every service. Preacher Trotter won my husband over to the Lord. If there was a weekly revival, we'd go without missing a single night. It seemed like after services we'd get home and, every time, the phone would ring with more jobs from one of the church members. I was so happy that Larry had finally straightened out his life. It was sheer joy to see him that happy. I was hoping against hope that he had changed for good this time. It was a relief to no longer worry that he would hit one of us again. He was still controlling, but in little ways that weren't so terrifying. I would have done well to remember my mother's words: "A leopard can't change his spots".

24

It was again getting close to Christmas. The year was 1963. Harvey was marching with his trombone in the Easley High School Band. On this particular day, they would be participating in the Greenville Christmas Parade. I had so many things on my mind that day that I completely forgot about it, even though it was one of the biggest events of the year in our tiny town.

Dean always went straight from school to work. Harvey rode home on the bus. When he didn't show up at his usual time, I called the television shop where Dean worked. He was busy, so I told the lady who answered the phone that I was looking for my son Harvey. She told me that she had just seen him on local television, marching with the band. Oh, my goodness! I was too embarrassed to even talk to Dean. How in the world could I have forgotten such an important occasion?

With some effort, and not a small amount of guilt, I went on to a meeting of the ladies at the church. It was about eight when I got home. Larry was already there. I was about to sit down and get comfortable, when Dean came bursting through the door.

"Mother! Where's Harvey? He wasn't at school today."

Immediately I went into a frenzy. Hadn't the woman at the television shop seen him in the parade? She said she had. If he hadn't been in school, why would he have been marching with his school band?

"Just you calm down now," Larry said to me. "He's all right. In fact, I was getting ready to tell you that he called earlier and said he wanted to talk to you."

I didn't understand. "Where is he?"

"He called from Walhalla."

"Walhalla? What's he doing in Walhalla?"

"Well, I guess we'll get the answer to that when we get there."

I couldn't imagine that anything could be more important to Harvey than marching with the band. I started carrying on like mothers do when they're confused and half frantic. Finally, Larry said, "For God's sake, why don't you shut up? Right there, that's what's wrong with them young'uns. The least little thing happens and you have a damn fit. You think they have to have everything they want when they want it. Sometimes, where they're concerned, you act like a damn fool."

When we got to Walhalla city limits, Larry said, "Harvey told me he'd be at the laundromat." He parked in front. "Go in and get him. I'll wait out here."

I found Harvey crouched in the back of the building, behind a row of washers and dryers. His teeth were chattering. It was cool outside, but he was having a nervous chill. I put my arm around his shoulders and could feel his body trembling.

"What in the world is wrong, Harvey? Why are you here?"

"I don't know, Momma. I don't know."

"How'd you get here?" He had no reason to be in Walhalla. He couldn't give me a coherent answer.

I helped him to the car and we started back home. I still had no idea what was going on with my son. I told Larry I was going to take him to the doctor first thing in the morning.

"Stop your worrying," he said, disgusted. "He just wants to have his way, that's all."

I hadn't heard Harvey ask for anything, so how could he be wanting something we weren't giving him?

We drove on for a while with Harvey in the back seat shivering and confused, and me in the front seat just as confused. Larry cast me another critical eye, then sighed like he'd had enough of my dramatics.

"You're his biggest problem," he said.

"How can you say a thing like that with him sitting in the back seat hearing every word?" Not surprisingly, Larry didn't answer me.

When we got home, I gave Harvey a couple of aspirin along with a cup of hot chocolate to try to get him warmed up. Then I helped him into bed. He was still shaking almost uncontrollably. I lay awake worrying the bigger part of the night.

The next morning when he got out of bed, he was so stiff he could hardly walk. I couldn't get him to eat any breakfast, though he did drink another cup of hot chocolate.

After Larry went to work and Dean got off to school, I told Harvey, "Son, how about you go lay down on the day bed in the living room?"

I noticed that he was only using his toes on his right foot to try to keep his balance. I realized there was something wrong and asked him about it. He said he didn't know, but that it hurt real bad, so I took a look.

One glimpse and I said, "It doesn't surprise me that you're limping! You have a huge thorn in your heel. How could you not know that?"

He wasn't aware he had a thorn in his heel, only that his foot hurt. It didn't make the least sense and I told him so.

"Harvey, you're sixteen years old and you're telling me you don't know why you went off like you did, without telling anyone, or that you had a thorn in your foot?"

His voice trembled when he tried to explain what happened.

"I woke up around ten-thirty last night. It felt like a drum was beating in my head and there was a voice telling me to go...I listened to the voice for a few minutes, then I got up and got dressed and started out walking. I went through the field to the right of the trailer, then I went on up to the woods. It seems like I walked miles in the dark, mostly through the trees, until I came to a road. It was beginning to get light. I realized it was the road to Six Mile. By then I was hungry.

"About nine o'clock I saw a turnip patch, so I went and pulled me up a turnip to eat, then I kept on walking. Some miles later, I came to a store. I was still hungry, but I didn't have any money." He stopped and hung his head. "Momma, I stole me a coke and a pack of crackers at that store. I'm so sorry. I never stole anything before in my life." I believed him. By now he was in tears. "Please, take me back to that store and let me pay the man, will you?"

I assured him that I would, but the immediate concern was the thorn in his foot. While I examined it, he went on with his story.

"While I was walking along, that drum just kept on beating in my head to go, go, go. My foot got caught in some underbrush. It caught my shoe, pulled it right off my foot. The drum was beating louder in my head. It wouldn't stop long enough for me to get my shoe, it made me keep going, so I walked on to Walhalla. That's when it stopped...and I called you. But you weren't home. Daddy said you were at church."

That explained why Larry was in such a snit; Harvey called home to talk to his momma rather than to him. But the whole story was so strange, it was almost unbelievable. If it hadn't been coming from Harvey, I never would have believed it. He had walked more than fifty miles, a good portion of it through woods, in the dark and all the following day–with a thorn in his heel and without a shoe.

Once at the doctor's office, I told Martha, the nurse, what happened. She immediately went to get Dr. Jamison. The doctor came into the room and Harvey related the story to him exactly as he'd told it to me and to the nurse. Not surprisingly, he said he was going to make an appointment with a psychiatrist.

"Let him run some tests," Dr Jamison said, "then let's see where we go from there."

The doctor asked to see me alone. Once Harvey was out of hearing range, he said, "My guess is that he could possibly have a brain tumor. Now, don't you go jumping to any conclusions. Just keep yourself calm and keep him calm until we know for sure what's going on here."

Dr. Jamison told me that he had found a dark spot in part of the brain that dealt with clear thinking. Two days later, I took him in to see the psychiatrist.

"What would cause that to happen?" I asked, referring to the drums in Harvey's head and the voices that he heard. Before he could answer, I went on to tell him about being in labor for so long and how the doctor had practically torn him out of my body with forceps. "Do you think his problem could be caused by those forceps?"

"It's more likely to have been caused by his head being squeezed in the birth canal for so long," he replied.

I didn't tell him anything about the beating that Larry had given the child when he was six years old. I never told him about the constant pressure we had all been under, and were still under to an extent, because of the fear of my husband.

The doctor prescribed a bottle of pills, then dismissed him. Harvey seemed much better while he was taking the medication, no doubt about it.

◘

After Larry's business got going, we had enough money to build the bigger bedroom for the boys and to add on a porch. Once that was done, he decided to plant fruit trees and grapevines. Things were definitely looking up. The business prospered beyond belief. It was a full-fledged enterprise. We had all the work we could handle and sometimes more than we could handle. We needed a station wagon to haul materials, so we purchased a '62 Plymouth Wagon. I was still wearing my back brace and, according to the doctor, would be wearing it for the rest of my life. Three years later I proved him wrong. One morning I got up and started to fasten the brace around me when I thought, *You don't need that brace, the weather's too hot.* I slipped it off, slid it to the back of my closet, and never wore it again.

Meanwhile, Larry found an older, green panel truck that he bought to haul his tools in. Things were much better financially and the future looked bright.

Four years went by rather smoothly. Harvey didn't develop a brain tumor, the voices never returned–and I made the fatal mistake of letting my guard down.

One Sunday the sermon was particularly fantastic. We got home and I was finishing up the dinner that I always started before leaving for services. In a matter of minutes, I'd have a great meal on the table, just as Momma had taught me to do. All of a sudden, I heard a gut-wrenching scream come from the bedroom. The shock sent shivers through my body. I turned to see Larry come through the kitchen carrying a broken branch from our plum tree. As he hurried out of the door, he looked at me with venom in his eyes and muttered through clenched teeth, "I'm going to get another one of these, then I'm coming back and I'm going to beat him to death."

I had a flash of the way his father looked the day he beat that poor old mule.

Larry no sooner slammed the door behind him than Dean came out of the bedroom, wincing in pain. He had been brutally beaten. I felt my breath catch as I said quickly, "Run, son, run! Get away from here! Whatever you do, don't let him catch you!"

The demons that had once possessed Larry had surfaced again.

He came back holding the fresh broken limb from the plum tree and walked by me without glancing my direction. When he saw that Dean was no longer in the bedroom, he stormed to me, his entire body trembling.

"Where the hell is Dean?" he demanded. "I want to know right now. Dammit, do you hear me?"

I shook my head. "I don't know where he is."

He waved the switch back and forth in my face. "If you know and you won't tell me, I'm going to put this on you."

The old terror was rising in my throat. "My God, Larry, what in heaven's name do you think you're doing? Why did you whip Dean? That child hasn't done anything for you to beat him like that."

"I'm his damn Daddy. If I want to beat him, I'm gonna beat him, and I wanted to."

His fury was building. "What I gave Dean is small compared to what I'm going to do to you. Now do you, or don't you, know where he is? Dammit, I'm waiting for you to tell me. Where is Dean?"

I didn't answer. He finally put the limb down and sat staring into space for some two hours without speaking a word. At last he got up and went outside. I heard his panel truck start up and he drove off. He was gone a couple of hours, then he returned. I made it back to bed and tried to ignore him. He sat around, fidgety, until late that afternoon then he seemed to get an idea. He went to the phone and dialed. After a moment, I heard him ask if Dean was there.

I was pretty sure that Dean had gone to my brother Carl's house. From the sound of the conversation, Larry had to be talking to my sister-in-law Gladys.

"Fine," Larry said. "Good! Go right ahead and take him to the magistrate! I couldn't care less where you take him! There's not one damn thing you can do about it 'cause I am his daddy and Dean's my young'un. I'll do whatever the hell I wanna do with him, do you understand me?" He listened for half a second, then said, "What?" He snickered and said innocently, "Who, me? Go to jail? You're crazy. I'm not going to any jail." And he hung up.

They kept Dean overnight and didn't let him come home until after school the next day. Larry had talked real brave on the telephone, but Gladys had touched a nerve in him.

Now that the boys were older, it was hard for me to keep them out of harm's way. Harvey was working with him. What scared me was that every time something would go wrong for Harvey, I saw the same urge to lash out that I saw in his father. Dean would confide in me, but Harvey was more secretive about what was going on with him.

When Dean turned seventeen, he asked permission to go into the navy.

"Dean," I said, "I'd rather you wait until you're old enough to sign for yourself. It won't be that long until you'll turn eighteen. If you're still determined to get away from home, you can go then."

He didn't say anything else to me, but instead he took the papers to Larry who was only too glad to get rid of him. He signed right away. Harvey was strong and healthy and pretty much knew how to humor his dad. Not so Dean. He hadn't forgotten that whipping and he never would. Nevertheless, when his basic training ended and he was being sent out, he called me one day and said, "Mother, I don't want to go."

"Why don't you want to go?"

"I'm scared."

"Dean," I said as gently as I could, "this is exactly why I refused to sign the paper for you to go in. I knew you needed more time to think it over." I was searching for the right words to reassure a frightened seventeen-year-old who only wanted to escape his father's insanity.

"I understand that you're scared. If I could do something about it, I would. Just get on the plane. The more you think about it, the harder it will be for you. As soon as you get where you're going, call me collect. You belong to the government now. Just call me when you get there. You'll be all right. Call me collect."

Three days went by, but he didn't call. On the fourth day I went to the mail box to find a postcard from a ham operator in North Carolina telling me that Dean had arrived safely in Great Lakes.

That following Sunday at church, one of my nephews told Larry about a house on eighteen acres of land that was for sale. He felt it would be a perfect place for Larry to run his business. Larry had started out only finishing hardwood floors, but now he had expanded to where he was contracting to refinish old floors. He had a huge inventory of floor tiles and linoleum, which required storage space. If he bought the house my nephew was telling him about, he could back his truck up to the basement door and load or unload his materials and equipment.

Nobody was taking into consideration the fact that we had just completed remodeling our own home. It was comfortable and it was paid for. Harvey had gotten married and, with Dean in the navy, we had more space than we'd ever had. Knowing the ups and downs of my husband's personality, the thought of taking on another debt terrified me.

Larry decided to go look at the property after Sunday dinner. The gentleman living there invited us to look around. The minute I walked into that house, I felt the angel on my shoulder trying to give me a warning. I had never felt vibes that strong before. The feelings were so strong that cold chills covered my entire body. I tried to stay calm. I didn't want to show what I was feeling. I knew I had to handle the situation with kid gloves.

Larry bought the house. I didn't understand what intuition was trying to tell me, but I had the feeling I would live to regret the move.

"What do you think about my house?" he asked me after the fact.

"Well," I replied cautiously, "I think it has some good points, but it needs quite a bit of work. I feel like we need to concentrate on the business right now rather than on buying a house."

He blew up. "I knew it! By God, I knew that's the attitude you were going to take!"

I used a calm voice to say reasonably, "Larry, we just got out of debt. We should be thinking more about having money come in rather than going out. Besides, we don't have any furniture. When the trailer goes, all of our furniture will go with it. Do you really think you need to take money away from the business to put into a house at this time?"

"It'll be nice to have a basement."

Evidently I had taught him well when he bought the commercial equipment. He didn't need my help making the deal.

Ever since the day he'd beaten Dean so horribly, he started the abuse with me again, slowly but surely. I didn't think about it then, but I came to realize that he was eager to move out of our community because he had confessed to Preacher Trotter that he had beat Dean.

Almost every day I had to make a trip to a wholesale house, I took Bev with me. It was such a joy to be with my little girl. Together we scavenged discount furniture stores. I was pushing my body beyond any reasonable boundaries, and work was getting backlogged. Carpenters in those days left their trash behind when they finished what they were doing. In order to keep our machines going as much as possible, and in order to meet deadlines, trash had to be removed. I was the only one available. While I wasn't physically strong enough to handle the workload, I was stubborn enough to give it a try. It wasn't that it was heavy that presented a problem, it was the constant stooping and lifting.

Old habits die hard. No matter how rushed or bone-tired I was, Larry still expected supper on the table when he got home. One time when I was running a little late, he said, "You know it just ain't fitting for a man to work hard all day like I do, then come home and have to wait for supper to be cooked." He never took into consideration that I was putting in as many hours on the job as him, maybe more. I knew that if I kept pushing myself, I would eventually destroy my health. I didn't have a choice other than to hire someone to help me with Deb. Aunt Mag was the first to enter my mind, but I knew she had gotten too old, and Ella Mae had married a man who kept her pregnant. During her last miscarriage, she hemorrhaged to death. Aunt Mag's other daughter, Elvina, had finished college, gone to New York City, and became a model. Any thought I may have had of hiring any one of those three was out of the question. I ended up with a wonderful woman named Liz.

I had to buy material each day for whatever job we were on. Then we'd get the work finished, collect the money, and take it to the bank. That would give us the cash needed to buy what we needed for the next job down the line. We were living day-to-day, financially. The stress was enormous. Even though Liz, the eldest of sixteen children, had another job and couldn't help me mornings, just having her there in the afternoons was a tremendous load off my shoulders. All we needed now was assistance on the job sites.

A young man about Harvey's age applied. His name was Steve. As usual, Larry was being stubborn and not wanting to do anything anyone else suggested.

"Larry, will you listen to me?" I asked in a calm, reasonable voice. "We're six weeks behind in our work. There isn't any way I can do any more than I'm doing. You know I've been pushing myself as it is. I'm lucky that my back's held up like it has."

He made a gesture of dismissal. "Then you just go on, do what you want to do, 'cause that's what you're going do anyway."

I didn't argue any further, but went ahead and hired Steve. Luckily, they hit it off pretty good. Like Red, Steve had a great sense of humor.

We were showing up on the jobs earlier and staying later, trying to catch up. Liz was a wonderful cook as well as a fine housekeeper. She took care of our laundry and the ironing, which took a huge load off of me.

Larry bought Bev a pony. He kept telling me how much he wanted to get post holes dug for a corral. I took it upon myself to ask our neighbor Bertha if one of her sixteen children could give us a hand with the fencing. I knew her older boys all worked at the cotton mill, but I thought maybe they'd like some extra money and might be able to help on their day off. When I got to her place, I found only one child at home, and he was just twelve years old.

"He works sometimes for neighbors," Bertha said when I told her the reason for my visit.

"Well," I said, "I doubt, just being twelve years– "

Her black face split into an easy grin. "Oh, no, Evelyn. He ain't a regular twelve-year-old. Donnie's strong. He could dig fence holes just like you want 'em."

Donnie had come into the room and had heard our conversation. He was watching me with big, pleading eyes, but I couldn't get past his size. He was a slender thing without much evidence of muscles.

I said, "You look real small for such a big job, Donnie."

"Yes, Ma'am," he replied earnestly, "but I'm strong. I'll do you a good job."

Those pleading eyes did it.

"In that case, if you're sure, let's go. I don't have any time to waste."

When we arrived back at the house, Larry's truck was parked in the driveway. Curiosity had gotten the best of him.

"You were gone so long I thought something must have happened to you," he said.

There wasn't any need to carry this conversation any further. I understood without him saying another word. I saw him check his watch before I left, his usual way of timing me. It was the same old story; he had to know where I was at all times. It dawned on me why he was so contented to work the whole time I was confined to that hospital bed; he knew where I was every minute of the day.

I could see that he was agitated more than usual. I wondered how I was going to break the news to him that I'd brought a young black boy to dig fence post holes. My timing didn't seem to be so good. I knew how he felt about Negroes and I knew I'd have to present Donnie in such a way that Larry would accept him. It turned out that he wasn't upset only because of the boy's color, but also because of his size.

"You know damn well he's too little! He can't dig them post holes. Have you lost your mind?" he raged at me.

"Larry, how many people told you that you couldn't do this or that because you have an artificial arm? How did you feel when they said that? Well, that's exactly what Donnie must be feeling now. His mother told me that he's dug post holes for other farmers. Is it so hard for you to give this boy the chance to see if he can do it?"

Larry stared at the ground, but he seemed to be taking in every word I was saying. Finally, he turned and walked to the house, then he came back out in the yard where Donnie was standing. Larry scratched his head, looked around, then he motioned to the boy. I heard him say, "It hasn't rained for a while. The ground's awfully hard and dry. Do you think you're strong enough to dig these post holes for me?"

"Yes sir, Mister Larry. I dug some for one of our neighbors before." Donnie had a real deep voice for someone so young. "All you need to do is show me where you want them dug."

Larry went about showing him where, and how deep, he wanted them. Indeed, the ground was very dry and hard. It wasn't going to be an easy job. As soon as Larry finished with his instructions, we left to go to work, Larry in his old, green, panel truck, me following behind in the Plymouth Station Wagon. When we got home that afternoon, the first thing Larry took notice of was Donnie sitting down under the oak tree in the front yard.

Immediately, we got out of our vehicles with Larry grumbling, "See there! See what I told you? Dammit, Evelyn, I told you he wasn't going to be able to dig them holes."

My heart was in my throat. I didn't know what to expect next. I didn't want him to hurt that young boy's feelings.

Larry went to his truck and got out his measuring tape. We could see there were some neat little fresh piles of dirt scattered around. It looked as if Donnie had just given up.

Larry looked down at the boy. "What's the matter?" he said. "I thought you said you could dig them post holes."

Donnie was braced for a burst of temper, I could tell. "Yes, sir, I did...dig 'em...Mr. Larry." He pointed to where he had been digging the holes.

Larry proceeded to measure every hole Donnie had dug. Surprise! They were exactly the depths he told Donnie to dig them! Every single hole was exactly where Larry had said he wanted it, and at exactly the right depth. Larry went into the house without an apology to the child, so I made it a point to apologize for my husband's bad manners when I took Donnie home.

25

It didn't seem to affect the child. Almost every night after that when I drove Liz home, Donnie would come running up to me, wanting to know when he could come do some more work for us. The only help we needed at that time was an experienced sander. Donnie wasn't old enough, or big enough, to handle a commercial size sanding machine. Nothing that I could say or do, however, could deter him. Donnie had a burning desire to work and he refused to give up on me. I kept telling him to be patient until he was a bit older.

"Miss Evelyn, won't you please ask Mister Larry for me anyway?" he'd say.

I knew there wasn't any need in asking Larry, but I liked Donnie's attitude. He was going to turn into a fine young man. I decided to go ahead and give the boy a chance at real work; I'd take the risk with Larry. I'd make Donnie my responsibility, so if things didn't work out, it would be my fault and no one else's.

Larry ordered another eight-inch commercial sander so that one of them could rough sand while the other did a finer cut. It amounted to getting twice as much work done in the same amount of time.

Donnie was even stronger than I believed him to be. We were really beginning to accomplish something. Customers were pleased. Despite Larry's dark side, he was still able to charm people with his charismatic personality. He gained the respect of everyone who hired him. Receiving all of those compliments and high praise was a real ego booster for him. Here was a man who, as a child, was told repeatedly by his abusive father that he'd never amount to anything, and Larry had finally proven him wrong. I truly believed that he had mellowed out. It had taken a long time and a world of patience, but he had finally become a good and decent man. God was blessing us both and letting us prosper. I didn't even question the fact that Larry was presenting me with more and more payment books. When it hit me that we were seriously in debt, I began to look at the number of payments we faced each month and I asked him about it. He told me that my job was to pay the bills, not to question them. He'd improved, granted, but he was still no saint. I never expected to be married to a saint, though, so I wasn't worried.

One day, before I left to go to the wholesale house to pick up supplies, I told him, "I'll probably be at least a half hour longer getting to the job this morning." We were working on a customer's house and it was a bigger job than either of us had anticipated.

"Why? What are you up to now?"

"I'm going to swing by Bertha's to pick up Donnie to help me."

"What for?"

"I need him to move lumber out of the house so you won't have to wait to get started sanding the floors. He can keep cables out of your way while you're working the machines."

Suddenly his temper flared. Through clinched teeth, he hissed, "Damn it, you aren't asking me, you're telling me what you're going to do. Don't come bothering me any more with your decisions when we both know damn good and well you're going to do what you want to do anyway. I want you to help, not somebody else. I haven't taught you a damn thing over the years, have I?"

"Just because I'm able to walk again doesn't mean I can get out there and do the work of a healthy man."

His attitude seemed crazy. Donnie had been working for us and doing an excellent job, yet today Larry was upset about him coming to help me out. That night he was still furious with me, so I brought up the subject again, deciding to get it over with once and for all.

"How many times have you told me to just go ahead and do what I thought best? I don't hire people to help you for the fun of it. I hire them to help get these jobs done so you can move on to the next one.

Your time is much more valuable running those sanding machines."

He sat staring at the television for about thirty minutes. I knew he was thinking over what I'd said. He'd grown accustomed to me working beside him and he wanted just the two of us to get everything done. I had to constantly remind him that I was limited in how much I could do.

"Evelyn," he said at last, "I been thinking it over. I guess you're right. You can go ahead and pick Donnie up again in the morning." He hung his head, then added, "You know I've never been around black folks until you brought Aunt Mag to watch the boys. Now, every time I turn around, you're bringing another one home with you."

"Wasn't Aunt Mag the best thing that ever happened to us?" I reminded him. "Let me ask you this; if you were in a wreck and hurt real bad, and the only person to come along was a colored person, would you rather they went on their way and leave you laying there to suffer, or would you be grateful for their help?"

"What the hell kind of question is that?"

"Well?" I persisted.

He was sullen, but he acknowledged that he'd be grateful for their help.

One day, Bertha, remarked, "Mrs. Evelyn I've never seen two people as much alike as Donnie and Mr. Larry. If I didn't know better, I would have to believe that Mr. Larry is Donnie's father."

We both laughed at that!

Not long afterward, Donnie came to me to ask if I thought Mr. B would let him run one of the big sanders. Steve had given Larry that nickname, and Donnie had picked up on it. Now Larry was Mr. B and I was Mrs. B, at least to Steve. Donnie always called me Mrs. Evelyn.

Steve was near enough that he heard Donnie ask about using the big sander, so he took it upon himself to give the child an answer.

"Donnie, you know Mr. B ain't going to let you mess with that big machine. Why, before you'd have time to spit, that sander would chew all the way through the floor. You'd have Mr. B buying his customer a new floor. Those machines are mighty powerful."

Donnie looked away, thinking deeply. The boy never said anything without thinking it over first. Finally, he looked straight into my eyes. "Mrs. Evelyn, I can do it. I know I can do it. I can run that sanding machine."

I shook my head and took a step back. "You're not getting me in the middle of this one. You're going to have to work it out with Mr. B yourself. Those machines are Mr. B's They're off-limits to me."

Donnie begged Larry for days on end to let him work the commercial sander, but the answer was always a flat no, so it was quite a surprise when Larry said to Donnie one day out of the blue, "Come here, Donnie. I wanna see if you're the man you think you are. Since you don't intend to let me alone about this, let me fasten this safety belt around you. I don't want this machine to run away with you." He turned on the power. "There you go. Take it away. Let's see if you can back up all that talk you been doing."

From that day on, Donnie did the job that a lot of grown men couldn't do, or didn't have the nerve to try. It didn't take Larry long to appreciate, and even come to love, Donnie. He, Steve and Donnie made a dynamic trio. They got a huge amount of work done. Quality work. I thought, with some satisfaction, "Now my husband's on track, operating his business the way it should be run."

One Sunday, we were having our dinner when the phone rang. The voice on the other end of the line sounded a little like Donnie's.

"Is this Donnie?" I asked.

"No, ma'am. This is Henry. I'm Donnie's older brother. Miss Evelyn, can you come and get me?"

I could tell there was something very wrong. "Where are you?"

"I'm at the country store where you turn to go to my house."

"Tell me what's wrong."

"Yes, ma'am. Well, we came home from church today and Daddy was drinking. He beat me and told me to go and never come back."

That's all I needed to hear. "Stay where you're at," I told him. "I'll be there in a few minutes."

Larry asked me who called and I told him it was Donnie's brother and that his daddy had beat him and thrown him out of the house. All the time I was talking, I was hurrying to get myself together to go get Henry. I'd learned a long time ago that when things of that substance come up, not to give Larry time to think about the situation. I couldn't turn Henry down.

It was as if history were repeating itself. What's wrong, I was thinking, with this picture of these fathers beating their sons? The beating that Dean once took came to mind. I felt like a knife had pierced my heart.

When I got to the little store, Henry was standing out near the road. I saw him before I got to him. He had a small bag of clothes in one hand. His Sunday best suit, was on a clothes hanger, along with a white shirt and necktie. He had them thrown across his shoulder.

As I drove up alongside him, he hurried to get in the car.

"I sure am glad to see you, Miss Evelyn."

"Does your mother know I'm picking you up?"

"I told her I was going to call you. Momma knew you'd come get me."

"What about your father? He's a big man. I don't mind helping you, but I don't want any trouble from him."

"He's the one what told me to get out of the house and don't never come back."

When we got home, I showed him the basement where he could stay. It had a bed in it and a bathroom, too. He grinned real big and I could see how much he appreciated everything.

"We don't have a bathroom in our house," he said. "We just have the outside toilet. You have a real nice basement."

"Well then," I said, "I guess it's settled. Looks like you have yourself a new home."

The following Saturday, while getting some shopping done, I ran into Bertha on the street. She couldn't thank me enough and I was quick to praise her for raising such fine boys. They were polite, smart, and hard working. What more could any mother ask?

Henry was sixteen years-old and ready to go to work. We didn't have enough to keep him on full time, but I found things for him to do to help out around the house when Larry couldn't use him on a job. Now that Donnie, Steve, and Harvey were working full time, Henry and I only had to work part-time to help them, so Henry and

I decided to plant vegetables. What started as a garden, however, soon turned into a small-sized field. Like Donnie, Henry was a hard worker with a green thumb. Everything he planted seemed to flourish. Donnie had found his niche with the sanding machine. Henry was much more comfortable helping me outdoors. That first summer we put out over two hundred tomato plants.

I had put a wood-burning cook stove in the basement that served two purposes: it came in handy when I canned fruits and vegetables, and it helped out with the heating expense during winter months. But, of course, a wood stove has to have wood cut in order to be used. Henry would fill a huge box with cut wood and he'd also lay out kindling for me.

"Now, Miss Evelyn," he said, "if I happen not to be here sometime when you need wood, it's right here, ready for you to start a fire."

One day after we got the tomato plants set out, we had to carry water from a nearby spring to irrigate them. My plants were all standing up straight, looking good. The ones that Henry had set out were every which-a-way.

I called Henry. "Henry, come here and look! How come your plants aren't standing up?"

He flashed his shiny, white teeth. "Don't you worry about that Miss Evelyn. They'll live, you'll see."

Henry and I kidded each other a lot. I missed my boys so much. Now that Henry and Donnie were around, they helped fill that void. Henry was the playful one of the two. Donnie was more serious, like Larry. Henry got a kick out of just having childish fun, especially when he realized there was still a lot of tomboy in me.

One day we were walking to the garden when I said, "Your tomato plants had best be standing up today."

"They'll be fine," he laughed. "You gonna see."

I figured that he didn't know much about planting tomatoes, but that I could show him. Once he realized that his plants were near dead, he'd turn to me for advice. I hadn't planted that many tomatoes, but I was good at everything else, so it only stood to reason to expect my tomatoes to be plump and red.

When we got to the plants that I had set out, a fourth of them were lying down. Every one that Henry had set out was standing up. Henry took one look and threw his hand over his mouth to choke back laughter.

"Why don't you go ahead and laugh, Henry?" I said. "It's all right if you laugh. Go ahead and enjoy yourself at my expense. You earned the right."

He practically fell to the ground, he laughed so hard.

I studied his plants and then I studied mine. Finally, I just had to ask. "What did you do different when you set yours out than what I did?"

He managed to stop giggling long enough to answer me. "You got to pack dirt real tight around them roots. If you don't, they'll go to sleep on you and die every time."

Of course he didn't share that tidbit of knowledge with me the day we planted all of those tomatoes. I couldn't resist picking up a clod of dirt and chasing him across the field. When I playfully threw it at him, he knew he'd gotten the best of me in fun. Henry never let me live that one down.

There was an old building on the property that had an ancient piano in it. The chickens had used it for their nest. It was covered in chicken poop from top to bottom.

"Henry, how about we check out that old piano? I want to see if you think it's worth cleaning up."

"Awww, Miss Evelyn, it sure is a mess, ain't it? Do you really think you want to do that?"

"I know it's a mess, but a little bit of chicken poop isn't going to hurt you."

I couldn't see but one broken string on it. The wood was good. All it needed was the poop off it and sanded down. A new coat of finish would do wonders.

Henry was standing there, scratching his head. He had a frown on his face. "Well, if you're sure, Miss Evelyn. If you really want to clean it up, I'll help."

"You don't look real enthused about our new job here," I said, but we cleaned it up. We'd gotten as far as stripping off the old paint when Harvey, Donnie, Henry, and Steve decided they'd make me happy, or at least shut me up. They slid that old piano onto a sled through the basement door. And there it sat for a good six months before we got around to doing more work on it. One Sunday, Larry was telling the brothers at church about my ordeal with my piano. He told them, "Why she's so determined to get it fixed, I'll never understand."

One of the men said, "If there's only one broken string, I know a man who can fix and tune it. He'll come to your house to take a look at it, and he's reasonable. He tunes most all of the pianos for the churches around here."

The man came out, and for thirty dollars, I had what amounted to a brand new piano. But it didn't set so well with my husband.

Larry was still on a spending spree. One day he brought in drywall finishers to refinish all the walls in our house. Once that was done, he brought in painters. I commented that we didn't have enough money to completely remodel the house, which is where it looked like we were headed. That's all it took. Larry was determined to make me eat my words even if it meant putting us in bankruptcy. He had a hard time waiting for the painters to finish so he could go shopping for carpet.

It wasn't too long after that he bought himself a boat. Granted, all of us loved to go boating, water skiing, the whole nine yards, but I worried about the bills.

"Don't you think you need to wait until we can get some of these other obligations paid off before you go buying a boat?" I said.

"Dammit, Evelyn, there you go again. All you ever think about is work." Gee, where had I heard that before? "I got credit now. I'm going to buy what the hell I want, so you may as well shut your damn mouth."

That made me mad. It was like we were going back to how it was years and years ago. I was older now. I was wiser now. I wasn't mousey and I wasn't afraid to speak my mind. So I said, "You know, when you go out and spend, spend, spend, there has to be lots of work, work, work if you're going to be able to meet the bills every month. You're making all these debts, then you bring me the payment books. You think just because I have the checkbook, all there is to it is to write checks. In case I haven't gotten around to telling you, there has to be enough money in the bank to cover those checks before they're written."

Nothing I said seemed to have any affect on his decision. Late spring of 1964, he came home pulling a boat behind his new work van. It wasn't anything extravagant, a fourteen-foot boat with a forty-horsepower motor. With the debt overload, I often thought God forbid if something unforeseen should come up, such as rainy weather or a slowdown in contracts. It seemed like the more he bought, the more he wanted. For the first time in his life, he was beginning to realize what it meant to have something. People in high places were showing him respect. His ego was inflated. He had become the last of the big spenders. The way I saw it, the hatchet was bound to fall.

Now that he had the boat, he was ready to go to the lake to try it out. That was the beginning of us going camping every weekend, which put a halt to Saturday work and Sunday morning church services. I have seen this so many times over the years, the way people turn to God when they're in trouble. He answers their prayers and blesses them and then His people forget Him. Larry had everything he needed and wanted, so he figured he didn't need God anymore. He was on an ego trip with only room enough for one aboard.

Albert and his second wife, Leona, had two boys and they all loved to water ski. We hadn't seen much of them in recent years and the children had grown like weeds. We made up for lost time with our weekend excursions.

One weekend a neighbor who lived about a half mile down the road from us, pulled into the campground with his boat. We were members of the same church and I was happy to see him–except for the guilt I was feeling. God had healed me. He had let me walk again. I'd promised Him that if He would heal me, I would spend the rest of my life serving Him, but here I was, at the lake. The only thing I served was potato salad and cold drinks to my friends and family.

Money truly is the root of all evil, just like the Good Word tells us; with money comes pride and with pride comes the fall. I couldn't help but feel that we were once again on a downhill spiral with the brakes no longer in service. I knew in my heart, and common sense confirmed it, that it would be much easier and faster to lose a business than it had been to build it.

When everyone else went out in their boats, I made an excuse to stay behind. I hadn't been in a boat since we left Newport News in 1956. On this day I needed time to think things out; I rarely managed to get a few minutes to myself any more. Lord only knows that, from the day the business got started, there had been very little rest. Besides running around to buy materials, then delivering them to the job site, it was also my responsibility to meet the contractors, measure the floors, and submit a cost estimate. I was aware that doing too much could destroy all the healing that had been accomplished. I momentarily forgot that, when God is in charge, He fixes things and I needn't have worried about it staying fixed. I was dealing with the human side of my nature, however, and that side is receptive to the devil who never sleeps. When I was younger, I often told God that I didn't want to bother Him, I felt there were so many others who needed Him more than I needed Him. Then I heard a preacher read from scripture: "You have not, because you ask not." I was sitting in front of my television, watching the evangelist, and my mouth just fell open. That quote was such an eye opener. I had heard the scripture before, but it had new meaning in my life at that instant and it just hit me like a ton of bricks.

Recent times had brought me no peace of mind. Things were deteriorating in what little relationship Larry and I had developed during the good times. Actually, ever since the Sunday when Larry beat Dean, nothing had been the same between us. Up until then I had my hopes up so high. My husband had accepted the Lord into his heart, surely he would become a better husband and father from that day forward. It seemed that we were financially secure–but were we? We were head over heels in debt. My father had often commented that some people just can't handle prosperity. Truer words were never spoken.

As I lay on my camp cot, I began to pray. I cried to God, pouring out all of my worries, and I began to feel the tension slip away. I knew that God would never turn away from me. It was the feeling you get when you know that God has heard your prayers. I reminded myself that God promised that He would supply our needs, not our wants.

Crying is a wonderful way to release stress. I've always felt better after a good cry. I hadn't made the effort to be alone and pray for a long time. I needed God's guidance then, I still need it now. I'll never forget the day I boarded that train to go to work in Charleston. I was on my own, just as if I had been twenty-one instead of thirteen. I had to make my every decision, pay my room rent, handle everything completely alone. I had no one near me to confide in. Thank God my parents had taught me well because, to my knowledge, I didn't make a bad decision–until I let Larry into my life.

I thank my parents to this day for teaching me about God's love. If only they had taught me there were people who would use me and abuse me to pleasure themselves, maybe things would have been different. In defense of Momma and Daddy, I'm sure they didn't have a clue there were people in the world like my father-in-law. I still shiver to think what could have happened to me, walking those Charleston streets at two in the morning. I know now that it was my prayers, and those of my parents, that kept me safe. We are God's children, God is our Father. So many times we walk away from God, but God never walks away from us.

I was thinking all of these things, praying all these things, when I heard our boat pull onto the bank. All of the campers had returned, most likely hungry. It had been like that since the last week in April. At first we camped weekends, then it turned into an entire week. From there it became two and then three weeks without leaving the lake. Larry left all of the work for Donnie to oversee, and Donnie never once let him down.

The Fourth of July was always our busiest week of the year. That was when our customers took their vacations. Somehow, I got Larry to work that Fourth of July week, mainly because it was next to impossible to find a place to camp anywhere near the water. Fall was right around the corner. Nights were getting cooler. I was glad because I felt it was bound to slow down the camping trips.

On one Saturday in particular, Albert was at home with his wife. He was as hard on his boys in a lot of ways, as Larry was on ours, but on this Saturday afternoon his children managed to talk him into letting them go to a movie. Leona had gone into the bathroom to take a bath and get dressed before time to pick them up at the theater.

Leona told me, "I had run my bath water and just as I sat down in the tub, I heard what sounded like a pistol shot. I called out to Albert to investigate, but he didn't answer me. I jumped from the tub, grabbed my robe, and threw it around me before opening the door. Albert had sat down on the side of the bed and placed the barrel of the pistol in his mouth. The bullet went through his brain."

◘

During the time we were in Virginia, Larry's favorite sister, Laura Mae, had died, too, though we didn't know it until months later. I never knew what caused her death. Now there was only Larry and his brother George left in their immediate family. George was living in Augusta, Georgia. We rarely saw him after Mrs. Barkley died. Larry had been so jealous of his brother and me in the early years that he preferred George not be around me.

One rainy Sunday after church, the choir director asked me to join the choir. I accepted without asking my husband's permission. Bad mistake. When we got home, I went in the bedroom to change clothes before setting out our dinner. Suddenly Larry came up behind me and swung me against the wall to face him.

"Now you explain to me how you think you're going to sit up there in that choir in front of all them men?" he said.

Before I had a chance to reply, he punched me in the stomach. I couldn't breathe for at least a minute. Finally, I was able to ask what in the world happened to him.

"I saw it on television, if you beat a woman in the stomach, the marks don't show."

I was too stunned to make sense of it. "What'd I do?"

"You didn't do nothin' in particular 'cept want to show yourself in front of a bunch of men. I just wanted to smack you. What more reason do I need?"

That ended my singing career.

My husband had been happy in the Lord for the greater part of seven years. Had he forgotten Colossians 3:19: " Husbands love your wives and be not bitter against them"? Maybe the only one he ever read was Ephesians 5:22: "Wives summit yourselves unto your husbands, as unto the Lord." I'm not finding fault with the scripture, I'm just saying to pay attention to both scriptures, not to just the one that suits you.

I didn't have any idea I was pregnant again on that Sunday afternoon when he punched me in the stomach. Three days later, I went to the bathroom with terrible cramps. Blood poured from me. I was hemorrhaging. I drove myself to the doctor who confirmed that I'd had a miscarriage. It was my second one since Bev was born. The other also came after a punch in the stomach delivered by my husband.

Once again, he started kicking me out of bed, just as he did when I was pregnant with Harvey. Most people kick a wall when things don't go to suit them. My husband liked the feel of flesh under his fists or his feet. I had definitely become his punching bag again. We were back camping on the lake, surrounded by so many people I couldn't even imagine how he managed to ask them along without my knowledge. It was like a big family reunion, with me doing all the work. When anyone offered to help, which was rare, my husband would tell them not to worry about it, that Evelyn would take care of everything. I understood they were there for some rest and relaxation. I had learned patience very early in life. I'd always been slow to anger, but the time comes when enough is enough. And I had flat out had it.

26

I was standing out in the water when my neighbor asked me if I'd like to water ski. He offered to pull me with his boat. I was the only one of our group still at the campsite. All of the others had gone to rest after a big meal. Everything in me shouted a warning. I almost knew what to expect if I tried to get up on those water skis, but I threw my worries to the wind and accepted the invitation.

I was still a bit hesitant, but I wanted to get back on those skis. It was the one sport I thoroughly loved.

The soreness in my stomach was gone, but I couldn't be sure that something I did wouldn't set Larry off again. My life had returned to that place where I was damned if I did and damned if I didn't.

I put on my skis. My neighbor, Mr. Duncan, threw me the rope. I told him to "hit it", and the boat took off across the lake. I was up immediately. Mr. Duncan looked back and gave me a big A-OK sign. He pulled me along in one long, wide circle, then brought me back to where we started. I let my rope drop. What a great feeling that was! I can't say who among us was the happier, him, his wife watching from the shore, or me. Best of all, there were no repercussions from Larry about my little escapade.

He was taking less and less interest in work. If a customer came to him on the job, and it happened to be a customer he liked, he would negotiate with them. If they asked to negotiate with him over the phone, sometimes he would talk to them, but most times he would tell me to take it. I was getting calls from customers, telling me that

Larry had been overcharging them and they no longer wanted to deal with him. That was fine with Larry. He didn't want any part of making decisions any more. The smoking was getting to his lungs and breathing had become a problem. He loved staying at home, watching television. He just plain didn't want to be bothered with work. Donnie and Harvey were left to run things. Larry worked against them, though, by blowing off contractors or jacking up prices to the point they walked away from him. Business was beginning to suffer.

Early spring of 1965, Larry decided we should pay my parents a visit. It had been more than six months since I'd seen them. Even though my mother had read him the riot act all those years ago, he still loved her. In fact, he showed her more respect than he did me or the children.

The morning after we arrived, two boatloads of men, including Larry, went fishing. Daddy wanted to stay home with Momma and me. He was sitting on the porch in one of the old rocking chairs when he called to Momma in the kitchen.

"What in the world are you doing in there that's taking so long? Come on out here and sit down so we can talk. We don't get to see Evelyn very often."

It was amazing to sit there and see how much he still loved my mother. My mind went back to the time when I thought all marriages would be like theirs.

While I was reminiscing, Mother came out and joined us. After she got settled in her rocker, we talked about old times and old stories and relatives, living and dead. It was good to be home again. It was good to hear their porch talk again. I was once more a child and they were my beloved Momma and Daddy.

It wasn't too long before the men returned from fishing. Larry confessed to me how much better he was breathing since we'd gotten there. He attributed it to the salt air. I figured it was because he was away from laquer sealers and other finishes he'd been breathing for so long. I had lived with him long enough to know that when he started talking like that, it was time to beware. He was looking for an excuse to stop working. I hoped he wasn't going to suggest we stay longer since he was feeling so much better. If he would wear the mask I got him and stop inhaling varnish fumes, he'd find how much better he could feel even at home, but that wasn't about to happen.

I'd been enjoying this time with my parents. I would love to have been able to throw everything to the wind and stay on a few more days, but we had those payment books waiting for us at home. I knew the longer we were gone, the more business would suffer, yet the child in me wanted to stay. I yearned to sit on the porch and talk to Momma and Daddy. For some reason, I just didn't want to leave them. It turned out that I was having a premonition; it would be the last time I'd ever see my momma alive. She died just past her eighty-fourth birthday. Daddy lived seven more years. He died at ninety-four.

On the trip back home after Momma's funeral, Larry slipped into one of his quiet moods. I tried to draw him into conversation, thinking to lift his spirits, but nothing seemed to work. Miles clipped by. Finally, to break the silence, I said something about the well needing some attention. He wanted to know what kind of attention since we now had city water.

"The other day I was upstairs and I looked out the window. Bev and her little friend was using the slab of concrete that's laying over the well for a table. They had their tea set on it."

"So? What can that hurt?"

"Concrete against concrete. It only takes a little pressure against it for it to slide. If that happened, the children could fall in the well and drown. What if we were away, like now, or on one of our camping trips? What if someone else's child came on our property and fell in? I'm just saying that it's dangerous to be left like that."

"I told Bev to stay away from that damn well!"

"Don't you think it's better to be safe than sorry?"

"I'll look at it when I get home."

"It's going to take more than being looked at."

" If it'll make you happy then how about the next time you go to Greenville you pick up a bag of mortar mix and I'll seal it off. I swear, Evelyn, all you do is sit around and dream up stuff for me to do."

We got home that night about nine o'clock, tired and depressed. I'd forgotten all about the conversation concerning the well when I dropped into bed. I hadn't been asleep more than a couple of hours when I landed sideways into the dresser. I hardly knew what hit me, though common sense and experience told me it was Larry.

I managed to pull myself up and went into the bathroom, hoping to give him time enough to go back to sleep. I thought about sleeping in one of the other beds, but that would only get a door smashed in. I'd actually made that mistake once. He forbid me to ever be stupid enough to think I was going to sleep anywhere except next to him. I wasn't about to repeat history.

I sat on the side of the tub and waited. Finally, I could hear him snoring, so I knew I could go back to the bedroom. I crawled under the covers wondering what in the world had brought on such an outburst when he never let on that he was angry with me.

The next morning, I was pretty upset, but I didn't say anything. I must have looked sullen, though, because he glanced up from his breakfast to ask what was wrong with me. Since the children were at the table, I didn't answer and he didn't pursue it.

That night, Liz had our supper on the table when we walked through the door. Larry was still in a gloomy mood. He walked by her without speaking and went into the bathroom.

Liz asked, "What's Mr. Larry's problem?"

I shrugged. His mood swings were flip-flopping in ways I hadn't seen in a very long time. It was not a good omen. We had dinner, then I took Liz home. When I got back, he was sitting in a recliner, glaring at me, but he didn't say anything. I went on to bed and don't recall him coming in, so I must have dropped off to sleep right away. The next thing I knew, my body was once again landing against the dresser.

Two nights in a row. Not good. Plus it was making me mad as the devil.

After that, I was afraid to go to sleep. The only time he ever touched me in bed any more was with his feet. He'd get his back braced against the wall and kick like a mule, hurling me through space and into the dresser. I began to do what I'd heard other people talk about; I slept with one eye open.

Something seemed to be going on between him and Harvey on

the job. Harvey threatened to quit on a couple of occasions. Knowing Larry like I did, he'd have to be pushing our son to the breaking point for him to threaten to walk out. I would question Harvey, but he wouldn't give me an answer. When I tried to talk to Donnie about it, he'd just give me his don't-get-me-in-the-middle-of-this look. I knew Harvey wasn't happy. I wanted to help him, but I couldn't help if he wouldn't confide in me. Then again, how could I help him when I couldn't even help myself?

It was a constant battle to keep Bev away from Larry so there was no chance he'd hurt her. He wouldn't hesitate to jump on her any more than he did Harvey or Dean. She didn't have much of a life, though she loved her daddy. I kept making excuses for keeping them apart. I'd say he was sick and we had to be careful not be under his feet. If he snapped at her, I'd take the blame. I didn't want her to grow up hating him, after all, he was their father. The children shouldn't have had to suffer because I got involved with him in the first place. I blamed myself for everything. I was ready to go to any lengths, short of murder, to keep everyone as happy as possible. I never stopped to consider the children overheard much more than I ever dreamed.

By this time Larry had lost at least half of the business. I decided to have a telephone put in at my sister's alteration shop, so I could do alterations when I didn't have to go to the wholesale houses. One day I was sitting at my machine, working away on a woman's dress, when that angel on my shoulder whispered in my ear to go home. It came clear as anything: "Go home."

I put aside what I was doing and followed the angel's instructions. I had no idea why the notion was so strong, but I knew I had to do what I was being nudged to do. I pulled in the driveway and stopped. For some reason, I glanced to my right and was greeted with the sight of my husband embracing a young woman half his age.

It wasn't like it took me by complete surprise. I had known of his womanizing for a good many years. I think it was God's way of letting me see for myself. Before this happened, all I had to go on was hearsay and sometimes a smudge of lipstick on his white shirt. I took a good look and went back to work. He never ever mentioned the incident to me. I never mentioned it to him. That was the type of thing his mother told me that Mr. Barkley had done for years.

By 1966, Larry was refusing to work on any kind of regular basis. He started his day with vodka and, if he did happen to venture off to work, continued with it approximately every thirty minutes from the time he got home until he went to sleep. My day started with picking up materials first thing in the morning, then I'd go on to the alteration shop and work there the rest of the day. Steve had quit long ago, but Henry was available most times when we needed him even though he was now married and working third shift in the cotton mill. This left Larry at home all day by himself. When I left in the mornings, he would be sitting in his recliner in front of the television set. When I got home from work in the afternoon, he would be in the exact same spot, as if he had never moved the entire day. He stuck to his story that he was too sick to work any more.

One day when Bev and I returned from the grocery store, I parked behind Larry's Chevy pick-up. Bev gave me a long, hard look, then she glanced at the house. I could see that she had something she needed to get off her mind. I waited.

"Mom," she said finally, "I know Daddy thinks I'm asleep at night, but I hear what he's doing to you. I want you to know that he don't stay here all day like he wants us to think."

"Can you tell me how you know that?"

"Well, sometimes I put sticks in front of the truck tires. He tries to park it back the way it was, but I can tell when he runs over the sticks. Sometimes I even look at the gas gauge."

I knew she was telling the truth. I had figured it out myself. Larry was staying home pretending to be so sick he wouldn't have to go to work. I was pretending that he was sick, because I had learned the hard way that as long as he left me alone, I could play like it wasn't happening. Even at the lake, rather than go out in the boat anymore, he would find himself a spot near the young women who stayed behind.

Since Larry was claiming to be too ill to work, I thought it was only right I get him to a doctor and get him checked out.

"Why do you think I need to go to the doctor?" he asked, indignant when I suggested seeing Dr. Rogers. "All I need is some vodka. It helps more than any doctor."

This went on for a couple of weeks before he gave in. I don't know why I bothered. The doctor prescribed a bottle of something for him, but Larry refused to take it. It was a wasted trip, wasted money. I felt myself coming apart. He said he was too sick to work, but he wasn't too sick to leave after I got off to work and go who knows where, with who knows who. He wasn't too sick to lift that vodka bottle every few minutes or to kick me out of bed in the middle of the night. He was getting lazier by the day, and I was getting more and more fed up with the whole thing.

One day I left him watching his soap operas and took a walk into the woods. It was one of those days when I just didn't see how I could go on another minute. Larry had taken to pretending he was nuts, just like a woman on one of his favorite daytime shows. I knew him well enough to know when he was genuinely nuts and when he was acting. I had to ask myself why he would bother pretending to be cuckoo and determined that it was simply a ploy to worry me.

The woods were so beautiful that day. I went beyond the hill where Henry and I had planted our tomatoes and into a forest of pine trees, the ground was covered with their soft brown needles. I scooped them into a long mound and made myself a bed where I lay down and listened to birds twitter and whistle. Water trickled in a little stream nearby. The sky was an incredible blue. I could feel the Lord's presence all around me.

"God," I whispered, "give me the recipe I need to straighten out my life. You gave me the miracle of walking again and You've shown me how to provide for my family, tell me what I've done that I have to keep enduring Larry's punishment."

While I was talking to God, a mockingbird found its way to a tree limb and was looking down at me. It started to sing. The Book of Job came to mind as I listened to the bird's sweet song. Job went through so much, such torment, yet he never lost faith. I felt so close to God at that moment. I realized that my problems were small compared to Job's. I knew that Jesus would see me through these tough times. He promised on the cross and He'd never broken his word. He said He would never leave me, never forsake me. Matthew 11:29-30 came to mind: "Come under me, take my yoke upon you, learn of me for I am meek and lowly in heart. You shall find rest unto your souls, for my yoke is easy, my burden is light."

I thanked God and I thanked Jesus for always being there for me, and I felt somehow stronger.

Deb had been begging me to let her sleep over with her friend Jane. I didn't mind, but Larry didn't think a child should spend the night away from home. I let her go, anyway, but I wasn't blind to the possibility that I had just bought myself a barrel of trouble. As I expected he would do, he ranted and raved about my defying him. The more I heard, the more I just got sick to death of his curses, his vodka, his soap operas, his "illness" that kept him from doing a decent day's work anymore. Finally, I marched myself into the bedroom where I picked up my purse and car keys, and I left without a word. I drove straight to the liquor store where I'd never been in my entire life. I bought vodka since it was the only drink I knew anything about other than moonshine, and that was only hearsay.

With the bottle tucked beside me on the car seat, I drove to a secluded spot and I pretended that I liked the stuff. I had two big swallows of it, choked, sputtered, coughed and then felt an amazingly warm peacefulness spread throughout my entire body. I drove on for a few more miles and decided to repeat the process. Which I did. And the glow was even nicer that time around.

Once back home, I parked the car, got out and went into the house. I didn't see Larry anywhere. I figured he was in the basement. I carried my bottle into the bedroom and hid it in the closet. There wasn't any way I was going to take a chance on him drinking my vodka. It was mine, all mine. After that, I went to bed, well, actually what I did was fall across it.

I woke up some hours later feeling a wetness around me. I was horrified to find that I'd upchucked all over myself. Aside from being grossed out at the mess I was in, I felt physically wonderful. I was relaxed. I'd heard of hangovers, but this didn't match any description I'd been given. Did God have a sense of humor? I was expecting to feel His wrath at my brazenness, but instead, I felt great. Maybe He was showing me mercy, as He is said to show fools mercy.

I got up and changed the bed clothes, then I went into the den to face my husband. I was braced for warfare, but again, he surprised me. He thought the whole thing was hilarious.

Something else was happening that wasn't the least bit hilarious, was Larry's strange attitude toward our daughter. He had become almost obsessed with the idea of harming her. For weeks he'd been hinting that he was "going to get her". He said the same thing in a lot of different ways, but the message never varied.

I'd taken a second job as a waitress at Huddle Restaurant, to help us meet our obligations. One Saturday I got home after a nine-hour shift and felt surprisingly good. Maybe it was because I'd made a side trip after work to take Bev to catch a plane. She would be met by Dean at Sky Harbor Airport in Phoenix, safe from harm. Larry had been on particularly bad behavior for the past several months; I was never sure what he was up to.

It was four-twenty when I pulled the station wagon into the driveway. I parked and went inside. As I reached the den, Larry came down the hall dressed in casual clothes, which was unusual for him that time of day. At this point, he hadn't worked in over six years.

"Give me your car keys," he said, covering the space between us in two giant steps.

I didn't argue. He took them without a word and walked out to his truck. Since we both had a set of keys, I assumed he'd misplaced his and I gave it no more thought.

I was exhausted and plopped down in the recliner thinking I'd watch a movie on TV. It wasn't long before I heard his truck pull into the driveway. He came through the kitchen door carrying a brown paper bag filled with three pints of vodka and ten packs of cigarettes. He put one of the bottles in the refrigerator and threw away the bag. The other two bottles he took to the basement, which struck me as odd. To my recollection, it was the first time he'd done that.

When he came back upstairs, he settled into his recliner near mine, and lit a cigarette. He hadn't spoken a word and I wondered if he was upset about something. He watched the movie for a few minutes, then got up and went to the kitchen. I heard the refrigerator door open and close. Then he came back and sat down. I was drowsy and felt myself nodding off, though I happened to glance in his direction and saw that he was staring at me the way a fox stares at a rabbit before it pounces. I tried to ignore him, hoping that he'd turn back to the movie on the TV screen.

Suddenly, I came full awake. Larry was standing over me with a pair of eight-inch sewing scissors raised, ready to strike. In a knee-jerk reaction, I threw my hands up in self-defense. He quickly moved in front of me and shoved one leg between mine, forcing the recliner upright. I was aware of a glint of lamplight on the tip of the shears and, for some reason, it triggered a rush of adrenaline in me. I grabbed his steel hook and fought savagely, trying to grasp his wrist and pry the scissors away. I'd learned that if I could just hold onto his hook, he was virtually powerless, but it was almost impossible to do. I was using strength I didn't know I had.

I finally wrenched the scissors from him, but not before he managed to stab me over and over again, not deeply, but small, piercing jabs that broke the skin and brought blood. I knew I had to hold on to that hook until I could get to my feet; I had no desire to feel its cold steel penetrate my brain. I had seen him drive a nail with it; he could even use it to pick up a coin. Slowly he forced the hook toward my face. I pushed with all my might. His body fell against mine. Even though his left hand was free, I was still hanging tight to the steel hook. Somehow, in an instant, he fastened his left hand into my hair and jerked so hard it brought me to my feet. In the distance, I could hear a scream. Then everything went black.

27

The screams were so terrifying, they brought me to my senses. That's when I realized the sound was coming from me. Larry was standing in front of me with a maniacal expression on his face. He held out his hand where I could see a huge clot of my own hair, dripping blood. A portion of my scalp had been torn loose from my skull. Looking into his twisted face so filled with hate, I knew that if I wanted to live another day, I had to escape.

He had made so many trips to the kitchen, I was positive that he was drunk. I depended on the fact I was catching him off-guard to get away and I ran out of the front door. I raced, without looking back, for the station wagon. When I grabbed the car door and jerked it open, I left a bloody trail. My heart was beating fast as I jumped in the front seat and slid under the steering wheel. Even though I was in shock, I was aware of the incredible pain I felt all over my body, but particularly around my head.

I locked all the doors and reached for the ignition when I remembered that Larry had my set of keys. I glanced up and, to my horror, saw him stepping unsteadily off the front porch. With dogged deliberation, he ambled to the passenger side of the car. A vile grin spread across his face. In the hand that once held my bloody hair, still remained a few limp strands along with my keys. He stood dangling them in front of me, like the pendulum of a clock. He was teasing me, tantalizing me with them, then he slowly, very slowly, slid the key into the lock. With much exaggeration, he casually pulled the door open. Then he leaned to me with a half-smile on this lips, as if nothing had happened.

In a low monotone, he said, " What are you doing sittin' out here like this? You come on and let's go watch television."

I cowered, trembling, against the door.

"You come on," he said more sternly. "Let's go inside. Don't make me tell you again." He never raised his voice. If a neighbor happened to be watching, they would never have guessed the drama being played out in that station wagon.

My mind was filled with terror. It raced in every direction at once, seeking an answer as to how I could defend myself and stay alive. I prayed a silent, desperate prayer, asking what I should do. I knew better than to open the door and bolt; Larry would have started the car and run me down. Besides, I didn't have enough strength to run. My purse with identification and money was in my bedroom. I'd actually been slipping a little cash aside whenever I could, anticipating that this day was bound to arrive sooner or later. I had accumulated just over four thousand dollars. It was hidden in my billfold.

Larry dropped the car keys in his pants pocket.

I tried to get past my fear and use reason. If I went back inside with him, if I played his little game as if nothing was wrong, maybe I could get to my purse. The real trick would be to get my hands on my car keys, though. If he took his trousers off to go to bed, I figured I might be able to grab them, but there was always the possibility that he'd sleep in his clothes. He did that when he got too drunk to change.

Back in the den, we settled into our twin recliners. And there we sat, me with my body throbbing in pain, him drunk and staring at me, daring me with his eyes to make a move. Finally, I convinced him that I had to go to the bathroom. I wanted to look in the mirror and see how much damage he had inflicted on me. My head ached horribly. He let me go to the restroom knowing there was no escape from there. He stood guard outside the door.

As I stared in the mirror, I asked myself if the mangled mess I saw in the reflection could possibly be me? I had felt something warm and liquid run down my neck and forehead, and had assumed it was blood, but now I could see that I was wrong. It was a clear, white substance rather like white Karo syrup. I cried at the sight.

The scalp itself was still there, but a large portion of it was torn from my skull. The only hair I had left was around my ear. As I stood staring, I felt a scream building in my throat. I thought, *My God! What kind of man could do a thing like this?* I choked back any sound that I might make, knowing it would only cause me more harm.

How would I escape? I had to come up with a plan, and soon. Lost in my thoughts, I nearly jumped out of my skin when he banged on the door. Fear once again gripped me. I quickly wiped away my tears. He mustn't see me crying. The sight of tears made him go ballistic. No matter how much pain he inflicted on the children or on me, we knew not to cry. If we gave in, he would only hit harder.

I opened the bathroom door. He stepped aside so I could get by, then walked one step behind me until, once again, I was settled in the recliner. I stared at the television screen, but I didn't see what was there. My mind was spinning.

I was desperate for a pain killer, but all we had was aspirin. The bottle was in the kitchen. I glanced at Larry. He appeared to be asleep. As I began to ease out of the chair, his eyes flew open and he leaped to his feet. His expression said that if I wanted to remain alive, I had better sit back down.

I told myself to stay calm.

I knew it wasn't going to be easy, but if I were to survive the night I would have to continue to be obedient, at least for a while longer. His look told me that he wasn't through with me yet. Nothing I could do, short of murder, would stop him.

I waited until he once again appeared to be asleep before I eased my way down the hall and into the bathroom where I locked the door behind me. I didn't hear any noise coming from him. I turned the water on and let it run until it was warm, then I splashed my face. Soreness had set in with a vengeance. As I attempted to bathe away the mess on my face that had hardened to the consistency of a scab, Larry pounded on the door again.

"Dammit! You've been in there long enough! Come on out!"

I didn't want to antagonize him further. Once more he marched me back into the den. He stayed in front of me, forcing me to walk backwards. I fell into my chair, breathing a prayer for God to help me through this horrible ordeal.

"Look at me, dammit," he commanded. "By God, you'd better look at me!"

I did as I was told.

He chuckled softly. "I guess you want me to apologize." When I didn't respond, his voice got harder. "I ain't going to apologize. I'll never apologize to you. I don't have any reason to apologize. Everything I ever did to you, I meant to do, so don't think for a damn minute that I'll ever apologize to you. If that's why you're sitting there pouting, you can forget it. Any man that's a real man won't ever apologize to a damn woman."

Time went by. Slowly. Agonizingly slow. A couple of times he pretended to be asleep. I'd ease out of the chair only to have him spring to his feet and shove me back down. It was now somewhere between three and four in the morning. I'd been held hostage in my own house for nearly twelve hours. I wasn't lying when I once again told him I had to go to the bathroom. My nerves were causing my bladder to nearly explode. When he asked me where I thought I was going, and I replied that I was going to the bathroom, he responded with, "You're going to hell if you don't straighten up your act."

I had to walk backward down the hall, so that I remained facing him. When I came out, he was propped in the doorway. He had his back against the door frame with his knee bent to keep me from getting by.

"Now where the hell do you think you're going?"

"Larry, please. Back off. Let me go to the den for a cigarette."

"No, by God."

He grabbed me and swung me toward the kitchen. With the palm of his left hand, he shoved me backward. Before I knew it, he slapped me open handed on the right side of my face. Just as quickly, he slapped me on the left side. The pain was so intense from the soreness that had set in earlier, I buckled. It was then he kicked me in the pelvis. I lost count of the number of punches he delivered. The next thing I knew, I was flat on my back on the kitchen floor. Larry was standing over me, about to jump on top of me. I drew my knees up to my chin and kicked him with every ounce of strength I had left in me. He staggered back against the kitchen wall, but I hadn't stopped him.

He came after me again. The look on his face told me that he was determined to finish what he had started. I scrambled to my feet and kept backing up until I was jammed against the sink cabinet. He had backed me into a corner. To my left was the stove, to my right the table. He was between me and the back door. Incredibly, at that moment, I heard a voice, and I do believe to this day that it was the voice of God. I heard, "Don't stand there. He has every intention of killing you."

I glanced at the table. Within my reach was a two-liter glass Pepsi bottle. I grabbed it and, as he came at me again, swung with all my might, catching him between his left ear and the center of his forehead. It made a deep gash about three-fourths of an inch above his eye. I had hit him so hard that I lost my grip on the bottle. It literally bounced off his head and flew across the table. He stood, baffled, and frozen in his tracks. Blood poured from his wound as if a main artery had been ruptured. When he realized the extent of the injury, his countenance changed dramatically. He broke out in wild, crazy laughter, something straight out of a Steven King novel, and he screamed at the top of his lungs, "LOOK! Just you LOOK, what you've gone and done to me!"

I did look and what I saw gave me shivers. I saw the demented expression of sheer joy in his eyes! Never before had I seen him so enthralled. He began to catch every drop of his blood that he could and scrubbed his face and shirt vigorously with it as if he was trying to bathe himself with his very own blood. Once the bleeding stopped, he grabbed my arm and swung me around. Using his right leg, he kicked one of the chairs out from under the table and slammed me into it.

"By God, you better sit there," he said narrowly. "Don't you move until I find something to tie you up with. I'm going to beat you to death."

As he spoke, he was desperately looking around, trying to find something to use as a rope. He was insane with determination. My only advantage was in his slowness of thinking.

"Larry," I said as coolly and rationally as humanly possible, "let me call the deputies to come get me." I knew it would never do to let him think I was going to call the Sheriff to come get *him*.

"What in the hell for?" he screamed.

I haven't any explanation as to what went through his mind at that moment. The only thing I can think of is that God must have appeared on the scene, answering my plea for help. Larry stood still for maybe a full ten seconds, then he turned and went into the bedroom where he picked up the phone and dialed the Sheriff's office. It was the first time he had let me out of his reach.

Once I heard him making that call, I got up and eased myself to within three feet of him. Amazingly, he handed me the phone the moment the dispatcher answered. I took the receiver and heard a voice on the other end of the line say, ""Sheriff's office. How can I help you?"

"I...I'm Evelyn Barkley."

Larry was pacing back and forth behind me, muttering to himself, "By God, let 'em come on, let 'em come on, 'cause you're going to be dead when they get here."

The dispatcher obviously heard him because he said, "Try and stay calm, Mrs. Barkley. I'm going to get someone out there right away. You do live in the Enon Church community, don't you?"

"Yes, sir."

Less than two minutes went by before there was a loud banging at the door. "Open up! Now! It's the Pickens County deputies!"

Larry stood staring at the door, then he slowly turned the knob.

Two deputies rushed into the room.

"Just you look here at what she's gone and done to me!" Larry wailed. When neither officer responded, he went on. " Damn it, I told you to look here at all this blood on me! See what she's gone and done to me?"

There was blood and broken glass all over the floor. The deputy looked at me propped against the kitchen cabinet with not enough strength left to stand on my own.

"You there," Larry said to one of the deputies, "you come with me." To the other deputy he said, "You stay right here and watch her."

The officers did as they were asked to do. Larry led the way down to the basement. Although they were only there for thirty minutes or less, the pain I was experiencing made it seem much longer. My entire body was in a state of shock. I don't remember the deputy who had stayed behind with me speaking a word the entire time. Every now and then he'd sneak a peek at me, as if he couldn't believe his eyes, but then he'd quickly look away again. Most of the time it seemed to me that he stared at the floor. To this day I have no idea what Larry and the other fellow did in that basement, though I do know that when they came back upstairs, the man said, "Well, Mrs. Barkley, there's nothing more we can do here. We've got to get on back to Pickens. Without a warrant, our hands are tied."

I was stunned. I couldn't find my voice.

They went out the kitchen door, to the back porch. I followed them. Larry wasn't to be left behind, however. He managed to get between the deputies and me. He put his arm out to keep me from getting past him. I thought my knees were going to buckle. I sat down on a brick planter, too dizzy to stay upright. As I watched the men walk away, I thought I would surely hyperventilate. I couldn't seem to catch my breath. And in that instant my fear vanished. In its place came a surge of anger.

"Hey!" I called out. "Just you wait a minute."

The men turned to me.

"I want you to listen to me because tomorrow when you hear that I'm dead, I want both of you to remember what I looked like, and I want you to remember it every day of your life for as long as you live."

I went closer to them. "You stood there in my kitchen and told me there isn't anything you can do without a warrant. Now you tell me how can I get one of those things because he's holding me here hostage. He's had me hostage for fourteen hours, and he's clearly told me that he's going to tie me up and beat me to death."

No one tried to interrupt or stop me.

"I know there's the law. I also know there's a way around the law if you look for it. You leave me here with him and go back to Pickens, he's going to kill me. I hope you live every day haunted by the stupid mistake you're about to make if you leave me here with him."

My timing was perfect because, before I got the last syllable out of my mouth, Larry chimed in with, "You can't do a damn thing about it until after it's done."

The deputy who had stayed with me in the kitchen, said, "No, that's where you're wrong, Mr. Barkley. I'm taking Mrs. Barkley into protective custody." He nodded toward me. "Get your purse. You're going with me."

Larry was suddenly fit to be tied. "By God, you take her, I'm going too."

I didn't stay to hear what happened next. I went back inside, to the bedroom, as fast as my battered body would take me. But my purse wasn't where I religiously kept it. I started to panic. Larry moved it! That's when a small voice inside me said, " Look under the bed." I didn't argue. I'd never kept anything under the bed, but I had to believe I was being divinely directed. I hesitated only a second, during which time I heard the small voice again instruct me to "look under the bed." I got down on my knees and looked, and lo and behold, there was my purse, pushed all the way to the center of the space under the bed.

Once back on the porch, one of the deputies helped me get down the steps. Larry was allowed to go along, but he was in the back seat, beside an officer. When I made a move to get in front, he yelled out, "No, by God, no. If you're going to take her, then she's going to ride back here with me."

I suppose they felt that with both of them to protect me, it would save a lot of hassle to let him have his way. "Go ahead, Mrs. Barkley," one of the men said. "Sit back there with him." When I hesitated, he nudged me gently. "Go ahead, get in. It's going to be all right."

Before the squad car pulled out of the drive, the deputy who had gone downstairs with Larry said to him, "Mr. Barkley, listen to me very carefully. If you put your hand on this woman just once before we get to Pickens, I'm going to stop this car and drag you out of there and beat the hell out of you with my nightstick. Do you understand me?"

We got underway without another word between us. There was almost no traffic out on the highway at that hour of the morning. We'd gone a few miles when we got to a stop sign but, with no other cars in sight, the deputy went on through it.

"Stop this car this minute," Larry commanded. " I mean you stop this car. I'm putting you under Citizen's Arrest for running that stop sign."

Of course the deputies ignored him.

Once at the jail, Larry said, " "Are you going to lock her up?"

A deputy replied, "Yes," while continuing to fill out jail slips.

Larry looked at them, puzzled. "You've got two made out in the name Larry. What's that mean?"

"One of them says Mrs. Larry."

Larry repeated what he had already asked. "You're going to lock her up, though, aren't you?"

And once again the deputy said yes, he was going to lock me up.

"Well then," Larry said, satisfied, "do it. Lock her up."

"I'm going to lock her up, but I'm going to lock you up first."

Larry was thunderstruck. "Me? Lock me up? What for? I showed you what she done to me!"

"Like I said, I'm going to lock her up, but first I'm going to lock you up."

The deputy took him by the arm and escorted him away, but Larry began to resist. One look from the officer and my husband immediately backed down. He was taken into another room and placed in a cell.

I wanted to sob in relief. I finally felt truly safe.

When the deputy returned, he nodded toward a very small holding cell, maybe two feet square. There was a seat built into the wall but nothing else was in there. He unlocked the door and held out his hand for me to enter. I wasn't sure what was happening, but I had no qualms about walking inside that little steel box. The officer shut the door behind me and turned the key in the lock. Then he unlocked it and offered his hand. As I came out, he said, "I couldn't lie to the guy. I did lock you up."

If my face hadn't hurt so bad, I would have smiled.

"Come on," he said, leading the way. "Let's get you to the magistrate so we can issue a warrant on this man."

Later, after everything had been done to get a warrant in motion, the deputy drove me back to my house. It was quiet. It was peaceful. I reflected on what the magistrate told me back in his office: "Be sure you get to the probate judge's office first thing in the morning. Tell her I sent you. She'll understand. If you don't file the proper papers within twenty-four hours, your husband will be released. So, make sure you put forth every effort to get it done as quickly as possible. He'll be sent to the Columbia State Mental Hospital for evaluation. You, being his wife, are the only one who can do this. He'll have thirty days in there to think over what he did to you on this night."

28

My head felt like a buzz saw had ripped through it. When the officer drove away, I went inside and turned on the overhead kitchen light. Looking around, my stomach did a flip-flop. The stench of dried blood was sickening. I put my hand over my mouth and nose, and made it to the bathroom. I hovered over the toilet bowl, vomiting my insides out. I have no idea how long I stayed there. Eventually I turned on the water in the bathtub and let it fill. I wanted to wash away all the dirt that I was feeling. I prayed that a hot bath would ease the pain and soreness. My scalp was another matter. My head felt as if it was keeping time to drum beats. There was nothing I could do to stop the throbbing. I'd have to somehow bear it until I could get to Dr. Roger's office later in the morning, after I visited the probate judge.

It felt so good to soak in the tub knowing that no one would bang on the door, no one would yell at me. It was peaceful, so peaceful. When the water turned cold, I got up and reached for a towel only to find that none were anywhere to be seen. I didn't think too much of it. In all the confusion of the past few weeks, it wasn't surprising that I'd neglected to put clean towels in the bathroom.

I kept my bed and bathroom linens in the drawer of a large mahogany buffet in the dining room. I made my way to the door, turned on the dining room light–and stood transfixed, staring at the sight before me. Larry had taken all the linens and thrown them in a pile between the buffet and the dining room table. Beside them was a five-gallon can of highly flammable laquer sealer and a box of matches. I reeled back, horrified at the reality of what he had intended. He was going to kill me, just as he said, then set the house on fire.

The hot bath did wonders for me. Despite the physical injuries and pain, my heart was at peace and I had an amazingly good night's sleep. The next morning, I was able to give thanks that Larry never had the opportunity to set those linens on fire or to kill me. I still felt like I'd been beaten with an ugly stick, but I was moving about and I was ready to go to the judge's office. My throbbing head was numb, which was a good thing. I wasn't able to feel the pain. A better thing was the knowledge that in just one hour, I'd have all the right papers in my hands to put Larry in the State Hospital for at least one full month.

I felt pretty good about the fact I would be facing a lady judge that I knew personally. She wasn't a best friend or anything like that, but one of my sisters had done alternations on her clothes for years, and Larry had once worked on her floors. Normally, when we met on the street, she would speak to me. My optimistic outlook was soon smashed into a million pieces when she studied the papers I handed her, then stared at me with a look of disbelief on her face.

"Why, Mrs. Barkley," she said as if she was stunned beyond belief, "Mr. Barkley is one of the nicest men I've ever met." She extended the papers toward me. "You're going to have to bring me more proof than this. I can't send him to the State Hospital with just this warrant."

I wondered if she'd gone blind. Surely she could see my condition. What about my hair, or places where I should have had hair? What about the marks on my face? All I said though was, "What more do you need?"

"I've heard that Mr. Barkley hasn't been doing too well health-wise lately. I need the name of the doctor who's been treating him."

I told the judge the name of the specialist I had taken him to in recent times.

"Well," she said, "you'll have to bring me a statement from him."

My mind went sort of blank so I can't quote the rest of her

dialogue, but I can tell you that she spent the next few minutes telling me what a great man she thought Larry to be.

That was the straw that broke the camel's back. I'd lived with this man for thirty years. How in God's name did this judge think she knew more about him than I knew! I heard about all I could handle. I was filled with rage and disgust and indignation. She had the power to do something about the situation and this is how she was going to use it? She just wouldn't shut up planting orchids on his character.

I lost my temper and started to lunge at her across the desk, then caught myself. I looked her straight in the eye and pointed my finger in her face. "My dear lady, if you think this man is all that nice, I suggest you go stay with him for six months. You take the beatings that I've taken and I'll be happy to go back and take another turn just to please you."

She didn't budge. "Like I said, you're going to have to bring me a medical statement from his specialist."

Now I knew what my daddy meant when he said there was no use in trying to fight City Hall. I didn't have much strength to go on before she got my adrenaline pumping, but I vowed that I'd do whatever it took to get Larry to Columbia for an evaluation. I walked out the door determined that this judge wasn't going to outdo me. If it was papers she wanted, by heaven she'd get papers.

The doctor was in Greenville about twenty miles away. I had less than five hours from the time I left her office to get those papers and get them back to the probate judge. I headed the station wagon toward Easley. My next stop on my way out of town would be the Huddle Restaurant. I had to let my boss know that I wasn't going to be able to work the lunch or even the night shift. Right now I had a challenge that I couldn't figure how to overcome: What if I couldn't see the specialist without an appointment? What if they couldn't make an appointment for me for days or weeks? I only had hours! It would take magic to get the job done. My thoughts were running wild as I pulled into the Huddle parking lot.

I parked the station wagon and went inside, embarrassed about the way I looked. Eleanor, my boss, came through the kitchen door to the front counter. She took a long hard look at me and stopped in her tracks. Seeing her expression, I lost all control. I began crying hysterically. I let go for the first time in years. I cried for Larry's mother, and for Edith, I cried for the beating Dean took, and for the children who had to take their father's abuse. And I cried for me. I cried a barrel for me.

That must have lasted a full three or four minutes before I pulled myself together realizing I had no time for a pity party. I had to get those blasted papers back to the probate judge before five o'clock. I managed to get the whole story out. When I was through, Eleanor handed me a tissue. "Here," she said. "Try to calm yourself. You're not leaving this building in your condition."

"Oh, no! You don't understand. I have to go to Larry's specialist in Greenville. I've got to get a medical statement from him and have it back in Picken's at the probate judge's office before five. I've got to do this! I have to do this. There isn't any way around it."

"I'm going to drive you where you need to go myself."

"You can't do that. It's almost your lunch rush hour."

"Stop your worrying. This place will be here when I get back."

Fifteen minutes later, we walked into the doctor's office in Greenville.

The receptionist argued just as I'd predicted she would do. I needed an appointment, he couldn't see me without one. I argued that it is was critical that I talk to the physician for just a very few minutes. She argued that it couldn't happen without an appointment. The nurse joined in, assuring me that they were all trying to be patient with me, but that without an appointment his full schedule just didn't allow for spur-of-the-moment conversations. I must have wore them down because I was finally ushered into an examination room. There I sat for five minutes, cooling my heels and watching the minute hand on the big wall clock slide slowly toward the hour of five.

When Dr. Cleary arrived, I stuttered and bumbled, but managed to get the whole story out. I told him about the beating, the stabbings with my scissors, the intent to burn down the house, the tearing out of my hair, which the doctor could plainly see for himself. He listened intently then got up and found a folder in his files, which he read silently.

"I see here that I've diagnosed him as schizophrenic," he said at last. He stuck his head out the door and called down the hall for his secretary to join us in the examination room. Once she arrived, Cleary began dictating a letter for me to take back to the judge. In a matter of moments, I tucked the envelope that held the letter into my purse and jumped back in Eleanor's car. I was becoming more and more aware of how much I needed medical attention myself. If Eleanor tried to make conversation, I don't remember what she said. I was racing the clock, fighting nerves and pain, and I was terrified that something would go wrong even with the letter from Dr. Cleary.

Despite my misgivings on the trip to the judge's office, I handed her the letter she had requested with a feeling of accomplishment. She read it carefully, then shook her head and handed it back to me.

"This still isn't enough proof," she said flatly.

I held my temper. "Can you tell me what more you need?"

"I'll have to have another statement from his family doctor. This just isn't sufficient."

I was in total shock. I glanced up at the clock over the door. Time was passing so swiftly. I knew the judge was giving me the runaround because she didn't believe me, but I couldn't let her get away with it. The family doctor was Dr. Rogers. I had only forty-five minutes to get to him, obtain his written statement, and get it back here. It seemed impossible. I had passed Dr. Rogers' office on my way back from Greenville. If I'd have known he needed to give me something for this judge, I could have gotten it then. Well, I'd never been a quitter and I wasn't about to start quitting at this late date. I'd keep trying right up until the last nanosecond.

Eleanor was a good sport and drove me to Dr. Roger's office. On the way, she seemed uncomfortable, like she wanted to say something, but wasn't sure how to begin. Finally, she said, "Evelyn, I think I need to tell you this. Larry called me a couple of weeks back. He wanted me to tell him who you were running around with."

This was news to me. "What'd you say?"

"Well, I asked him, I said, Larry you tell me just when Evelyn has time to run around. What you're accusing her of takes time, much more time that Evelyn has, I promise you."

I asked myself why in heaven's name Larry would ask her a stupid question like that. He knew where I was twenty-four hours a day, seven days a week, year in and year out. He, with his trusty pocket watch, kept me on my toes. He was on my trail our entire married life.

When we reached Dr. Roger's office, I felt like I was falling apart. My strength was fading fast. Martha, the nurse, greeted me with, "Good Lord, what on earth happened to you?"

"I don't have much time to explain. Larry is in jail. I have to get a statement from Dr. Rogers and have it back to the probate judge before her office closes or Larry will be released. The magistrate gave me a warrant to have him arrested and sent to the mental hospital for evaluation."

"You stay here. I'll talk to the doctor."

Dr. Rogers walked past the door where I was waiting and saw me there. Before he could come into the room, Martha called to him. He walked out of my line of vision, though I could hear them talking in the hall. I couldn't make out their words, but I could tell that Martha was talking fast and in an urgent tone. Dr. Rogers glanced at me again as he passed by. His expression made me curious, so I went to the door and watched him. He went over to the nurse's desk, picked up the phone and dialed. In a moment I heard him say rather gruffly, "I'm going to bring you your papers. Evelyn isn't going anywhere except home or to the hospital, I haven't decided yet which it will be. I'm damn sick and tired of her coming in here every week or two all beat up. You just have the county doctor meet me at the jail at eight o'clock tonight. Larry is going to Columbia where he should have been sent a long time ago."

It was almost dark when I completed and delivered all of the paperwork that needed to be done, then I returned to the doctor's office for some much needed personal attention. By the time I pulled into my driveway, hours later, the pain killer I'd been given was beginning to take hold. Physically, I was feeling much better, but the sight of the house gave me eerie goosebumps. When I opened the kitchen door, I was once more greeted by a smell more repugnant than before. I hadn't had time to mop up the blood and that, combined with the house being closed up, gave off the most incredible stench. I became nauseous. The room began to spin. I made it to the bedroom where I sat on the side of the bed until my head cleared. When I was sure I could manage it, I showered.

I awoke the next morning sore, but on the slow road to recovery.

Dean called from Phoenix to tell me that he was having difficulty with Deb. I knew her main problem was that she was worried about me, but I didn't want to concern Dean about our mess at home, so I just told him to put her back on the plane and send her to me. Bev was twelve. She knew her father was abusive and mean-natured, but she had no idea he wanted to kill us both. I couldn't possibly tell her a thing like that. She arrived the next night. I was glad to have her with me. With her father in the mental hospital, I knew we were safe at last.

Within the week a state hospital administrator called to give me instructions on how to go about visiting my husband. Of all the things I didn't want to do, that topped the list. I wanted thirty days of peace and quiet. I could tell from the tone of the person calling that Larry had won them over. He had their complete sympathy. The fact that I had a job and had to earn a living was of no interest to them. It was my duty to visit my husband and to be supportive, I was told in no uncertain terms. I guess I didn't sound enthusiastic enough for them, because a day or so later I got a letter from the hospital going over the same information. They detailed how I was to visit Larry and gave all the reasons why I should. Their attitude seemed to be that if he didn't get well, or respond positively, it would be my fault for not providing the necessary support he needed. I made the hundred and twenty-mile trip to Columbia, gritting my teeth the whole way.

When Bev and I got there, I was surprised to see there were no gates or fences on the grounds. So, I found myself thinking, *this is why I hear so much on the news about patients escaping from the mental hospital.* Then I had to wonder why they call it an escape when all a patient had to do was walk away.

Larry was seated on an outdoor bench, waiting for us. Bev and I walked up to him. Her small hand trembled in mine. His expression said that he was playing a role and enjoying it to the hilt. It was an expression that caused me to be as terrified of him as Bev was.

I sat on the long bench, about three feet from him, trying to stay out of his reach–just in case. He didn't greet either of us, so we three just sat there. It was a very long two-hour visit. He didn't even comment on the wig I was now forced to wear, since I had no hair on the crown of my head.

The hospital refused to let up on me. They called and wrote, demanding that I visit my husband. I was frustrated. I had to keep money coming in, so I had to work. Eleanor was wonderful about giving me time off, but that wasn't the point. I needed the income and I needed to be away from my crazy spouse. I knew that if he was released, he would come back and finish the job he had started. I was determined to prevent that from happening.

The second visit was as devastating as the first. This time I let him know in no uncertain terms not to look for me to be back, because I had neither the patience nor the time for the long trip. I told him that if he continued to keep up the charade with the hospital staff, then the house he professed to care so much about wouldn't be his when he got back. Somebody had to pay for it and, so far, that somebody was me.

I was in a turmoil with so many different kinds of emotions. He still had me brainwashed, I knew that. At the same time, even though I knew it intellectually, I didn't know how to break away. Like he'd bragged for so many years, he married me young so he could bring me up the way he wanted me to be. It was over six years ago he told me that he wasn't going to work any more. Now that he was drawing Social Security disability, he no longer needed me. If I were dead, he would have it all and he'd be free to marry again, if he wanted to. Divorce wasn't even an option in his mind.

The days and weeks raced along and soon his thirty days in the State Hospital would end.

It was on a Thursday. He wasn't due to be released quite yet. I was working the day shift at the restaurant. Bev was to get out of school about four-twenty and I always picked her up. It was no different on this day. We went directly home, but when I started to put the key in the front lock, the door was open. That is, it was closed, but I could tell that it was unlocked. Just something about the feel of the key in its groove didn't set right. Fear grabbed at my throat with evil fingers. I quickly eased my key out of the lock and started moving backward. I put one finger over my lips, indicating to Bev that she mustn't make a sound. I took her hand and, as quickly and casually as we could, we got back into the car. I felt that if we ran, he would come storming out of the house and run after us. Even though Larry was supposedly still in the mental hospital in Columbia, somehow I knew he was in that house. I can't explain how I knew, I just knew.

Once back in the station wagon, Bev wanted to know what was wrong.

"The door was unlocked," I said, trying not to sound as alarmed as I was feeling. "If I don't miss my guess, your father's in the house."

"What makes you think that?"

"Nobody else has a key but him."

"But he's in Columbia."

"Well, that's where he's supposed to be, but I know your dad."

"How would he get here?"

"I wish I knew the answer to that one myself."

"What are you going to do now?"

"I'm going to call the sheriff's office and have somebody come check out the house before I take a chance on us going inside. If he's escaped the mental hospital, I have to report it."

I called the sheriff from the nearest pay phone. They said they'd meet me where I was, not to move. In a matter of minutes, two squad cars pulled up. I got out and went to a deputy. I told him what happened and that I was certain my husband was waiting for us back at the house.

"You pretty sure it's him?" he said, his brow raised in thought. He was no doubt considerinh the ordeal around this whole situation.

"I'm confident it is."

"Well," said his partner, unconvinced, "the hospital's supposed to keep him thirty days and his time's not up yet. Besides, even if he escaped, they'd never allow him to have keys in his possession."

I shook my head. "All I know is that I locked my door when I left for work and it's unlocked now. Look, he's not as crazy as he claims to be. He knew enough to win the hospital over and to set me up in the past. He's in there. I'm here to tell you, he's in there."

The deputies exchanged glances, then looked at the men in the other car. They seemed to come to some sort of silent agreement.

"You follow us," the man I'd spoken to first said, "but don't get out of your car until we tell you to."

Both squad cars continued on to my house with Bev and me bringing up the rear. All four deputies went inside. They searched every nook and cranny, but all they found the least bit suspicious was that the back door was also unlocked. Even at that, they told me they'd stay around for a bit to see if he returned, if it had been him in the first place.

"Wait a minute," I said, alarmed. "Do you think he's crazy enough to come back in this house with two squad cars parked in the driveway? If he's out there watching, then he knows you're in here. You might think he's crazy but, believe me, he is crazy like a fox. He's just crazy enough to outsmart you and me."

One of the deputies thought that over for a moment before he said, "You're right." Then he told two of the deputies, "Take both cars and leave. Park far enough away that you can't be seen. I'll wait here. If he shows up, I'll call the dispatcher and she'll alert you."

By now it had gotten pretty late. The deputy told me to make the place look as it always did at this time of the evening, as if things were perfectly normal. The two squad cars drove away. To all appearances, Bev and I were now alone in the house. The deputy that remained took up a post out of sight through any of the windows.

I got busy turning out the lights the way I did every night before we went to bed. Then Bev and I sat clinging to one another, our hearts racing, scared to death. The only sound was that of the deputy snoring. I shook him. He woke up.

Exactly forty-eight minutes later, I heard the screen door on the opposite end of the house rub against the floor. Deb, the deputy and I leaped silently to our feet. Another deputy had magically appeared and they rushed to the door, but whoever it was, disappeared into the darkness of the pine forest out behind the house.

It was now well after midnight. The deputies decided to go back to their office. When they called the state hospital, they waited on the line while a nurse checked Larry's room. She came back to the phone to report that he was nicely tucked in, sound asleep.

What no one took into consideration was that he could have dashed into the woods after spotting the second deputy coming into the house. He had plenty of time. Had the second deputy been more discreet in his arrival, they would have had him.

A week later I got a letter from the hospital informing me of his release and instructing me on when I should bring him home. It was the letter I had dreaded. I had gone through all the pros and cons of whether or not to pick him up. Dr. Rogers had advised me against signing him out, and that was what I wanted to do, but it was more complicated than that.

29

The day of his dismissal came. I wasn't there, so of course Larry called, demanding to know why I wasn't there to pick him up. I knew that he had the ability to sign himself out, and that he had acted on that ability. He had been standing in the parking lot with his things, waiting for me. While he ranted, I went through a thousand things at one time in my mind: The sheriff and all of his deputies knew Larry had beat me and had planned to kill me, the doctors knew that he had threatened to kill Bev and me, the entire justice system knew the truth, so where were they now that I had reached this cross-roads in my life? If I picked him up and brought him home, I was dooming myself and Bev to certain disaster. If I didn't pick him up, he'd just get someone else, probably a lady friend, to bring him home and he'd be furious; the situation would be even more volatile. I couldn't see that I had a choice in the matter. There was nothing to do but to go get him.

The tears I shed as I prepared to leave covered a multitude of emotions. I was furious, I was hurt by the system, I was afraid for myself and for Deb, and I was so frustrated I could have screamed.

There he was in the parking lot, just like he said. His things were in a brown trash bag. He got in the car. I fought with all my might not to follow my instinct and wrap the station wagon around an oak tree, putting an end to everyone's misery. The report would call it an accident. Easy out for all concerned. I passed by the oak, feeling I had just let my last opportunity slip away.

About four miles up the road, I turned to him and I said, "You sure you want to come home?"

"Yes."

"Well," I said, setting my jaw in determination, "then you'd best fasten your safety belt." Of course it was just a figure of speech in those days; we didn't yet have seat belts in our cars.

I revved that old station wagon up to its highest notch and drove like a bat out of hell, looking all the while for another oak. Any kind of timber would do, actually. Every time I found one, another car would be approaching, or the tree wasn't in exactly the right spot. I didn't want anyone else to get hurt, I just wanted out. I drove and I watched for a place to end it all, but before I knew it, I was in my own driveway. Larry hadn't said a word, but the blood had rushed out of his face. I think he was glad to feel ground under his feet.

The second he got out of the car, and retrieved his belongings, I threw the car in reverse and shot out of the drive.

"Hey! Where you going?" he shouted after me.

"Back to work," I said through clenched teeth.

I wasn't in the restaurant ten minutes when he called. One of the waitresses answered the phone, then held the receiver up for me.

"When you coming home?" he asked, as if everything was just ducky.

"The usual time, around eleven-thirty."

"I want you home now."

"You know I can't come home now, I'm working."

It was as if he never heard a word I said.

"If you don't come, I'll come there and drag you home by what hair you have left on your head."

The thought sent chills over my body and I caved in. Without the legal or the medical systems to back me up, what could I do, I wondered? "Give me time to get somebody in here to take my place."

I had Bev with me, of course. When we got home, he was sitting in his recliner. I had instructed Bev on the way there to go straight to her room and get in bed as soon as we arrived, but that wasn't to be.

Larry got up when he saw us. He looked at Deb.

"Take your clothes off," he said.

"Why in the world would she do that?" I asked him.

"'Cause I'm going to beat her."

That's when I saw the tree limb lying across the coffee table. It was the size of the one he'd used to beat Dean.

My heart cried out, Dear God! Please save us!, but I remained calm when I said to him, "Now why would you want to do a thing like that, Larry?"

"Just 'cause I want to." The veins in his neck bulged out and were pulsating.

I had my arm around Deb, holding her close. I looked Larry in the eye. "I'm not telling her to take her clothes off and you're not whipping her."

"Well then, by God, I'm going to put it on you."

I stuck my chin out and stayed cool. "Well then, by God, you're going to have to put it on me, because you are not whipping her."

He looked kind of like a balloon when the air goes out of it. Then he sat down in his recliner. I nudged Bev toward her room. She went quietly and quickly. I stood there waiting to see what would happen next, but all he did was go to the refrigerator and take a long pull out of his vodka bottle. I could see by the way he walked, it wasn't his first trip to the frig. I stayed just where I was until he finally fell asleep in his chair.

The next day Bev went on to school. I was getting ready to go to work, though I didn't have to be there until ten. Larry was acting as if nothing happened out of the ordinary. With a great dramatic flair, he pulled an envelope out of his pocket and sort of waved it around in front of me.

"Sit down," he said.

"I can't right now. I have to get ready for work."

He opened the envelope and pulled a sheet of paper from it.

"You see this here piece of paper? It says there ain't a damn thing wrong with me."

I reached for it. "Let me see that."

"Hell no, you won't ever touch this piece of paper."

"Why not? You're showing it to me. I assumed you wanted me to see what it says."

It came to me as clear as if I could read his mind. Even though the hospital found him sane, if he did kill Bev and me, the most he would get would be maybe thirty more days in the hospital. Just because he failed once to kill us, didn't mean it wasn't going to happen.

Somehow we managed, the three of us, to exist under the same roof for another six months. Larry spent his days watching his new color televison set, and I worked. Bev stayed close to me as much as possible. In fact, she had started helping out some at the restaurant. When Dean called, asking me to come to Arizona to give him a hand with his new drapery business, I knew I couldn't, but Larry jumped on the opportunity. He loaded up his truck and off he went to Phoenix. It wasn't ten days later Dean called me at the restaurant to warn me that his father was on his way home, and in a nasty mood.

"What happened, honey?" I asked.

"Daddy got in a fight with my partner, threatening to hit him in the head with a hammer. I took it away from him, then I ordered him out of our house. I told him I'd put up with his meanness as a kid, but I didn't have to do it now. I can't let my wife or stepdaughter be exposed to that kind of thing, Mother. I told him this was my house and it just wasn't going to happen here."

I assured him that he'd done the right thing, told him I loved him, and we hung up. Dean felt that Larry would be pulling up in about two hours and he nailed it right on the head. I was working at the restaurant, dreading the passing of time. He always blamed me when one of the children didn't do things to his liking. With Dean telling him to pack his things and get out, I knew he'd be beside himself.

History repeated itself, as it had been repeating itself over the past thirty years. Larry arrived at the restaurant, but this time he put a little spin on history. He came inside, which was unusual. I was making a sandwich for a customer, and the two teen girls who worked with me were busy with other orders. Larry reached across the counter.

"When you coming home?" he asked.

"Usual time. Eleven-twenty or so. After I get the place cleaned up."

"No. You're coming home now."

"I can't leave the girls here by themselves."

Suddenly he made a grab for my wig. I dodged. The girls let out a squeal. He just stood there, staring at me, then he said, "I want you to know your young'un run me off. What do you think about that? Your son running his own father off!" Then he walked out, got back in his truck and left. He must have broken all speed laws getting home, because it seemed like only two minutes passed before he called on the phone.

"By God, I want you here and I mean now! Not just now, but right now, dammit! Do you understand?"

"Larry, I've told you enough times that I can't leave the girls here alone. We'd all wind up in jail. These are high school kids. There has to be an adult on the job."

"I'm giving you twenty minutes. If you and Bev aren't here in twenty minutes, by God, I am coming back up there and when I do–"

He slammed down the receiver without telling me what it was he was going to do. As if I didn't know.

All things considered, I knew the best course of action was for me to get home as fast as possible, even though I'd just as soon have been going to the gas chamber than face him in his drunken state of mind. One thing for sure, he meant every word he was saying.

Same ol', same ol'; Bev went to bed, I stood and listened to Larry rage about Dean. Finally I said, "I don't know what to say to you, Larry. I wasn't there so how about you telling me what you did to cause him to run you off."

"I didn't do a damn thing. I knew all the time you were gonna take his side. Doesn't make a damn to you what he does 'cause anything he does you think is all right." It took him a few seconds to get into high gear, but when he did, the words came out in a flood. "I don't blame Dean as much as I blame you. All of it's your fault for not listening to me! You wouldn't let me beat those damn young'un's like I needed to. I knew he wouldn't ever turn out to be anybody, but you were so damn proud of him! Dammit, I told you in the first place that I didn't want any damn young'uns but, no, you had to go get pregnant anyway. Then you always took their side against me. You never did want me to beat 'em, dammit. I wanted to beat 'em like they needed to be beat, so they could grow up to be a man like me!"

Surprisingly, he got up and went to work with Donnie the next morning, and actually worked a couple of days straight.

On my next day off at the restaurant, he handed me a list of supplies he wanted me to get at the wholesale houses, just as I had been doing for the past seven years. By the time I got home it was almost dark even though it wasn't quite seven o'clock. I noticed a lot of strange cars in the driveway and I thought it odd that every light in the place seemed to be blazing, but I wasn't prepared for the sight I saw when I walked in. An all-female party was in progress. Some woman sort of sallied up to me when I walked into the kitchen, trying to collect my thoughts. She said she sure did appreciate Larry being so sweet to invite her to this wonderful little celebration.

I told her to have a nice time. If he was partying, he wouldn't be giving me grief. And while I didn't care about his female guests, I was concerned about his motive. It was definitely out of character for him.

I was alone in the kitchen, putting something away when I noticed him standing behind me. With so many people in the next room, I wasn't afraid.

"What do you need?" I asked casually.

"I need you to bring up the laundry that's still in the dryer."

Without giving it a second thought, I replied. "Yeah, sure."

The dryer was in the basement. Larry went back to his guests. As I opened the door to go downstairs, the television blared out real loud. I thought, *Good Lord, who could have jacked up the television that loud?* Larry hated for the TV to be even the least bit loud. Sensitive ears, he said. I guess it didn't bother him this time, however, because the sound continued to blast away.

When I reached the bottom of the stair steps, I was annoyed to find it almost dark. It appeared that only one of the six or so lights down there was working. That, too, struck me as strange, but not so strange that I went racing back up the stairs. I made my way in the dimness, to the dryer at the back of the room. Suddenly, I began to slip and slide. Once I got myself steady, I realized there was a large sheet of plastic spread on the floor in front of the washer and dryer. It was like the kind we used at some of the job sites once in a while. Again, no huge warning bells, but a little nagging voice that wondered why it was there in the first place.

I reached out for the handle to the dyer door and was immediately jolted by a violent surge of electricity. I couldn't let go. I screamed at the top of my lungs, but the television set was too loud for anyone upstairs to have heard me. I called out, "Dear God in Heaven, won't someone please hear me? Please! Will somebody come help me?"

It seemed like an eternity that I was stuck to the dryer with electricity jolting and stabbing my entire body. I pulled and tugged, but I couldn't get loose. An electric monster had taken over with a fury. Over to my left was an old kitchen chair, but it was just out of my reach. I thought that if I could only catch hold of it, it would give me the leverage I needed to help tear me away from the dryer. I saw the chair had been used to hold a corner of the plastic in place. That chair became my savior. I stretched out as far as I could, still being twisted and jerked violently by the electricity coming through the handle I couldn't let go of. Finally, a miracle occurred. I was able to get a grip on the plastic back and tip the chair toward me. It did, indeed, give me the needed leverage to break the dryer's deadly grip. Once free, my knees went out from under me. I fell to the floor.

I put my hands to my face and was surprised to find them wet. I staggered to the basement steps and sat down to get my bearings, to try to make sense of what had just happened. That's when I noticed blood dripping from the hand that had been sealed so strongly to the handle of the dryer door. There was a bathroom in a dark corner of the basement. I went in and washed away the blood, then I went upstairs, one agonizing step at a time. I shook violently, realizing that once again Larry had failed in his attempt to kill me. He had straight-wired the 220 electric dryer. What saved me was the sheet of plastic over the concrete floor, plus the plastic on the back of that chair.

Two weeks later, on Saturday night, Bev had gone to spend the night with a friend and Larry was watching TV from his recliner. He was drunk, but it wasn't a terrifying drunk. There were certain times in his drunkenness that he would actually mellow out. Over the years I'd learned that if I could time a question to hit him at precisely the right moment during this mellow phase, I'd get a truthful answer out of him. This seemed like such a time.

"Larry, there's something I've been wanting to ask you."

"What's that?"

"Well, a couple weeks back when I went down in the basement to get the clothes out of the dryer, I can't figure out what was your reason for having that sheet of plastic spread out in front of it like that."

He laughed. "Why do you want to know?"

"Because I slipped and almost fell on it. It was so dark down there I didn't see it until I was teeter-toting around. You remember me telling you that the dryer had a full charge of electricity on it and that you needed to fix it?"

He chuckled lightly, almost to himself, before he answered. "Now, why do you want to know a crazy thing like that?" His tone of voice told me that my timing wasn't all I thought it to be; he was playacting.

"Hmmmm, no reason actually, just being a little curious as to what you would need with a large sheet of plastic like that on the basement floor. Being so dark down there, someone could slip and fall."

Once again he chuckled softly. He was enjoying himself. He wanted me to know he thought it was funny.

"You really want to know? Well, if you want to know so badly, then I'll tell you. I was gonna use it to wrap you in and put you in the well." After a moment's hesitation, he said, "Both of you."

"Oh, so you straight-wired the dryer to electrocute me?"

"Yeah, by damn, you got it." Then he got quiet.

I acted like nothing unusual had been said.

"It's nice to see you in such a good mood tonight," I said conversationally.

"I'm always in a good mood." He snickered and gave me a broad grin.

"While you're in such a good mood, how about telling me how you left the mental hospital that night and got back without any of the nurses missing you?"

He really got a bang out of that question. I could see the wheels turning in his brain. "You really want to know, do you?"

"Yeah, sure I do. Seems like it might be interesting to hear."

"Let me make a deal with you."

Oh yes, a deal. Sure. "Just what kind of a deal?" I asked.

"I tell you if you'll tell me how you knew it was me in the house."

"Oh my dear, that's one is easy. I'm the only one knows how smart you really are. You forgot to lock the door back after you went inside."

He turned as white as a man could turn. "Well, I'll be damn. You don't miss a damn thing, now do you?"

"The moment I put the key in the lock, I knew. You were the only one who would, or could, have unlocked that door. Had to be you. So, now, tell me. How'd you leave the hospital, come here, and get back without anyone missing you?"

"I had my buddy to cover for me. I kept all my things under my mattress. I took them out and made my bed up like I was asleep in it. I seen that one time in a movie."

I laughed a little like I meant it. "You sure pulled a good one. That answers part of it, but how'd you get back to Columbia without anyone seeing you?"

He was just drunk enough to think, and he was having fun at my expense. He sat up straight in his chair, put his arms between his legs and started rocking back and forth. Then he got quiet for maybe five minutes. I just let him be. I let him think over whatever he had on his mind, though I wondered if I had pushed a bit too much.

Finally, he said, "You got a private detective watching me?"

"Oh, come now. How could I have somebody watching you with you being locked up in the hospital?"

"Well, then...just how the hell could you know somebody brought me and took me back?"

"Doesn't take much figuring. All of our vehicles are here."

He was highly amused. I might even say he seemed to have a begrudging admiration for my thought process. "You're damn right. You're right, but I can't figure out how."

"Now we've got the whole story out in the open except for one tiny bit of information."

"It seems to me like you know everything."

"Who kept the extra set, my set, of house keys for you? Was it the same woman who brought you and took you back to the hospital?"

That one caught him off-guard. "Just what the hell makes you think it was a woman?"

"Simple. You don't know a man who would do a thing like that for you."

"Well, that's the one thing I won't ever tell you. You're so smart, you can figure that one out for yourself."

That last question sobered him up some. It was the first time I'd ever mentioned a woman to him.

"So," I said, pushing my luck, "you were going to do even better than your daddy did. He just got away with one murder, but you were going to commit the perfect double murder, weren't you?"

That kind of threw him. He didn't answer any more questions, which was just as well since I didn't have any more to ask. Now I knew the truth. I'd always known it, but now he was at least confirming it. And there was no one I could tell, no one I could turn to. Not the legal system, not doctors, not the law. No one. If Bev and I tried to run away, he'd find us. No doubt about it, he'd find us. He'd threaten Dean until Dean told, because I'd never go where I couldn't see or talk to my son. Dean wouldn't want to tell, but if his daddy was going to harm Dean's wife or stepchild, he'd have to tell. Or kill his own father, which I knew he wouldn't do. No, there was no place to hide, and no protection from my husband, not in this whole wide world.

◘

Our business had come pretty much to a halt, despite Donnie's best efforts. One day I got a call at home, on my day off, from a man who said I'd been highly recommended as an alteration lady. He owned a dry-cleaning establishment. The woman who had been doing the work had quit on him with no notice. He was in a real bind.

I was stirring something on the stove and had the phone to my ear with my free hand. "If it's not too much out of your way," I said to him, " why don't you run by here? I'm cooking supper right now and my husband's here. You're welcome to eat with us, then we can sit and talk business."

He said he'd see me in about five minutes. I didn't think any more about it. It was the way I'd been cutting business deals for the past seven years. Most of them had been done out of our house and consisted of me meeting with contractors.

The man arrived as I was setting our meal on the table. He and Larry shook hands, I introduced them, and things seemed to go pretty well. When we finished eating, we went into the den to make ourselves comfortable. We hadn't yet got around to talking business. Larry sat in his chair, I gave mine to the gentleman and took a place on the sofa. The fellow began to tell us about his problems at work, about the alternation lady leaving with no notice, that sort of thing. He told us that he was between a rock and a hard place, a position I knew very well, but I never said anything. When the man got around to quoting a salary for me, Larry suddenly took great exception.

"She ain't working for that little bit of money. If she works for you, you're going to pay her more than that."

The man looked at my husband, then back to me. He made me an offer of more money.

Larry shook his head. "Hell, no. She ain't working for that little bit either."

The gentleman wasn't liking what he was hearing. "Mr. Barkley, I'm willing to pay her what it's worth only because she's been recommended very highly. I'm not saying she isn't worth more money, but that's all I can afford to pay. If I give her any more than that, I'll be out of business."

What was wrong with Larry, I wondered? The man was offering twice as much as I was making at the restaurant. The work was easier and I needed the job, I was the sole breadwinner. I didn't realize I was going to say anything until the words seemingly popped out of my mouth. "Larry, why don't you shut up? I'm the one who'll be doing the work."

He came out of his chair like he had been ejected.

In a reflex action, I jumped to my feet.

He slapped me up side the head so hard that my glasses flew off my face.

I snapped. Everything went black. The next thing I knew, Larry was spread eagle, belly up, on the floor, using the baseboard for a pillow. The gentleman jumped up, leaped over Larry and the last I saw of him, he was out the kitchen door. I heard the engine kick to life on his truck and the screech of tires as he sped away.

Everything had happened so fast, I honestly don't know if I hit, slapped or shoved Larry. I'd only hit him once before and that was the night with the two-liter Pepsi bottle.

He continued to lay on the floor, belly up. It was taking him some time to come around. After he finally did, he pulled himself up on his chair and sat down. He remained in his chair for several hours, staring at the television, without any conversation. What the aftermath of this little fiasco would lead to would be anybody's guess. I didn't hear any more from him. He slept in his chair that night. I thought it was a safe bet that I didn't get the alternation job either.

His reactions were sometimes slow in coming, but he never forgot anything. He would plan and plot and then, one day, he'd hit you with it.

One night not long after that incident, I came home from the restaurant exhausted. I started to lie down on the sofa, when he began arguing for me to sit in my recliner. I didn't want to sit up, I wanted to lie down. Larry never would let the children lie down on the sofa; it was for sitting, he always insisted.

The argument went on and on and the longer it went on, the more exhausted I became. Finally, he stood over me with narrowed eyes.

"I've had it with you, Evelyn. You get yourself up from there and go get a suitcase. I want you to get the hell out of my house. Now!"

I thought, Thank goodness, this is my chance to get as far away from him as I can. I got up and went to Deb's room to tell her to get her things together, that we were leaving. Before I could say anything, though, Larry was standing behind me.

"You're not taking her anywhere. Now get on in yonder and pack your things. I told you once to go and that's what I mean."

Deb was terrified. I knew if I argued in front of her, Larry was apt to do worse than the night that sent him to the state hospital, only this time I couldn't turn to the hospital; they had already said he was fine. His look was getting darker and more dangerous with every moment I delayed. It would be just like him to begin beating Bev in front of me, just to show me that he could do it. The thought of her taking what I'd taken that night when he'd pulled my hair out of my skull was just too much to bear.

I was nearly out of my mind with panic. Throwing clothes in my suitcase, I kept thinking it through. I had nowhere to go. I didn't know which way to turn. I did know Larry well enough to know one thing for certain, however; he wouldn't have the nerve to kill Bev while I was on the loose. He would have to wait now until he got both of us together before he could carry out his perfect murders. Part of his sickness was that he stuck to whatever original plan he devised, and his plan had been to kill the two of us.

If I left, he'd make sure everyone knew it. If I managed to get back and spirit Bev away with me, he'd kill us both for sure, and then he'd tell everyone that I'd gone and taken Bev with me. They'd believe him. He would have gotten away with it, after all. He had me at the brink of insanity. This was the straw that almost broke the camel's back.

It was a little after one in the morning. I drove for hours not knowing where I was most of the time. My mind was telling me to keep going. I thought about going to Phoenix with Dean, but I would have to get Bev first. I dismissed the idea of Dean. I couldn't put him and his family in harm's way like that. Other than that, I remember very little about the night other than headlights and telephone poles as they whizzed by.

I spotted a small country motel ahead, to my left. I stopped. I knew I wasn't in any shape or condition to be behind a steering wheel. I had to rest.

30

I checked in under the name of Elizabeth Fort, Elizabeth being my middle name, Fort being my maiden name. I paid the desk clerk for two days. Once in bed, I tossed and turned and cried until my head ached as deeply as my heart ached. I had convinced myself that Bev would be safe with me gone. I had argued to myself that he wouldn't dare do anything to her without me there to witness his abuse. He knew that hurting the children was the one sure way to kill me without causing death. Yet, I couldn't get the picture of him alone with her out of my mind. Sometime about daybreak I drifted off to sleep only to have a nightmare. Larry had Bev and me tied up in that sheet of plastic and he was dumping us in the well. I was hanging onto Bev for dear life, praying, sobbing hysterically, when suddenly I was awakened by the sound of my own screams.

About noon the next day, I dragged myself up and got dressed. I didn't check out, but I wanted some hot chocolate. I hadn't eaten in so long I couldn't even remember. As I pulled away from the motel, I hesitated, trying to decide which way I should go. To my right was the way I came in. I decided to check out the opposite end of the road, so I hooked a left and was soon at the Georgia state line. It wasn't long until I reached the city limits of Toccoa. I drove until I came to what appeared to be the center of town, where I found a small café. Fortified with hot chocolate, ham and eggs, I left an hour later with no plan and no idea where to go except back to my motel room to do some more heavy thinking.

The first thing I saw when I went in, was that someone had been through my suitcase. *Oh, my God!* I thought. *Larry has found me!* I told my racing heart to be still. I looked around quickly, half-expecting to see him sitting in a chair, grinning at me. But he was nowhere in sight. With weak knees, I sank to a chair. That's when I heard a car pull up outside. I looked out the window, but I didn't see Larry or anything that made me think he was there. The man who had checked me in the morning before, was sitting in a lawn chair, staring at my door. It scared me. I got a straight-back and propped it under the door knob. I remembered the way he had looked at me when I checked in. It was the kind of look I'd seen from my father-in-law so many times before, the kind that sends chills along a woman's spine. I didn't feel safe any longer.

I'd already paid in full, so I didn't have any reason to go back into the motel office. I waited until the man left his lawn chair to race out to the car and take off. I drove on to Toccoa where I found another motel room. I only came out twice that day for food.

I was trapped and weary. I kept thinking what's the use? I was his wife and there was no law in the land that prohibited a man from beating his wife or his children. It wasn't illegal. I thought, not for the first time, of simply killing him. The downside of that was, since beating me wasn't illegal, I'd end up going to the electric chair and that didn't seem to me to be solving anything. He'd have half the community cheering the executioner on; everyone thought Larry was such a fine, upstanding man. A real charmer. The tag line of my thinking always turned out to be the same: God put us here, it's up to God to let me know when and how we should go. If he hurt my little girl, however, I knew I'd be forced to turn the tables on him and put him away, electric chair or no electric chair.

I stayed at the Toccoa motel for three days, sifting all of this through my mind. Then I packed my things once again.

The next clear thing I remember is coming into the city limits of Walhalla. Of all the places for me to be, I was in Larry's hometown. What in the world led me there?

I passed the store where his folks had found that ugly blue dress they had me wear to tie me into the mess I was in. I kept driving.

Outside Walhalla, I took a left and headed toward Pickens. About then I spotted a sign on the edge of the highway that read, "Trailer for Rent." I pulled over and parked long enough to write down the telephone number. Then I went off in search of a pay phone. A woman answered on the first ring. I told her I was inquiring about the rental trailer, and she told me it would cost twenty dollars a week or seventy-five dollars a month. Following her directions to her office, I walked in a few minutes later and rented the place for thirty days. Now all I had to look forward to were sleepless nights until I could get Bev away from Larry. For four nights I suffered one nightmare after the other.

My thoughts when I was awake weren't much more of a comfort. I found myself thinking back to something I was told years ago. A family member had confided to me that Larry's grandmother was a child of incest. The remark had been about inbreeding in the family. It was the first time I'd heard the word. "Anyway," the relative had said to me, "everyone in the community is afraid of her. They say she's the cause of their cows going dry." That didn't make much sense to me and I said so. "She's a witch," the relative said as if further explanation wasn't necessary. I had no education in the details and ramifications of inbreeding, though it didn't seem to me that it would cause witchery. On the other hand, what did I know? I knew this: Incest seemed to be a way of life on Larry's side of the family. I also realized that this kind of thinking is what made my parents so overly protective of me, so protective they went so far as to send me, at thirteen, far away from my brothers and their friends.

I realized that I had to stop thinking about the past. I had to get back to my own problems and find a way to protect Deb. I decided to test the water and call Larry at home. I found a pay phone and dialed. He answered. I asked to speak to Deb. He refused. However, he did say that I could talk to her *if I'd come home*. Then he had the audacity to accuse me of "running off".

"What are you talking about?" I said into the phone. "If you think back, you didn't give me any other choice. How can you accuse me of running off when you're the one that told me to pack my suitcase and get out of your house?"

Even as I said what I said and he said what he said, my mind kept telling me that his intention was to get me back so he could roll Bev and me up in that plastic sheet and cram us down the well. I knew I was right in my thinking. That wee small voice inside my head told me to beware.

I hung up the telephone with a heavy heart and went back to the trailer. I walked the floor constantly, day and night, worrying, stewing, planning, and scraping each plan as worse than the one before.

I spent a lot of my time in that trailer praying. It was the only thing that seemed to clear my head. I knew I had to listen to the still, small voice inside me that said, "If you wait around for him to trick you again, then what more can you expect other than to walk into another one of his traps like you did in the basement with the dryer? You've got to get Bev and get away from him." I also knew I had to force Larry's hand one more time.

I had to call Eleanor. She was kind and understanding, but she was my boss and she needed to hear from me. Maybe I'd luck out and Bev would be working at the restaurant when I called. Eleanor told me that, yes, Larry was letting Bev work some, but she wasn't there at the moment. I hung up filled with despair. Bev was never off of my mind. Once back in the trailer, I fell to my knees in prayer again. I was nudged to call Larry once more. I did and found him to be in a better mood. He agreed that I could talk to Deb, but at the house, and with him present. Something told me to go along with it.

I moved back in. At least I was close to my girl. What the next move would be, was anyone's guess. I'd just have to keep my eyes and ears open for opportunity.

I was relaxing in my recliner with my purse on the floor beside me, tired after a long day at work, when I must have dozed off because first thing I knew, Larry was pilfering through my pocketbook. My heart leaped to my throat. I had my savings in there; my get-away money. I'd never known Larry to go through my purse before and had always felt that it was the safest place to stash my savings. Fortunately, he tossed my billfold aside and found what he was looking for, a motel receipt. He held it up triumphantly. With an expression that said ah-hah, I caught you, he demanded to know why I had gone to Georgia.

"You run me off," I reminded him. "Why do you care where I was?"

In his confusion, he got it in his head that I was with Etley and the children when in reality I was miles from them. Nevertheless, if it satisfied Larry to believe that, then so be it.

We went on like that for a few days, then he did another about-face. He started walking around with his rifle in his hand, telling me that he was going to kill himself. Bev had gone to spend the night with her girlfriend, so we were home alone. At first I thought he was joking. For two weeks he had been in an exceptional mood, almost pleasant. Anyway, it didn't take me long to see that he wasn't kidding. The rifle was making me nervous, but I didn't want him to know it. It would be just like him to threaten to do away with himself, then turn the fool thing on me. He was taunting me with it. No matter where he sat or stood, the rifle was right there with him.

That went on for a couple of hours. He never threatened me, never said anything out of the way, but the careless manner in which he was moving that rifle around, I knew that anything could happen. It dawned on me that maybe he was aiming to cause an 'accident' like they say happened to my mother-in-law and to Edith. Whenever these thoughts would pass through my mind, I could see the pleasure in Larry's eyes. He was enjoying making me nervous.

I made myself busy washing collard greens to cook for dinner and doing my best not to lose my temper with him. I hoped he'd give up and find a western movie on television, but for some reason he wasn't interested in TV. This thing about him killing himself was beginning to sound like a broken record. I was to the point that if he said it one more time, I would be forced to scream or better yet, take that rifle out of his good hand and beat the living day lights out of him with it. I was sure I couldn't possibly stand to hear any more of his low, monotone whining about suicide. Sure enough, the next time I heard him say "I'm gonna kill myself", I picked up the rifle by its stock, and with the barrel pointing straight up, threw it at him with all my strength. He made a perfect catch.

"Larry, if you've made up your mind to kill yourself, here then, just do it. Go on, get it over with. I'm sick and tired of hearing it. It's time to either put up or shut up."

Larry put the rifle away and went to the den to watch television. Thirty minutes later he was back on the "I'm gonna kill myself" kick again. This time I didn't stay around to listen. I went to the telephone and called an old friend, Jeanette, to come get me. Her husband, Walt, was a deputy. He knew about Larry's trip to the mental hospital, although he hadn't been involved in the drama of that night.

It didn't take Jeanette long to arrive. She tooted her car horn out front.

"Who's that out there?" Larry asked, peering out the window.

"It's Jeanette."

"What the hell's she doing here?"

"She's come to get me."

I grabbed my purse and went out the door without waiting for him to respond. No sooner were we in Jeanette's house than Larry called. Walt answered the phone, which in no way intimidated my husband. He demanded that I be brought home that very minute. When he hung up, Walt said to Jeanette, "Larry told me that if I didn't bring Evelyn home, he was coming over here. I told him, if he wants to come here, he's more than welcome, but he'd better behave himself, that I wasn't taking Evelyn anywhere until she says she's ready to go."

Jeanette asked how Larry responded to that.

"He hung up on me," Walt said.

He no sooner finished telling us about their talk than Larry called back. The conversation went pretty much like their first one and ended with Larry slamming the phone down in Walt's ear. But then Larry called again. And again. Walt answered the phone each time. Larry threatened to come over and burn their house down with all of us in it if somebody didn't bring me home. This time Walt hung up on him. This went on until I finally gave up and said that the next time Larry called, to tell him I was on my way back. Sure enough, two minutes later, Larry called and Walt told him to calm down, that Jeanette was bringing me home. But then he added, "Before you hang up, I've got one more thing to say to you. If you hurt her, I will personally come and take you to jail myself. You won't get by me as easy as you did those other deputies."

When Jeanette pulled her car into my driveway, we could see Larry standing under the porch light with the rifle in his hand.

I said to Jeanette, "He wants to make sure we see him."

She pulled the car up as close as she could to the porch steps, parked and rolled down her window. "How're you doing, Larry?"

He answered her as cool and calm as one person can be. "Oh, I ain't doing too bad myself. How about you?"

Jeanette went on making small talk with him while I got out of the car. When she pulled away, and I went on into the house, Larry could not have been in a better mood. He had accomplished something that made him very happy. He had caused a deputy sheriff to yield to his demands. That made him feel powerful, and any time he won a battle, it calmed him down. It was like he'd had a bath in tranquility. Relieved to know there would be no battle on this night, I walked into the dining room–and was stunned to see that all of my linen had been piled on the floor, just like before. Beside the stack was a five-gallon can of lacquer sealer. On the dining table was a box of matches.

I showered and went to bed as quickly as I could. I didn't have any desire to take a chance on getting him upset again. If he followed true to course, it would take him a couple of days to get that inferno of hate and resentment that was inside of him blasting away again, but rest assured, it would erupt. Guaranteed. He went to his chair in the den and clicked on the television set. He was totally peaceful. He had worn himself out.

Deb was just this side of thirteen and threatening to kill herself if I didn't find a way to get us out of this horrible nightmare that we were in. But I had to time everything just perfect or we'd be in a worse mess than we'd ever been in before. My chance came just a few days later.

It was Sunday and he was in a pretty good mood again. That's when I said, "Larry, we need to talk."

"What do you want to talk about?"

"I think it's time we think about a trial separation."

"Just what the hell is a trial separation?"

"It's when two people have been together as long as we have, but nothing's ever right. That's the place we've reached in our life. You're not happy, I'm not happy. I think it best we come to an understanding and go our separate ways. Then, after awhile, once we get ourselves together, we can discuss if we want to continue on with this relationship."

"Woman, you must have lost your mind."

He sat down and appeared to be thinking over what I was saying.

"You know," I went on in a reasonable tone of voice, "I think two people can live together too long. Sometimes it's better when they decide to just part company."

He seemed totally taken by surprise. He was baffled.

"Well," he said slowly, "if you're that unhappy after all I've done for you, then you go right ahead and get yourself a trial separation. I want you and everyone else to know that I've given you everything you ever wanted. Now you tell me you want a trial separation. Well then, if that's what you want, that's what you're going to get 'cause all I ever wanted was to make you happy. So I am telling you, yes, I'm going to let you have that, too."

I knew better than to shout with happiness quite yet. I just couldn't picture him giving in. I had caught him at a moment when he hadn't, in his foggiest notion, thought that I would bring up something like that. I had used the word separation on purpose; I didn't dare to say divorce. That was the one thing that would have gotten him riled up real quick. I happened to catch him at the right moment, and he had agreed. The one thing I could count on with him was that when he told me something good or bad, he always kept his word. I knew I had to get things moving fast. If I messed around and gave him too much time to think it over, things could be disastrous. I would have to handle this as if I were walking on eggs.

Even though I doubted that he understood the full meaning of the term 'legal separation', or else he didn't think that I would go through with it, come morning I intended to get the ball rolling. First, I needed to find a place to live. That would have to be handled very carefully. The actual moving out would be a dangerous time.

Next morning, as planned, I started out the door when he stopped me. "Just where do you think you're off to now?"

I had always told him where I was going, every time I left the house. I never lied to him about where or why I was going some place.

"Don't you remember? Yesterday you agreed to a trial separation. I've taken the day off work to get it started."

He didn't say anything else.

I hurried to the liquor store where I heard the owner had trailers for rent. The gentleman was a quiet sort, with hair graying around the temples. When he finished with a customer, he asked what he could do for me.

"I heard you own a trailer park."

"That's right."

"I'm looking for a trailer to rent."

"What's your name?"

I told him.

He took a good look at me through squinted eyes. "You Larry's wife?"

"Yes, sir, I am."

He kind of shook his head. "I have some empty trailers that I need to get rented, but I just don't know about this."

"Why do you say that?"

He scratched his head, taking time to think about his reply. "I don't know the man personally, but from what I hear, he can get pretty nasty."

As far as I knew Larry had bought his vodka from the other liquor store in town, but this was proof of what my daddy had always told me. He said, "It pays to live right and to be honest because it doesn't matter where you go, or how far you go, your reputation will be there before you get there."

I was so afraid the proprietor wasn't going to rent to me. "Please. We're separated. I've got to find a place for my daughter and me to move into. Won't you reconsider and let me see what you have for rent?"

The old gentleman got real quiet, then he said to me, " I don't know ... That husband of yours—"

"He's agreed to a trial separation."

"All right. I'm going to take a chance, but before I do, you have to make me one promise."

"What's that?"

"Promise me that I'm not going to have to clean your blood up from all over my trailer."

31

When I got back home, Larry seemed to still be in a pretty good mood. My mind was racing, wondering what to do first. My sewing machine was the main large item on my list of things to be moved. It was probably the only piece of furniture that he'd let me take. I kept it in the dining room. If he stayed in the den in front of the television set, I'd have a good chance of getting it out of the house. It was awfully heavy. I prayed that Bev would be able to help me lift it.

I kept myself busy all afternoon doing some sewing. I stopped to cook his supper, trying to keep everything normal. For the first time in a long time he sat down at the table to eat. Most times I had to take his meal to him in the den where he could watch television, but that night the three of us sat at the table to eat our last supper together. About halfway through the meal, he said, "Well, did you find what you were looking for?"

"Yeah. I found a trailer, but I've got to go clean it in the morning."

He didn't say anything else.

The next morning I got up and cooked his breakfast just as I'd done for the past thirty years. We sat down at the table to eat, just as we always had. He finished his breakfast and went into the den, like always. Bev and I quickly washed the dishes and put them away then we gathered up our cleaning supplies and left. As I drove to the trailer park, I thought, *So far, so good.* My luck seemed to be holding up.

When I pulled back into the driveway three hours later, I parked the Plymouth directly behind Larry's truck. Before we got out of the car, I said to Deb, "Listen to me carefully. You know the first thing I have to do is cook your daddy's lunch before I can do anything else. I want you to go to your room and start throwing things together. I put a couple of sheets on the dresser. You'll have to use them to tie your things up in. I can't take a chance on bringing in boxes. That would get him going real quick. We'll just have to make do. Don't worry about your things. If they get wrinkled, we can iron them later. Just move as quietly as you can. I'll try to occupy your daddy to keep him from going off the deep end. The quicker we can get everything loaded, the better our chance will be of getting most of our personal stuff." I doubted that I would get hardly any of my own belongings, but I wanted to make sure that Bev got hers. I knew that once we were out of the house, we'd never get another item.

I went on. "I hope your father eats in the den. He probably will. You know how he loves his soap operas. If he's in there, I'll start getting my things loaded as soon as I get him served. If he chooses to eat at the kitchen table, we'll have to sit there with him like we always do, until he gets up and goes back to his TV."

"What about your things?"

"Don't waste your time worrying about that, Deb. I can make do with whatever I get."

He decided to eat at the kitchen table. It had been pretty quiet until he said, "That must have been an awful nasty place you're moving to."

I tried to smile. "Why do you say that?"

"Shore did take you'uns long enough to clean it and come home."

I agreed with him. "Yes, it was pretty bad at that."

He finished his meal and went back to the television. I washed the dishes and made sure I left the kitchen clean.

Deb was loading her things into the car when I went into the bedroom to grab some of my clothes. I wouldn't be able to take much. I just focused on what I needed and didn't think ahead to fall or winter. The station wagon was almost full when Larry came to the kitchen door.

"Hey!" he called out. " Is that it?"

"What do you mean?"

"I'm asking you if you got all you're gonna get?"

"No, not yet. There are some more things I want to take with me. I'm going to need my sewing machine."

He went back to his favorite chair and his soaps.

Deb asked me, "How are we going to carry that big sewing machine in the station wagon?"

"Quick as you get the last of your things loaded, we'll bring it out. All we have to do is let the tailgate down, then we'll pick up the machine, lay it on its back and slide it on in. It's heavy, but I'm hoping it won't be all that hard if we heave together."

Larry kept his cool, that is, until I made the mistake of getting a brown paper bag for pecans. There was a box of them that his brother, George, had given us a couple of weeks earlier. "Whoa!" he said. "Wait just a damn minute. That's it. You can stop right there, right now. You aren't taking another damn thing out of my house. By God, what's here is mine. What's more, it's going to stay right here. If you touch one more thing in my house..." He turned and went back into the den without finishing the sentence.

He wasn't gone too long before he came back and sat down at the kitchen table. "Both of you come here. Listen to me. Before you leave, I want you to give me your house key, both of you. I want my damn house keys and I want them now."

I took my key off my key ring and laid it in front of him on the table without a word. Bev also put her house key on the table in front of him. Then we went out the door. There were no goodbyes. I just turned my back on thirty years of pain and shame and off we went, me and Deb.

Less than a week after we moved, the woman who had been clerking at the liquor store quit without giving the proprietor, Lacel, notice. He asked if I'd take her place. I'd never thought about working in a liquor store. I considered what it might do to my reputation, but I also considered that he was offering me more money than I was making at the restaurant. The work would be less strenuous and Deb's education would be guaranteed. That was important to me, that she have the schooling I wasn't able to get. With the wages I'd be getting from Lacel, I could pay bills and take care of my girl the way I should.

I worked at Huddle's at night, at the liquor store during the day. Every bad thing I'd ever heard about liquor stores was quickly dispelled. I learned that it was illegal to allow any bad language on the premises and that the deacon's son was one of our steadiest customers. I even found out that some churches had bars! They were our best clients.

My first Friday working there, a sudden thunderstorm appeared out of nowhere. The wind was taking everything in its path. It was nearly dark as night. When I saw how bad things were outside, all I could think about was Bev being alone in the trailer. A neighbor had agreed to let her stay with her while I worked, but she, too, lived in a tiny mobile home. The storm had all the makings of a tornado.

Lacel looked out the window. "Soon as this cloud blows over, you best take off and go see about that young one of yours."

As I reached for my purse and started out the door, a bald headed man I recognized as Lacel's friend came in. He had Bev with him. I must have looked stunned, because he said in a rush of words, "I'm G.W. Stewart. I was out on my riding mower, cutting grass, when this storm hit. I saw her–" he pointed to Bev "–coming toward me. The dark clouds were coming up fast. She was pretty scared. I didn't know who she was, but when she told me that her mother worked here, I thought I'd better bring her on over so you'd know she's all right."

I said, "Whoa! Wait up. How about slowing down enough so you can catch your breath? I sure thank you for seeing after her, and I appreciated you taking the time to bring her over, but it's against the law to have minors in here. I'm going to have to ask you, if you don't mind, to take her back to our neighbor who's offered to sit for me till I get home." Now that I knew Bev was all right, I figured I should finish out my shift.

G.W. was smiling. "I'll be glad to take her back, but I was on my way to Pete's Drive-in to get me something to eat. If you don't care for her going with me, I'll be glad to get her a bite while I'm there, then I'll take her back to the trailer park."

I agreed. "I should be home in a couple of hours." I didn't have to work at the restaurant that night.

One day I asked Lacel, "Who is that man?"

Lacel look surprised. "You don't know who he is?"

"No, I sure don't."

"That's G.W. Stewart. He's my best friend."

"What's he do for a living?"

"He drives for W. R. Grace Trucking."

That didn't ring any bell with me. I wasn't familiar with trucking companies or truck drivers, for that matter. G.W. was a big man, six foot three and a half inches tall, and weighed about two hundred fifteen pounds. He was a handsome older man even though he'd lost most of his hair. The blue of his uniform brought out an even deeper blue in his eyes. He was three years younger than me.

I'd been working for Lacel for three weeks when he knocked at my door one morning while I was dressing for work.

"Evelyn," Lacel said in an excited voice when I opened the door, "Walt called my house and asked me to come tell you that Larry's house is on fire! It's burning down!"

I was so stunned that I couldn't speak.

"You need to hurry and go see what it's all about," he added.

The fire truck was there along with some others looking on, when Bev and I arrived. Larry wasn't anywhere to be found. Later, when there was an investigation into the cause of the fire, Larry assured everyone that he was in Augusta, Georgia with his brother.

I drove away from the smell of the smoke thinking, *My God, he's won again!* I remembered the day he waved a piece of paper in my face, giggling and drunk. "Lookie! Lookie what I got!"

"What have you got?" I asked him.

"I've got the deed to my house."

"What are you doing with the deed to the house?" He was making no sense. I didn't even know he knew where the deed was. He never could find the drawer his underwear was in.

"Well, I was just curious to know if there was any name on here besides mine."

"What difference does it make?" I said. "We're man and wife. I guess we'll both live our whole lives here."

At that, he kind of laughed. "I don't think I told you, but if I die first, I'm going to see to it that you or your damn young'uns don't get a thing that's here."

As I stood and watched the fireman, I decided to go and see if I could open the front door. My French Provincial living room suite, the dining room furniture, all my nice linens, everything was turned into ashes. All I could do was thank God for the little I had managed to get out of there when I did. I couldn't help but think about all those years of hard work and now we were both back to nothing. I was forty-seven years old.

The next day when I got off work at the liquor store, I went home and, as I unlocked the door, noticed a new, yellow Ford pickup stop out front. I knew it was G.W.'s truck and I thought to myself, *Wait just a minute. I hope G.W. isn't planning on making this a habit.* The last thing I wanted, or needed, was to get involved with a man. I couldn't have him coming to my trailer. I'd just have to put it to him straight. About that time Bev got out of the truck, from the driver's side, and ambled up the walk.

"Where's G.W.?" I asked.

She casually told me, "He's at home."

"Oh, my Lord, you're not telling me that you drove that truck, are you?"

Again, as casually as she could, she said, "I am"

"Oh no, no, oh nooo-nooo! Come now, you're not telling me you drove that truck here all by yourself? Tell me you didn't."

She was laughing, but she knew I was more than upset. The very thought of her driving terrified me. She was only thirteen, too young even for a permit.

"Mom," she laughed, "G.W. sent me to get you."

"He must be out of his ever-loving mind to let you drive that truck. And when did you learn to drive, anyway?" She had no idea what the consequences of a thing like that could turn into–but G.W. certainly should have.

Deb didn't answer me direct, but went back to why she'd come after me. "G.W. wants to talk to you about renting us his house trailer. Oh, Mom, it's really nice, much nicer than this one. It's lots bigger than ours is, too. You know we need the room."

I was suspicious, thinking he was using her and his trailer as a ploy to get to me. I couldn't see that I had a choice other than to go to make sure that truck got back safely, and to make him understand that my child was not to drive it ever again. We pulled up and parked in his muddy driveway. It was so slick that the truck wanted to slide back down the hill, even with the emergency brake on. We finally made our way in through the back door. As we went into the hall, we collided with G.W. attempting to hide his dirty rugs to keep us from seeing them. He blushed to the top of his bald head.

"Come in," he said, scooting the throw rugs aside with his foot. "How are you?"

"I'm not sure if you want me to come in or not, as upset as I am with you right now."

He laughed. "Why are you mad at me? Go on, you can tell me."

"As if you didn't know. G.W., how stupid can a grown man be, letting a thirteen year-old drive your new truck, not even old enough for a driver's permit?"

He took one of my hands. "Look at that little old hand. You couldn't hurt anybody, so why are you pretending to be so mad at me?"

G.W. and Bev both laughed. It wasn't funny to me. I was trying to set him straight. "You don't turn children loose with a new truck, or any vehicle. Come now. You're old enough to know better than to let a child drive. What if she wrecked that truck? I don't have the money to get it fixed. You'd end up hating both of us."

He grinned easily. "That's why I got the thing insured."

The words were scarcely out of his mouth when Bev said, "Look, Momma, look!"

I looked out the front window as Larry drove by on the main road. I thought, *Oh, my Lord, how long has he been following us? Now he knows what part of town we live in.* I knew he didn't want me back, and he didn't want Deb. He only wanted to frighten and torment us.

I knew he was on a tracking mission. It was up to me to outsmart him if I intended to keep Bev and myself alive.

I thought it only fair to tell G.W. some of what was going on so he could know what to expect if he planned on being our friend. He listened and took it with a grain of salt. Later, he told me that he figured it was just a thing that husbands and wives go through when they separate, and that it would go away in a few days. He confessed that during his divorce, he'd done his share of idiot acts. He had no idea what Larry was capable of, and I didn't get into those kinds of details with him. Not then, anyway.

"This isn't the first time that truck's gone by," he said, when I finally stopped talking. "I've seen it quite a few times."

Since the road dead-ended after about two miles, Larry had to make the trip past the trailer park twice, once coming and once going.

Deb was so nervous, she was shaking like leaves on a tree during a sixty-mile an hour wind storm. G.W. put an arm around her in a protective sort of way. "You stop your worrying now," he said. "If he comes up here, I'll take care of it. You can count on it."

While the words were still on his lips, Larry drove back by.

I thought, *I sure am glad my car's in my driveway. The lights are on inside the trailer, too, so I'm pretty sure he thinks I'm home...unless he saw me get out of G.W.'s truck a few minutes ago.* It was only about seventy-five yards from our place to his, but I'd driven the truck, not walked. Surely Larry didn't see me go in G.W.'s trailer.

I felt like a trapped animal. Here I was in a strange man's house. I needed to get home and get Bev settled down. She had school the next day and I wanted her to be rested.

I could take it no more. I broke out in tears. "Can someone please tell me how I'm going to get back home with this man running up and down this road like he is?"

G.W. said, "I promise he's not going to hurt you."

"I lived with him for over thirty years. You have no idea what he's like."

G.W. remained quiet for a moment, thinking. I saw him as someone who'd never back down from a fight, and who would probably come out on top every time. He finally insisted that I take Bev to his spare bedroom to get some rest. Then he and I stayed up with his shotgun nearby. I was too exhausted, mentally and physically, to keep from falling asleep. When I woke up the next morning, he said that Larry had driven by again around four a.m., but hadn't been back since.

When I got home from working at the liquor store that afternoon, there was a note on my door. It was from G.W., asking me to come to his trailer. Bev had just gotten in from school. She insisted we go.

When we got there, he wanted to know more about what led up to the situation Bev and I were in, so I told him what we'd been through. When I finished, G.W. said, "If the man is what you say, and I believe you're telling me the truth, he's apt to try anything."

I thought about Larry driving back and forth in front of the trailer court. It wasn't a good sign. He was still keeping his eye on me. In truth, he was stalking me. "Evidently he's keeping a pretty close watch over us," I said. "Deb and I can't go to the Pizza Hut that he doesn't circle the building."

"I didn't have any idea it was so serious," he said.

Deb had a question for me that I couldn't answer. "After our house burned down, he brought you the key. Explain to me what that was all about."

G.W. raised his brows. "He brought you the key to a house that no longer existed? Did he bring it out here to the trailer?"

I shook my head. "Deb and I were working at the restaurant a couple of weeks after the fire when Larry pulled up in his truck. He parked where he knew I could see him, but he didn't get out. Finally, Bev said I should go see what his problem was or else he might come in and cause a scene like he'd done before. I didn't want to go, but she was right. He didn't say a word to me. He just handed me the house key and raced out of the parking lot. It was eerie."

Deb said, "I think he was setting it up to look like Mom had set the fire."

G.W. was silent for a bit, then he said, "I have a confession to make. The reason I sent Bev to get you was because I knew you wouldn't come here any other way. I figured you'd return my truck to me." He leveled those blue eyes at me. "Mad?"

I shook my head. "Daddy always said that confession's good for the soul. You were right, I wouldn't have come here, but it's okay now. I feel much better. I just don't want Larry giving you trouble."

"I can see that both of you are scared of him. I tell you what. If you'll give me a ride to the terminal where I pick up whatever rig

I'll be driving that day, I can leave my own truck here. I've got a feeling that as long as my truck's parked in my driveway, he'll think I'm home. Your husband's a bully and a coward, but he won't tangle with a man. What do you say?"

We set up a plan whereby I'd take him to and from the terminal whenever he needed to go. He suggested that we stay in his trailer when he was gone, if it would make us feel safer. Even though he was away from ten days to three weeks at a time, I knew I wouldn't feel right in his place, so I turned him down, but the offer was certainly appreciated.

Things went along without much excitement or trouble for a period longer than any I'd ever known. But like Momma always said, "All good things must end" and my peace of mind was about to explode into sheer panic once more.

32

I came home from work and put the key in the front door lock with no warning that I was about to get the shock of my life when I stepped inside. The trailer was practically empty!

My heart was in my mouth. What was I going to do? What could I do? I was scared out of my mind. About that time, Bev came driving up in G.W.'s truck. I turned on her with a fury.

"If your daddy don't drive me crazy, you're gonna get me for sure! I told you not to be driving that truck! I told G.W. not to let you drive that truck! Can you not understand the danger you are putting both of us in?"

To my amazement, she burst out laughing.

"Why are you laughing? I don't see anything funny here. Everything we have is gone and you stand there laughing. I assure you, there's nothing amusing about any of this."

She wiped the grin off of her face and gave me a look that only a daughter who's being so reasonable it's disgusting can give a mother. "Mom, it's all right. I moved our things to G.W.'s place. I was trying to get it all done before you got home. I wanted to surprise you."

"Surprise me? You scared the living hell out of me!" I took a deep breath and tried to calm down. "Just how did you come to make that kind of decision without my knowledge?"

"Mom, you know we can't go on living like this. We can't sleep at night, never knowing where Daddy is or what he might do next.

G.W. and me talked it over before he left on his road trip. We agreed that you and me would be safer in his trailer, at least as long as Dad's stalking us like he is." She reached into her pocket and produced a set of keys. "Keys to his trailer," she said with a twinkle in her eye. "We both wanted to surprise you."

"Of course he told you not to tell me. He knew if you told me it would never happen." I tried to act indignant, but actually I was grateful. Nevertheless, I told her that if I wasn't so tired, I'd march myself right up to G.W.'s trailer and put everything back in our place the way it was. At another level, even though the man appeared to be doing all he could to help us and to show us that he was our friend, I couldn't help but wonder if he wasn't manipulating my daughter. He had certainly gained her confidence. She trusted him completely. He was everything to her that she wanted her father to be. In truth, I was more scared to stay in our place than she was. I hadn't told her yet, but I had every intention of finding us another place. I didn't have *any* intention of moving in with another man.

We loaded up the last few things and went on to G.W.'s trailer. Bev had done real well, most of our belongings were already put away. We hadn't been there ten minutes when the phone rang. I answered it. G.W. was laughing like he knew the best joke in the world as he said, "I just called to see how you like your new home."

"The two of you really think you're smart, don't you?"

He was suddenly serious. "Evelyn, I do care about what happens to both of you. It's driving me crazy out here on the road, not being able to be there to take care of you. I just want you to know that you're safe."

"Deb says you told her that Larry won't go to your trailer even if he sees my car up here. How could you make such a promise? You don't know the man."

"I did tell her that. What I didn't tell her was that I called Larry and told him that he'd better stay away. I told him never to lay a hand on either one of you again, that if he does, I'm going over there and I'm going to pull him out of his house and beat the hell out of him."

I was stunned. "You didn't."

"Oh, yes, I did."

After that, G.W. called almost every day to check on us and to make sure we were all right. That was the first time in my life I'd ever had a man show me that he cared for me as a human being. It brought tears to my eyes.

During the time he was gone, an attorney I'd contacted about insurance on our house informed me that he had finally received a settlement. The astounding part was the sum. The house had been insured for fifty thousand dollars, so why did the company issue a check to him for only eleven thousand? Because, they said, the house didn't burn to the ground. There was still some of it standing. I'm no mathematical genius, but it seems to me that any fool should be able to figure there's more to be gotten from insurance than eleven thousand dollars when the house is engulfed in flames. I reminded the attorney that there were also eighteen acres of land to be considered when we're talking about dividing things up. I wanted one half of its value; not a cent more, but every cent I rightfully had coming. In the end, the lawyer agreed to give Larry a call and see if something better financially couldn't be worked out. I didn't bother reminding him that it was me who had been paying Larry's way for the past seven years while supporting Bev and myself at the same time.

What the attorney didn't know because I hadn't told him, was that G.W. had put me in touch with a divorce lawyer after convincing me that Larry was never going to leave me alone unless I ended it once and for all, legally.

Even with all I'd been through, that was a tough call for me. My religion didn't believe in divorce. My family didn't approve of divorce. In fact, every one of my brothers and sisters, aunts, cousins, nieces, nephews, all of them were dead set against divorce. None of them had ever liked Larry, but still I knew that if I took this step they would turn against me. I weighed all of that very carefully before setting foot in the divorce lawyer's office. It was one of the most painful decisions I'd ever had to make.

The lawyer heard my story then assured me that I would indeed get one half of everything we owned, which included the dollar value of the eighteen acres. I was astounded that he could do that. I was even more astounded to hear that he would file charges on the grounds of physical cruelty, and that it would be granted in thirty days. My entire life I had been told in no uncertain terms that the only grounds for divorce was adultery. Pentecostal preachers had pounded that into my head since I was a child. I never forgot what was said by men of God–and now I found that they were wrong. Good Lord! If they were wrong about that, what else were they wrong about, I wondered? The news really boggled my mind–I was eligible for a legal divorce. Amazing.

When the lawyer told me that he intended to file for child support, I knew we were looking at a lost cause.

"Larry hasn't worked in seven years, so you can forget child support," I told him. I knew how child support worked in our state; fifteen dollars a week was top pay, if that much. I felt certain that all filing for it would do, would be to force me to give him the right to walk into my house any time he felt like it. Thank you for being so thoughtful, I said to the lawyer, but no thanks. I'd supported Bev to this point, I could do without his ten or fifteen dollars a week. There was no amount of money worth going through hell again. If that wasn't the way the law worked, no one bothered telling me about it.

The attorney said, "There's nothing for you to worry about. He won't be able to abuse or bother you any longer because I'm going to get a restraining order against him."

"Your restraining order just might be the instrument that detonates his anger to the point of eliminating the two of us. Listen to me, please. I don't believe there are enough restraining orders in Pickens County to stop Larry from doing anything he makes up his mind to do. He'll stop when he, and only he, decides to do so. A restraining order will only challenge him to prove to you that he'll do what he wants to do, regardless."

The attorney wasn't to be discouraged. "I'm going ahead and have a deputy serve him this afternoon. You'll see, like I told you, he won't be bothering you once he's been served." He came around his desk and gave me what he probably thought was a reassuring smile. "You've let him instill fear in you, that's all. It's going to be fine, you'll see."

I'm thinking, yeah right, we will see. We'll see his sorry rear end at my front door, making all kinds of threats and daring the law to do anything to stop him.

Another thought had given me concern and it had to do with my reputation. I'd always been mindful of it and worked to protect it as best I could. I'd heard stories about men in divorce situations paying guys to get up on a stand in a court of law and swear they'd had sex with their wife. I knew women who stayed married rather than be put through that kind of shame.

Two days later, the attorney dealing with the insurance company brought me a check in the amount of ten thousand dollars. Bev and I went shopping for a new trailer. We found one that we liked and the price was right. The next problem was where to put it.

When G.W. came in off the road that weekend, I told him about our purchase. He suggested we park it on his property and said he wouldn't think of charging me. He even helped install a six-foot high, chain-link fence around the yard. I bought a lock for the gate and had to admit, it did give me a feeling of security. A feeling that was short lived.

Our very first night there, and for many nights thereafter, someone standing in the woods across the way threw pebbles at the side of our trailer. Bev and I felt the familiar chill of terror once again. We worked hard all day, then came home to rest only to find there wasn't going to be any rest. We'd turn out the lights and peer into the woods, but we never saw who it was, we only saw the red tip of a cigarette as someone stood in the shadows, watching us. I finally came to the conclusion that whoever it was only wanted to scare us and keep us awake. To this day we don't know who threw the pebbles. My guess is that Larry paid someone to do it.

One night, three or so weeks later, G.W., Bev and I went out to dinner in my car. G.W. was driving. Afterward, on our way to my trailer, we were almost to a place where we had to turn off the main road when I spotted Larry's truck parked in front of my gate. Bev saw it, too. Although he was facing away from us, we could see him sitting in the truck.

G.W. stopped the car and backed into a stand of cedar trees and vines that would block Larry's view and keep him from seeing us. I glanced in the backseat to find Bev curled into a fetal position on the floorboard. *My God,* I thought, *how much more can this poor child take?* She's terrified.

G.W. asked what I wanted to do. "I'm going to find a pay phone and call the police," I replied. He got out of the car. "You take the car. I'll stay here and keep an eye on him."

Deb raised up on one elbow and said, "No, no, Mom! Please don't let him stay. If he stays, he'll hurt Daddy." Is there no limit to a child's loyalty, I wondered?

"No, he won't," I assured her. "He just wants to see if he can tell what your daddy's up to."

I drove to the nearest phone booth and called the Pickens County Sheriff's office. They told me to stay put, they would get a squad car out right away. Not more than two minutes later, a sheriff's car pulled in near the phone booth where I stood waiting for them.

One of the deputies said, "Follow me in your car, but make sure you stay behind me."

We got to the road leading up to my fence. Larry's truck was still parked within three feet of the gate. A deputy went up to him and found that Larry was asleep. He woke him up and put him in the squad car. I knew they were talking to him, but I couldn't hear what was being said. Then one of the officers walked away from Larry and came up to me.

"Mrs. Barkley, I've radioed for handlers to bring in track dogs."

"Why?"

"We have every reason to believe that your husband has hidden a rifle some place nearby. It's our belief that it could be in the woods where he has easy access to it." He pointed to a place where our mysterious someone had been throwing pebbles. "We think it's possible he plans to come back and use the gun to sniper-shoot you and your daughter."

I couldn't comprehend what he was saying. It was too much to take in. "Did Larry tell you that?" "Ma'am, I'm not at liberty to tell you what he said to us. All I can say is that we feel it necessary to get the track dogs brought in to do some checking."

It didn't take the Pickens County Sheriff Department long to arrive with their canines. The animals made a circle across the road, then through the woods. Even though they did this several times, they never found a gun.

One of the deputies asked what I wanted done with Larry's truck. We were walking past the squad car. I happened to glance in the backseat and saw Larry doubled over in laughter. That did it. I lost it.

"I don't give a tinker's damn what you do with his truck," I said, doing my best to keep my voice level, "so long as you get it out of here. While you're at it, I have one more thing I want you to understand. Whatever you decide to do with him, you need to educate him. I'm telling you here and now, before God and you deputies, that if I catch him in my trailer, I promise you I will kill him! You can call it pre-meditated murder or whatever name suits your fancy, I leave that to you, but one thing is sure, he can consider himself a dead man if he crosses my threshold. Enough is enough. I've had it up to here!" I held my hand to my neck and made a slicing motion across my throat.

Two weeks later, I went to court and my divorce became final. Larry refused to appear for the hearing.

The following Christmas, Bev bought her father a present without my knowledge. She told me about it on Christmas morning. "If it's all right with you," she said, "I want you to take me over to Daddy's. I want to spend half of Christmas Day with him and the other half with you."

That was a real shocker, as terrified of her father as she had been. I told myself that Christmas is a time of miracles and that I should expect anything.

"All right, I'll take you, but just remember, this is your decision. You're thirteen years old, a big girl. You work hard and you've earned your own money. Regardless of what's happened between your father and me, he's still your father. So, I'll take you over there, but I won't stay with you."

She got his gift and, with much apprehension on my part, we left to go see the man I'd gone to so much trouble to get away from. She had taken extra special care to give his gift a beautiful and distinctive look.

Larry had been living in a camper since the house burned. It was in the process of being remodeled. I parked in the driveway. With trembling knees, I stayed behind Bev as she stepped into the camper.

Larry was sitting on a cabinet that covered a thirty-gallon water tank. Bev was so excited, like all children at Christmastime. She stood two feet in front of him, wanting her father to reach out for a Christmas hug. He remained motionless and didn't acknowledge her. He was staring at me. Bev glanced at me, then handed him the gift. With a slight sneer, he tossed it over his shoulder, onto a king size bed above the camper cab, tossed it as if it were a piece of garbage. Then he jumped to his feet, shoving Bev aside and knocking her backwards, making a grab for my wig.

I sidestepped him and leaped to the ground as Bev shouted, "Run, Mom! Run, run! Hurry! Let's go!" And run we did! We jumped in the car and off we went.

Somehow we overcame that just as I was managing to overcome the last thirty years. Larry had always said that if anything ever happened to me, he'd be married again in three weeks. It was a bit longer than three weeks, but he did remarry. For some time, even after his marriage, he continued to stalk us, but I was no longer afraid of him. The stalking stopped with another letter from my attorney, threatening jail.

On May 15, 1974, G.W. persuaded me to marry him. The private ceremony took place at the Spartanburg Courthouse. About a year after that, I began putting on weight. A lot of weight. And I wasn't feeling good most of the time. G.W. insisted that I go for a medical checkup. Imagine my astonishment when I heard the doctor proclaim me pregnant! I argued, but he argued even more. I couldn't be, but I was. Grandma Evelyn was going to have a baby. To my way of thinking, Dr. Reinovsky was one of the greatest doctors who ever lived. If he was convinced that I was pregnant, then I agreed I must be pregnant.

By the time I reached my eighth month, I knew in my heart there was something wrong. When I saw the doctor, he gave me a puzzled look and said, "I've been a little concerned for you lately." After his examination, he referred me to another doctor on the other side of town. It was this doctor who gave me news no woman wants to hear: I had a tumor the size of an unborn baby in my womb.

G.W. broke down and cried; he'd been so excited about the coming child. As for me, I thought I'd had all the breaking of a heart that one could suffer in a single lifetime, but I found that I had room for another. They operated and removed a seven-pound tumor. Despite the fact the nurse told me there was not one place on my female organs that didn't have a tumor, none of them were cancerous. But her concern didn't end there.

"Mrs. Stewart," she said, "Dr. Hardin and I could see that your stomach has been severely bruised. How did that happen?"

In searching to give her an answer, that little voice inside me said, "Why not tell her the truth?" I had kept it to myself, like Larry taught me to do, since I was sixteen years old.

"Yes, I've been bruised in my stomach many times."

"Would you like to tell me about it?"

"No," I replied honestly. "Not really, but if you insist, I will."

"Why would you hesitate to talk about it when you're lucky to be alive?" "Because I'm ashamed. Ashamed to admit that my first husband beat me horribly in the stomach."

"That's odd. Why the stomach?"

"He saw on television that if a man beat a woman in her stomach, the marks will never show."

She thought for a long moment. "Mrs. Stewart, the doctor and I feel that you should bring charges against him. He deserves to be punished for what he's done to you."

I refused to even consider such a thing.

"My mother always told me, 'The more you stir a stink, the more it's going to stink'. Besides, I'm married now to a man who's good to me, and I have my children to consider. Growing up with their father was hard on them. It's time to put it to rest, not stir up another hornet's nest of confusion."

Some months later, I was working at the restaurant when my ex brother-in-law, Etley, came by. I hadn't seen him or the children in months, and I missed them. I'd always liked him, though of course I was closer to Louise. I think one of the reasons it was hard to feel close to Etley was that he had kept a distance from Larry. Louise confided that her husband really disliked her brother. So, even though they only lived about six miles away, we didn't visit very often.

"My goodness, this is a nice surprise," I said when I saw him at the take-out window. "It seems like ages since I saw you last." When he didn't answer right away, I noticed that he seemed to be troubled and didn't know how to say what he wanted to say. "Are you all right? Is something wrong?"

"Yes, there is. I need to talk to you."

I wasn't all that busy, so I told him I'd be outside in a few minutes. We could talk in the parking lot where it would be private.

My first concerns were for his children, so I asked him if they were all right. They were. Finally, I asked him point blank to tell me what was wrong.

His voice gave away to a slight tremor. "I come close to killing Larry last night."

That was one I wasn't expecting.

"Oh, my God! Did I hear you right? You almost killed Larry last night?"

"I came real close."

To my knowledge, there had never been a confrontation between the two of them. Etley Dills was quite tall. Larry would had to have gone off the deep end to go up against this big strong backwoodsman.

"You know Larry is crazy as hell. Well, he came to my house with his rifle and he told me that he was going to kill me." He took in a deep breath before he continued. "He didn't just threaten, he pointed the riffle at me. Before he could pull the trigger, I grabbed it away from him. It went off, but nobody got hit. I threw it in the corner behind me."

"Then what happened?"

"I knocked the hell out of him. I told him that he'd better have a good reason for coming in my house and pulling a stunt like that. It was dumb luck that one of us didn't get killed." He looked away and shook his head. Then his eyes met mine. "I don't know how to tell you this, but I think you need to know."

"For heaven's sake, Etley, spit it out."

"Larry has it in his head that I'm Deb's father."

Oh, my God, was all I could think.

Etley went on. "When he accused me of that, I slapped the hell out of him."

My head began to spin and my knees almost went out from under me. I was so sick at my stomach, I felt like I was going to throw up.

"Are you all right?"

"No, but I will be."

I meant it. I would be fine. I was getting more fine every day, but then every day it seemed like I'd learn something new that brought it all back again, like I was never going to get out from under Larry's dark cloud of ugliness.

For instance, when Bev was sixteen I happened to notice a scar on her foot that I'd never noticed before.

"Where'd that come from?" I asked, mildly curious.

She didn't answer me right away.

"Deb?"

Finally, she confessed that one day, out on the lake, when she was very little, her daddy had beat her with a tree limb. She never told me. I never knew. And it broke my heart as if it had happened only five minutes before.

◘

Larry Barkley died October 12, 1982, of emphysema. When I received the phone call, it was like a burden had lifted from me. That night, for the first time in I couldn't remember how long, I slept peacefully.

Harvey had bought an eighteen-wheeler truck, and was driving long distance with Bev as his co-driver when they got word. They drove back for his funeral.

Dean flew in from Phoenix, which was a surprise, though I was glad he did. He was the one who had received the worst treatment of any of our children. When he got to the house, I asked if he wanted me to go to the funeral home with him.

"No, Mother. You don't have any business there. I want you and everybody else to know that I didn't come here for Daddy, I came for myself. I didn't want to say six months down the road that I wish I had."

The evil that Larry's father had begun, and perhaps even his father before him, had been put to rest. The cycle ended with Larry. Neither of our sons have ever lifted a finger against others in anger or meanness. How they came through all of that to be the fine men they became is another of God's miracles. Deb, too, turned out to be sweet-natured and filled with the kind of empathy one can only have when they've overcome pain and hurt themselves.

That chapter is closed forever, but the book has not yet ended. I live every day of my life grateful to have survived what so many young women haven't survived. Maybe I had to tough it out in order to pass along some of my history to those who feel that they, and they alone, are in such abusive situations that no one will ever understand. My message to them is to believe in miracles. And to believe in yourself. With God, all things are possible. I'm living proof of the truth of that statement.

Epilogue

I debated about passing along something Dean said when he returned from his father's funeral, but then I decided that I should. He said, "I hope that Daddy burns in hell for the way he treated us." Bev wasn't sure I should confide that to you, but I think it brings home a serious fact: children never, ever forget. They are molded and shaped by what happens to them as little ones. It changes them, for the good or not for the good, forever. Dean never forgot, but I thank God that he never let the abuse hold him back or turn him into an abuser. His statement meant that he hoped his father received his justice, if not on earth, then in front of God.

Larry kept his word to his children. He made sure they never got anything that had been his, however, he did do one decent thing. He left Donnie his truck and his tools. To hate black people as much as he did in the beginning, I felt I had accomplished one positive thing with him: I got him to recognize African Americans as human beings. To my knowledge, Donnie was his one and only true friend who stuck by him until he died. Today Donnie still runs Larry's company. He's a husband, a father and a loving, kind gentleman.

G.W. Stewart died February 10, 1985, of intestinal cancer.

Not quite two years later, on December 20, 1986, Dean flew to the Greenville-Spartanburg airport from Phoenix. I picked him up in my Dodge van and we rented a truck to move me to Scottsdale, so I could be near him. We got there on Christmas Eve. It was one of the best holidays I ever had. A few years later he had a wonderful opportunity to go into the pole barn business in Elizabeth, Arkansas, so off we went to one of the most beautiful spots on the planet. I settled in Mountain Home, and his business took off beyond all expectations. As he said to me one day, "Mother, I've finally found my niche."

On Saturday before Mother's day, 2002, I stopped by to visit with him and commented that he looked tired. He said he'd been cleaning the camper in preparation for an upcoming trip to Kentucky and then on to Florida to see his brother. When I left, I gave him a hug and a kiss on the cheek, followed by the usual, "I love you, son". As I walked away, he called out to me to wait a minute. He hurried to catch up with me. He had something he wanted to hand me.

"What's that?" I said.

"I just remembered I haven't given you your Mother's Day present."

It was a one-hundred-dollar bill. Not once since he left the navy, had he ever missed a Mother's Day, or Christmas, or my birthday, without giving me a one-hundred-dollar bill.

The next day he called from Kentucky to wish me Happy Mother's Day again. A couple of days after that he called from some place in South Carolina to ask for his brother's phone number; he had misplaced it. He was on his way to Florida to see Harvey. We talked a few minutes, then he had to go.

"I love you, Mother," I remember him saying. "Take care of yourself. I'll see you in a week to ten days."

I said I loved him, too, and to be careful. It was the last conversation I would ever have with my son. On Monday morning, June 3, 2002, there was a pounding on my door. The moment I saw Dean's best friend, Denny, standing there, I knew he was a bearer of bad news. Dean had made it to Florida. He and Harvey set up the camper then, on Wednesday, sometime in the afternoon, Dean went in to take a shower. He dressed and went to the living room where he no sooner sat down than he suffered a heart attack. He died Saturday, June 2. Over the years I've heard so many women comment on how they wish they had a son like Dean. I was, and am, so very proud of him.

Deb is married to a fine young man and has a grown son, Shanen, who lives in Phoenix, Arizona with his beautiful wife, Angel, and my great-grandchild, Kaila Marie. God gifted Bev with an incredible singing voice. She was a country-western singer and had her own band for fourteen years.

Harvey lives in Deland, Florida with his lovely wife Barbara. He works for a telephone company.

My family of fourteen is down to three: Stanley, Margie and myself.

Stanley and I lost contact and only recently reunited at a family get-together in South Carolina. When he read the first draft of this book, he said, "Sis, you should have told me. I would have kicked his damn ass." He retired from the navy yard as an electric welder, then went on to teach it. Married and widowed, then married again (to the terrific Susan), he managed to amass a fortune and opened a nursery business, which is still thriving. We have vowed never to lose touch with one another again.

My sister Margie suffers from Alzheimer's and lives in a nursing home, though she's in excellent health.

My beloved Nanny Eve lived to be well past one hundred years old. Her words, however, will never die. I remember them as if they were spoken only yesterday.

In summary, I can't say it enough: Abuse breeds abuse.

I pray that women who read this will take the time to find a good man when they think about marriage. Check out his family. Know what you're getting into before you bring innocent children into this world, so that you won't sentence yourself to misery and abuse. How I wish I could scream to every young girl who says, when a man tries to control her, "Possession and control isn't love!"

Husbands, love your wives as God loves the church, remembering that the word "church" doesn't mean a building, it means people.

I have chosen to turn my life into an open book because God has so wonderfully blessed me throughout all of the trauma. Those blessings are nothing short of miracles. It has been over fifty years now since my mother-in-law was executed by my father-in-law and my sister-in-law was killed. I feel compelled to let the world know that these women did not deserve this and neither did their children. It didn't have to be the way it was. If only they had known they were women with rights, maybe not in the eyes of the law at that time, but in God's eyes. If only I had known that I would not burn in hell eternally if I divorced a man who beat me and the children. If only, if only …

It's too late for me to undo the damage Larry caused me, but it's exactly the right time for me to tell you, dear reader, that your life is valuable and that if you are in an abusive situation, you must get out. If you have children, it's even more important that you find the courage to leave. It's difficult, but it's not impossible. God meant for life to be sweet. Let no one rob you of your divine right to enjoy each moment, each hour, each day.

Abuse has been going on since the beginning of time. No doubt the cave man batted around his cave lady. Only by the loving mercy and grace of God, am I alive to tell my story. My desire is to reach out to let the thousands of women, and men, living that kind of torturous life, know that they are not alone. I made it, you will, too.

Evelyn Fort Stewart
www.evesDVhelp.org
412 Cooper St.
Mountain Home, AR 72653

How to Order

"Behind Closed Doors"
by
Evelyn Fort Stewart

$23.95 plus $5.00 s/h

(CUT) ....

Please send me _____ copy(s) of "Behind Closed Doors" by Evelyn Fort Stewart. I have enclosed my check or money order in the amount of $_____ .

Send to: (name) _____

(address) _____ Apt_____

(city/state/zip) _____

Phone: (_____) _____ – _____

email: _____

Send check or money order to Evelyn Fort Stewart,
412 Cooper St., Mountain Home, Arkansas 72653

Allow 3 weeks for delivery
Special discount for bulk orders. Contact Evelyn Fort Stewart for details.